LI ZHIGANG

THE
JD.com
STORY

AN E-COMMERCE PHENOMENON

Published by
LID Publishing Limited
One Adam Street, London WC2N 6LE

31 West 34th Street, 8th Floor, Suite 8004,
New York, NY 10001, U.S.

info@lidpublishing.com
www.lidpublishing.com

A member of:

BPR
Business Publishers Roundtable

www.businesspublishersroundtable.com

Copyright licensed by Li Zhigang and arranged with Shanghai CEIBS Online Learning Co., Ltd.
The JD.com Story is translated from the original Chinese edition [－创京东]

© 2016 Li Zhigang
© 2016 LID Publishing Ltd.
Photo credit (Sim Chi Yin/VII)

Printed by CPI Group (UK) Ltd, Croydon CR0 4YY
ISBN: 978-1-910649-71-8

Page design: Caroline Li

LI ZHIGANG

THE
JD.com
STORY

AN E-COMMERCE PHENOMENON

LONDON   MONTERREY
MADRID   SHANGHAI
MEXICO CITY   BOGOTA
NEW YORK   BUENOS AIRES
BARCELONA   SAN FRANCISCO

Contents

Author's Note to English Edition

I am extremely happy to see The JD.com Story translated into English so that it can be read by international audiences. As a top-selling business book in China, with sales exceeding 300,000 copies, this volume contains many insightful interviews with JD employees, including Richard Liu, the company's founder and CEO.

I believe audiences worldwide are curious about the Chinese business environment. Thanks to ambitious reform policies and a general opening of Chinese markets in the 1980s and 1990s, China has helped drive global economic integration. Along the way, it has become the world's second-largest economy. With their huge, acquisitive populations, China and the US are the two poles of the internet world. To date, four internet giants with market values of far more than $10 billion each have emerged in China: Alibaba, Tencent, Baidu, and JD.

All these companies are aggressively pursuing globalization. JD set its globalization strategy in motion in October 2012. It has since entered diverse overseas markets, including Russia and Indonesia. Still, JD has a long way to go on the global stage. In the eyes of Richard Liu, earning money in China alone makes for a good Chinese company, but what he dreams of is a truly great company that conducts business, and succeeds spectacularly, on a global scale. When he's traveling in the US, Chinese students who are studying abroad often ask him: "When will you start doing business here?"

Many Chinese companies want more than success in the Chinese market alone. Some have set their sights on the global market from the very beginning, and in the future, more and more Chinese companies will get serious about expanding internationally. The entrepreneurs and visionaries behind these enterprises will be anxious to tell their stories to audiences far and wide. And these companies' leaders, in turn, will put considerable time, effort, and resources into getting to know their new global customers.

As an entrepreneur focused on the development of Chinese companies, I've long shared in that dream: to learn, grow, and go global. For me, the release of this English edition, in English-speaking countries, represents a pivotal step in that direction.

My deepest gratitude goes to Li Xi, JD's public relations VP, with whom I discussed the possibility of publishing worldwide before I started work on the original Chinese edition in 2014. Thanks also to Gu Xiaoman, PR director, and Wang Xiaodong and Qi Shanshan, PR managers, for their assistance on this English edition.

I'd like to thank Bai Wenge for her tireless work on translating the manuscript from Chinese to English.

My gratitude goes to Hu Zhifeng, publishing director of CEIBS Publishing Group, who contacted me the moment he learned about the book in June of 2015, hoping one day to promote it globally.

Finally, special thanks to Shi Tao, who reviewed the English manuscript and offered invaluable advice and counsel. Shi is a respected global e-commerce expert who was a VP at Amazon.cn before becoming JD Group vice president responsible for the media product categories and JD's global business.

Li Zhigang

A Return to Retail's Roots

By Richard Liu
Founder and CEO, JD.com

R ecently, I wrote a preface for the autobiography of Sam Walton, founder of Wal-Mart. Today, I find myself writing the foreword for this book, about my own company, JD.com.

To be honest, I prefer sharing my thoughts on Sam Walton, because Wal-Mart is the benchmark for the traditional retail industry and an inspiration to many. Reading his story was like talking to a chieftain of the industry, very inspiring and encouraging, and I hope to continue to use what I learned from his book, both with my team and for my own self-examination.

Today, I can say with pride that some see the JD model as a new industry benchmark. Yet it's far from time to sing its praises. We are still on our journey and the future still holds infinite possibilities. Besides, it is easier to know others than to know oneself. Although I often talk about JD's accomplishments, it is out of character for me to praise myself.

Therefore, when Li Zhigang offered to write this book, my only request was that he record the successes and failures of JD so far, without hiding or whitewashing anything.

He has succeeded and I am proud that this book shows not only the excitement and joy that those who helped create JD experienced along the way, but also the hesitations and anxieties we faced, the public questioning, and our setbacks.

In our early years, after working overtime into the night, the JD team often gathered at small pubs and food stalls. Several rounds of drinks later, the fatigue and depression accumulated during the workday would be largely defused. And when we toasted each other, frictions related to work evaporated. Most importantly, in this relaxed atmosphere, we could freely discuss the twists and turns of business, such as what problems had been addressed, what difficult customers we had won over, and all of the other issues, big and small, that had popped up that day. During these sessions we identified and analysed problems in detail and set bold sales targets. The next day, we returned to the fight fully charged, developing JD by leaps and bounds.

Today, more and more friends have come to JD. We have a growing catalogue of memories; however, we drink less and less.

Now, with JD's rapid expansion, we have trouble finding a place big enough to hold a meeting for all the staff. We've improved our organizational structure, established institutions and systems, standardized and coordinated internal communications, and improved assessment and incentive mechanisms. As a listed company, JD can no longer handle matters as loosely as it did in its pioneer days. Today, what I worry about is rigorous organization, smooth-running systems, and timely response to customer demands. Yet I challenge myself and my team to hold on to our entrepreneurial spirit, our unmatched sensitivity to market changes, and the rapid and powerful execution that distinguished JD from the start.

That's the foundation of JD, our original starting point.

In 2004, most Chinese people were more interested in the achievements of Liu Xiang – known as "the flying man" for his pole-vault and hurdling titles – than the shifts in retail. No one noticed when a group of guys selling magneto-optical recording equipment in Zhongguancun suddenly decided to move their entire business from a physical, bricks-and-mortar storefront to online. We were already the largest retailer of magneto-optical products, and there was room to grow if we had wanted to continue investing and enhancing the physical store. But under the traditional system, with layer upon layer of intermediaries, retailers had little room to reduce costs and improve efficiency. It was increasingly difficult to innovate in response to customer demand. Ultimately, it was the consumers who had to pay for the low efficiency and high costs of retail channels.

Today, we dare not say that JD emerged at the right moment to solve consumers' problems, but the rise of online channels did allow us to see the huge potential to be had by breaking away from traditional retail to create more value for consumers. In 2004, I slept most soundly, because we could finally face our customers directly and fully realize our ambitions.

Years later, Xu Xin, our earliest investor and the founder of Capital Today Group, surveyed 3,000 people. The results showed that

JD's rise was in step with the times and met the huge online-quality-shopping demand of the Chinese middle class that grew up with the internet.

We weren't analysing our data in any systematic or particularly innovative way at that time. It was only when we saw significant contrasts between our online and offline businesses that we discovered how online channels would reduce costs for consumers, which in turn would make us more competitive.

Therefore, JD's growth can be explained simply: it is nothing more than making constant ground-breaking innovations to a business model to meet new consumer needs and leveraging the internet to reconstruct the supply chain system, reduce costs, improve efficiency, and, ultimately, create value for consumers. This still follows retail industry principles. JD has been sticking to these principles in its growth and expansion and will continue to do so as we move forward.

In 2007, despite opposition from investors and senior management, I decided to launch a full-category strategy. My reasoning was simple: consumers wanted to buy a variety of goods, not just 3C products (computers, communication, and consumer electronics). I thought that if JD could satisfy those needs, we'd keep the consumers.

That same year, I decided we would build our own logistics system, integrating warehousing and distribution, partly because most of the customer complaints we received were about slow delivery and damaged products. Analysis showed that these pain points could not be fully addressed through the logistic services provided by third-party companies, so I concluded that the problem could only be tackled by building our own end-to-end logistics system. Again, we did not carry out professional, systematic cost estimates. In fact, as a company starting from scratch, we had little idea of how to go about that.

The sole objective was to provide better customer experiences. However, with better customer experience and a resulting increase in new users, JD's self-operation model also became increasingly heavier, with procurement, storage, distribution, customer service, and other links included. The industry questioned our approach. But what these sceptics failed to see (or perhaps willfully ignored) was the great reduction in costs and substantial increase in efficiency created by our model. What mattered in the end was not whether our model was as streamlined as others, but the value we created.

When the rapid expansion of JD's high-efficiency, low-cost operation inevitably collided with the traditional retail system, criticism exploded. Detractors accused us of destroying the original pricing system and affecting jobs, and JD was labelled an unwelcome "spoiler". I do not need to point out an inexorable truth: the efficient and advanced replaces the inefficient and backward. My goal was, and is, to return to the traditional foundation of retail and reassert that consumer satisfaction is the basic value of our existence. Frankly speaking, what concerns me most is consumer satisfaction, not competition among peers in the industry.

The good news is that, along with the gradual deepening of JD's market exploration, more and more manufacturers and brands have begun to appreciate how the reduced costs and better efficiency of e-commerce provides them with fast and effective low-cost sales platforms, as well as new precision marketing tools based on mass consumption data analysis. Trust is the basis of cooperation. Many manufacturers gradually accepted e-commerce companies like ours as their mainstream channel.

It is particularly worth mentioning that JD's recent exploration in IT manufacturing has also greatly enriched cooperation between e-commerce providers and manufacturers. JD's big-data platform can facilitate the transformation of traditional production. And, with the help of JD's equity crowdfunding financial platform, innovations can be exposed to the market earlier and more effectively. JD's exploration has enabled many manufacturing enterprises to embrace new transformation and upgrade opportunities. As we expand JD's platform, our supply-chain systems will continue to become more and more open.

Through interviews with many knowledgeable people, including nearly 260 JD employees holding a variety of positions, this book reveals our true selves to the public, hopefully dispelling doubts some may have about JD and helping potential partners to know more about us. In the future, JD, as a successful practitioner of China's "Internet Plus" initiative, will doubtless contribute to the transformation and upgrading of traditional industries across the country.

Of course, having strong faith in the value of JD's business model, I never worry when others question us, and I am even less concerned about whether external pressure will affect JD's share price. What I do fear is being infected by the complacency that takes hold in some large companies, because this would hinder us from perceiving customer demand in time and making targeted innovations.

Recently, we have been trying to fulfill new consumer demand by developing overseas and rural markets. We've also launched the "JD Door-to-Door Delivery" service by connecting off-line service and pioneering O2O (online to offline) programs to meet consumer demand for daily necessities. By expanding customer coverage, we hope to establish stronger customer loyalty and achieve full coverage of e-commerce retail services, step by step. In this process, through the adoption of JD's own IT advancements, we've upgraded and reconstructed the traditional commercial distribution system. We are committed to improving quality of life by offering genuine products with low prices and effective services to both rural and urban consumers.

We attach as much importance to the implementation of innovations as to making the ground-breaking changes themselves. Being innovation-driven is an important way for JD to attract, foster, and train talent. As Sam Walton said, the way to cultivate talent in retail is to hand the cart loaded with goods to a guy who just showed up and train him to be a capable, action-oriented doer. Faced with a rapidly growing e-commerce ecosystem, JD has done much more than focus on changes in consumer demand; we've cultivated talent and promoted from within.

For example, each year JD relocates 40% of its warehouses, which is unimaginable both for traditional delivery companies and offline bricks-and-mortar businesses. But for the employees working in JD's warehousing system, this is routine. As a result, everyone from executives to entry-level employees has been trained to move stock on short notice, and without affecting day-to-day operations. Our colleagues in R&D say upgrading large-scale systems is like "replacing a tyre while driving on the highway" because they have to execute rapid expansion without interrupting everyday business.

The key is that brilliant ideas – which can be as far-reaching as designing an open platform for third-party sellers or as basic as coming up with new shelving skills – take root and bloom in each and every business line and constitute the core of our competitiveness.

Over the past decade or more, I'd like to think that my openness with our employees has won their trust and faith in the company's future. And by sharing the company's success with them, I want to create a kind of cultural atmosphere of brotherhood in the company, so we can maintain the entrepreneurial passion for innovation together.

In 2015, JD's e-commerce business began its 12th year. And that represents an opportune time for the publication of this book. My hope is that it helps our veterans review the past and sustain their passion, and helps our new employees understand our history, so that every one of us can learn from the past to create a better future.

I would like to take this opportunity to thank our investors, shareholders, employees, partners, and customers for their great support. Without them, it would have been impossible for JD – and for me personally – to achieve so much. Of course, it is regrettable that, for their own reasons, many key players who appear in this book have left JD. But no matter where they are, I give them my gratitude, my blessing and my sincere hope that their lives grow ever better.

PREFACE

Why JD?

By Li Zhigang

I come from a village in Hubei Province. When I was growing up, shopping in my hometown was typically inconvenient. At the small stores, more often than not what we bought were counterfeits of brand-name beverages and instant noodles. If we wanted to buy home appliances, we had to travel 20 kilometres to a county where the distributors had stores. Even there, the choice of brands and models was far more limited than in China's first-tier cities. Later, my parents moved to a town. When I wanted to send things home, China Post was the only choice, because general express delivery companies did not yet deliver to small towns.

For a long time, retail development in China was unbalanced. Even China's largest retail chain, Suning, found it cost-prohibitive to set up stores in small county-level towns. In constructing a cross-country retail network, Chinese manufacturers relied on a distribution system that placed general national agencies at the top, followed by regional agencies at provincial, city, county, and town levels to cover the whole Chinese market.

In this distribution system, the flow of information, goods and capital was inefficient and quite unfair to consumers. Lack of information led to significant price-range differences in home appliances. For example, an electric rice cooker that sold for 99 yuan in first-tier cities was 119 on the outskirts, and 139 in village stores. For home appliances, the turnover period for major agents might be two or three months, but a year or more for smaller dealers, so the profit margins had to be high enough to sustain their existence.

Over the past few years, this seemingly solid distribution system, built over three decades, faced unprecedented challenges from e-commerce. JD built its position as an e-commerce company over 12 years of development. The company purchased directly from manufacturers and stocked the goods in JD warehouses. After consumers placed their orders via the JD website or mobile terminals, JD delivered to their door.

JD's 2014 annual report showed net income reached 115 billion yuan, representing year-on-year growth of 66%; Suning's turnover was 109.116 billion yuan, with year-on-year growth of 3.63%. This was the first time that JD bested Suning, and that milestone deserves to be recorded in the history of the Chinese retail industry.

It seems that the scent of gunpowder still lingers from 2012's "August 15 Price War". That year, Richard Liu launched a lightning raid using the Weibo social media platform and provoked a competitive skirmish in home appliance categories that targeted Suning and Gome. Subsequently, JD's competitors in e-commerce joined in and the price war turned into an all-out brawl.

JD was pushed into a tight corner for some time, but from a long-term strategic view, the company benefited. The price war attracted public attention to the e-commerce industry and many consumers became aware for the first time of the price differences in major appliances online and offline. Since then, sales of JD's major appliances experienced sustained growth, year after year. These events also marked the beginning of fierce confrontation between online and offline retailing formats. For China's traditional retail industry, the wolf had finally come to the door.

This is why I wanted to write this book. In my eyes, JD is a prime example of this business revolution.

First, it shook up a decades-old distribution system as well as the retail chains, and helped lift Chinese retailing formats from low- to high-efficiency mode.

Second, it enabled a fairer and more efficient information flow in society.

There will be detailed discussions of these two points in the book. Unlike other startup companies that subverted existing business models or patterns, the JD.com story is special because it embodies a brash upstart's "counter-attack" on a traditional industry. Liu started his business as an offline wholesaler. Later, he turned to retail chains. He delved into e-commerce almost accidentally; the internet and venture capital helped propel JD into the ranks of the world's top 10 internet enterprises.

Over the past 30 years or more, demographic changes, capital investment, and open markets created a golden age for Chinese manufacturing, foreign trade and export, real estate development and other businesses. However, the demographic bonus has been disappearing, overseas market demand has shrunk, and return on capital investment has fallen, forcing China to find or develop new drivers of economic growth. In Wenzhou, a shop owner told me a vivid story: a factory owner who lived across the street from him one day jumped from his balcony to his death. It was a day the shop owner would never forget; he even marked it on his calendar. That factory owner who committed suicide in Wenzhou symbolized the pain of economic transformation in China.

The key to China's economic growth lies in innovation, in enabling entrepreneurs to use new technologies and new models to achieve business transformation through equity financing – the most important catalyst for innovation. Over the past two years, I've talked or written about China's internet-driven business transformation on many occasions, and it is an extremely popular subject these days. Just like e-commerce in the retail industry, new technologies and new business models will subvert existing patterns in finance, healthcare, education, entertainment, energy, and other fields. Those who fail to meet customer demand, who stick with low efficiency, high transaction costs and over-regulation, risk being subsumed by innovation in the future.

Pioneering entrepreneurs – the visionaries behind today's business transformation – are digging the grave of traditional industries and blazing the trail toward a new order. They start by asking how to help users get better service and higher quality products at a lower cost. They stand ready to disrupt and reform anything that reduces efficiency in the traditional industries.

Three strategic decisions have played a decisive role in the development of JD. The first was to transition to e-commerce in 2004, when JD seized upon long-term consumer trends; the second was to expand to a full-category product portfolio by moving beyond a limited 3C products platform to a one-stop consumer superstore; the third was to build a logistics system, integrating warehousing and distribution into one. The latter two strategic decisions were made in 2007 and were ideas that Richard Liu fought for despite strong opposition from investors and management.

From 2007 to 2013, JD zeroed in on two imperatives: increasing the variety of online product offerings and making its own delivery capability broader and faster. JD gave customers nationwide a uniform price. E-commerce meant fairness in price, quality and information. For a long time, a brand that could be bought in a Beijing store was simply unavailable in a small county town in Sichuan. But through e-commerce, a person anywhere in the country could click the buy button and have that brand-name product quickly delivered to his or her home. The more remote the area, the more expensive the commodity, and the greater the value of JD, because it had upended the distribution system that raised prices at each stop along the path.

This process was like a game between JD and its suppliers, but it mapped to the general trend. A more efficient retail model was bound to replace a less efficient one. Manufacturers shipped their products to a JD warehouse and then to the customers with only JD in between. Links were cut and efficiencies enhanced.

Liu realized that "all innovation modes of the last ten or 20 years are related to transaction cost reduction and efficiency improvement. Only by lowering transaction costs or by making transactions more efficient can the new mode survive and develop. If the innovation mode fails to do so, then the innovation is meaningless."

Behind its improved transaction efficiency and reduced transaction costs was JD's powerful, sophisticated control over the supply chain.

It was easy for people to ignore the technical strength of JD, although research and development was its third-largest area of investment, behind only logistics and marketing. JD's innovative technology could be likened to a spring rain that moistens things silently. It covered everything, from the sales forecasting system, to the automatic replenishment systems that the buying and merchandising departments used, to the management system, and to maintaining the normal operations of warehousing and delivery.

The crux of an efficient retail business comes down to understanding what the consumer needs and reducing inventory costs by making good predictions of future sales. In traditional retail, operational efficiency was relatively difficult to control, mainly because it was hard to accurately predict fluctuating sales volumes. In 2001, when JD first engaged in retail, it tried to predict how many computer mice could be sold every year. Its forecasting proved to be sketchy at best. But by applying technology to the challenge, the company could record every aspect of consumer behaviour for data analysis. Big data drove JD's entire supply chain and distribution system. The accuracy of sales forecasting directly affected automatic procurement and vendor shipment as well as the inventory system downstream in the supply chain. Predictive sales tools also helped address the problems that plagued traditional retail: how to obtain the correct number of products to meet consumer needs via the right suppliers at a lower price, in real time, while maintaining product quality.

While it was possible to track and reflect the number of customers and their degree of activity and preferences online, it was difficult to do offline. A Chinese retail chain once installed recording devices at its stores' front doors to record foot traffic. However, the data obtained was far from relevant because it could only record how many people had entered the store, not whether or what they bought. As it happened, the foot traffic count was tied to employee performance evaluations, which led to fraud in some stores.

As JD's network connected suppliers, consumers, and entrepreneurs across the country through information, logistics and finance, it evolved into something more than a retail operation. It had become a technology-driven open platform that supported a rich diversity of consumer-facing businesses.

Parked next to Hualian supermarket near my home in Beijing, there was always a red Iveco van, painted with a white smiling dog and customized for a special purpose. The red-uniformed employees there were as busy as bees, handing one package after another to young customers emerging from the subway. The rush hour after work was the peak period for collecting packages. The van served as JD.com's product pick-up site.

In many Chinese cities, JD was already a household name. On its website one could order goods at a cheaper price than offline and have them delivered via its own logistics system. In addition to door-to-door delivery, JD also gave customers the choice of self-collection, at a time that was convenient to them. JD had become an enterprise with an annual turnover of 260.2 billion yuan, with nearly 70,000 employees and logistics covering 1,862 districts and counties across the country. (There are 2,860 districts and counties in China.) In the spring of 2012 I visited an e-commerce investor. "JD wants to become Amazon plus UPS," he said. "It's chasing a rainbow." It just goes to show that there are times when you can make the impossible possible and reap unimagined rewards.

In 2014, Amazon started to build its own distribution system and, like JD, attempted to control the crucial "last mile" to the customer's doorstep.

Liu accomplished many things that others said were impossible. If everybody thought a thing could be easily done, then what was the value of it? JD was a company engaged in some of the world's most toilsome work, and it eked out razor-thin profits.

In recent years, as the business landscape has been reshaped, there have been both fierce clashes and unprecedented cooperation within traditional industries. Companies with new technologies and new models became more deeply involved in the supply chain. For example, competition among video websites had been limited to on-line content purchase and broadcasting. Before long, those sites not only participated in content production upstream, but also stretched themselves downstream to the production and sale of player devices, like internet television hardware.

Companies became heavier and heavier by stretching in this way. Investors began funding emerging companies that were taking this path.

For young entrepreneurs, this meant more challenges. In the past, they just needed to know about the internet, how to write code, how to manage engineers and product managers. But now they needed to develop expertise in disciplines like supply-chain management and offline team management. For those geeks immersed in the 0 and 1 binary world, an offline team was like another world. Put another way, the engineering team and the ground labor force were like China's urban-rural binary opposition structure, and skillful managers had to bridge the gap. That's what entrepreneurs could learn from Liu. Faced with such conflicts, how did JD integrate people with different ways of thinking into a whole? That is also what this book is about.

In the pages that follow, I've divided JD's history into three broad, evolutionary stages.

The first stage stretched from 1998 to 2006. During this period, Liu put in place the basic structure to attract users, acquire capital and build the teams he needed to transition from offline to online retail, and gain a foothold in the e-commerce space.

The second stage was from 2007 to 2010. It was during this time that JD secured its first venture capital. This investment provided JD a doorway through to the internet and propelled it into a period of rapid growth. The first batch of professional managers started to join the company, and two major strategies were pursued: expansion to a full-category catalogue and creation of a logistics system that integrated warehousing and last-mile distribution.

The third stage extended from 2011 to the present day. This period saw JD continue its rapid expansion. New levels of capitalization not only supported JD's enormous logistics investment, but also broadened Liu's horizons. He became determined to move beyond China and embrace the global marketplace. JD's businesses diversified. "Opening up" became the new theme. Meanwhile, JD continued to strengthen its internal organization by hiring more experienced executives, optimizing organizational structures, and crafting a culture that rallied the workforce into a team with a common vision. JD had undeniably become a large corporation.

"This entire process requires updating and upgrading the team," said Liu. "That can be difficult for entrepreneurial types. An entrepreneurial team is unlikely to find the very best talent at the outset. But with entrepreneurs that's almost unnecessary. If there is an opportunity and a mutual recognition between team members, they will just do it."

However, once the company began to mature, expand and add new personnel, it faced the inevitable problem of weak management. The ability to learn quickly was essential in this era, but not everyone had the ability to keep up. What was to be done when veteran team members could no longer match the pace of this energetic, hard-charging company?

I found that some start-up companies remained in the hands of founding-stage veterans, even though their management shortcomings had become a bottleneck. I also found that some start-up companies aggressively introduced professional managers but failed to properly manage the older veteran workers. New culture conflicted with the old culture, producing internal friction. Management was never about feelings, and rationality had its cruel side. The process of building and upgrading the team tested every entrepreneur's management skills. JD started from a sales counter, a stall in Beijing's bustling Zhongguancun market. Very few internet companies had such a modest beginning. But this company faced the test of dramatically upgrading its team, and it passed with flying colours.

From that small counter in Zhongguancun to a company that approached $45 billion in market value, JD's development could be understood by examining three key elements: strategy, execution and corporate culture.

Strategy: JD was not created by Richard Liu alone. But its core strategies absolutely originated with him. Transforming to e-commerce, expanding to a full-category portfolio, and building independent logistics were JD's three foundational strategies. These imperatives did not emerge following rigorous calculation, but from focused business insight. The starting point was elevating the customer experience above all else. JD began drilling down into logistics because customers complained about the terrible service provided by third-party carriers. With an overriding goal of satisfying customers, the team stepped back through the ways it could re-balance costs and efficiencies. The desired end-point was, without exception, customer satisfaction.

Execution: JD's execution was perhaps the strongest and most efficient of all the companies I have seen. And that had everything to do with the fact that JD started in retail, and retail was all about a rigorous organizational chain and resolute execution.

Corporate Culture: The efficient executive force combined with employees' embrace of the company's vision to create a cohesive team. The complexity of managing JD was staggering, due in part to its rapid growth from 1,000 to 70,000 employees in just six years. Adding to that complexity was its shift from selling entirely offline to entirely online. As mentioned earlier, JD had to build a bridge spanning China's urban-rural social and demographic divide. At the heart of JD's culture, Liu created a fair and just environment in which talented people earned rewards – pay, position and status – based on performance.

When I first approached Liu about this book, he said he was in a transitional period – moving from entrepreneur to business leader – and it was too early to write the JD story. I agreed with him. But I also knew that if I didn't begin to record this story then and there, many living testimonials would never be heard. Memories would fade with time. Eventually, all that would remain would be dry spreadsheets and boring meeting transcripts. If we start the clock at 2004, then JD had been engaged in e-commerce for 12 years. There must have been some experiences and lessons worth sharing with others. This was my original intention in writing this book. I hoped it would give readers a better understanding of JD, and perhaps even some inspiration.

Introduction

On 22 May 2014, the NASDAQ Stock Exchange in New York City was covered in scaffolding. The place was a mess. Billboards with a red background and the white letters "JD" were everywhere.

In a first floor studio, a presenter was broadcasting stock quotes of NASDAQ-listed companies: Apple, Baidu, Cisco, Facebook, Google, Intel, Microsoft, Amazon. Virtually every listed company in science and technology you could think of flashed by, one after the other, before my eyes.

At 9:30 am, Richard Liu, sharply dressed in a suit and in high spirits, rang the opening bell. His company, JD, with $3.1 billion in financing, was officially listed on NASDAQ. Its market value that day hit $28.6 billion.

A huge LED screen in New York's Times Square displayed Liu's face. At the same time, across the Pacific Ocean in Beijing, a night-time crowd cheered wildly in an open atrium of North Star Century Center, JD's corporate headquarters.

Liu began his stock-exchange remarks by addressing "JDers", but immediately realized he was now speaking to a broader global audience and changed to, "ladies and gentlemen". It amused the hundreds of people assembled before him, including many Chinese investors and business executives.

After the listing, by virtue of the public offering's structure, Liu retained 83.7% of voting power with his shareholding ratio of 18.8%.

In 2009, Zhou Wei, partner at KPCB China, had considered investing in JD. But at that time, JD experienced a major drop in profits, so he declined. In 2011, when he finally decided to invest, the share price was more than 10 times higher.

Zhou said, half-jokingly: "My hand was shaking when I signed the contract." Then came the internal debate over whether JD could grow to the size of Amazon, or even eclipse it. "Liu and his team can endure hardship," said Zhou. "He can survive with razor-thin profits. This is the value brought from his past experience. E-commerce is an extremely hard job and no one compares with Liu. If it were a pure internet company, he might not have excelled."

Back then, many people had argued with Zhou about 's prospects. They worried about its gross margin. If JD were a second-tier e-commerce company, Zhou thought, it would have needed to focus on gross margin. But it was already a marketplace leader. The leadership, scale, and potential of the company were evident to him.

On 22 May, Liu announced that the first portion of the $3.1 billion obtained through the IPO would be invested in developing business in third- to sixth-tier Chinese cities.

That had Xu Xin, who invested in JD in 2007, smiling from ear to ear. "Imagine, returns of 150 times my original investment," Xu said. "But what pleases me most is helping an enterprise develop into a great company. JD will become a great company. I still own 7% and I won't sell it. I want to hold it for the long term. There are not many great companies in the world. I am lucky to have found one." Liu had told her: "The current share price is not important, but it will be after 10 years."

Back in 2007, when JD received its first infusion of venture capital, the company hosted a feast to celebrate. Drinks flowed freely. Everyone hoped JD would someday go public and become a great company. At NASDAQ, Sun Jiaming, vice president of JD Group and general manager for the General Merchandise Division, represented the company's very first employees. He stood in the front row, appearing unexcited. The most exciting moment for him was when he'd had the vision, years earlier, to join a company that was destined for greatness.

Upon listing in the US, JD had received the largest IPO financing of any Chinese company to date. (The record was beaten by Alibaba when it went public in the US later that year.) NYSE and NASDAQ vied for the IPO; JD chose NASDAQ only two months prior to the listing. Robert Greifeld, NASDAQ CEO, and Zheng Hua, NASDAQ's chief representative for China, had reached out to Liu many times. "Richard Liu is a very ambitious man," said Zheng. "He devoted himself to the company for more than ten years. He is formidable and persistent. He has great and lasting ambition. He is also very patient." Zheng saw Liu and his achievements as embodying the spirit of the bronze charging bull statue in the heart of New York's financial district. And who could argue?

At that evening's IPO reception, Liu spoke in English marked by the accent of Suqian, his home town in Jiangsu province. "I walked from the small village of Suqian to Beijing, which took 20 years. Then I took another 20 years to walk from Beijing to New York," he said. Everyone laughed. "What is our new target, our new goal? I hope that in the next 20 years, our customers or partners will be found in every city and every country in the world."

On 10 April 2015, JD's market value reached $45.4 billion, making it the fourth-largest internet company in China.

PART I

1998-2006

In 2004, Liu turned to e-commerce from the offline retail chain business, making the most important strategic move in the history of JD. The decision was driven by both accidental and inevitable factors. Liu showed that it was necessary, with the advent of the internet revolution, for a traditional enterprise to be brave enough to abandon a successful past.

Starting Up at a Market Stall

"Nothing is more miserable in the world than boating, blacksmithing and tofu-selling," goes a popular local saying in Suqian City, Jiangsu Province. The Grand Canal from Beijing to Hangzhou runs through Suqian from south to north, and many of the local families survive on boating and shipping.

One night in the spring of 1998, walls of waves crashed into a 40-ton iron freighter. In the cabin, Wang Shaoxia bailed furiously as more and more water rushed in. The ship was sinking, with all Wang's family belongings in it. Seeing that 20 years of painstaking efforts would be washed away, she felt helpless. She wanted to hold on to the bow and just go down with the ship. At that moment, she suddenly thought of her children and her elderly mother. Out of instinct, she jumped onto an adjacent boat to save her life. Ten seconds later, the bow of her vessel disappeared under the water. Because it was unlucky to cry on someone else's ship, Wang worked hard to control her tears. She remained on the vessel for three days, silent. Only when she was ashore and saw her sister did she burst into tears.

After the shipwreck, Wang stayed at her mother's home and kept the news from her son, Richard Liu, who was working far away in Beijing. When Liu called his grandmother's house, he found it strange that his mother always answered. "Mum, why are you at home instead of on the boat?" he asked. "Our boat ... has sunk!" Wang replied. "And Dad?" Liu sounded very anxious. "He is all right," Wang replied. "We want to borrow money to buy a new boat."

"As long as you are alive, everything's all right," Liu said. "Please don't go boating any more. I will repay the money!"

On 18 June 1998, with 12,000 yuan he had saved, the 24-year-old Liu rented a 4m² stall in Haikai Market in Zhongguancun. He bought a used computer, a second-hand tricycle, and started his entrepreneurial journey. JD Multimedia, the predecessor of JD, was thus founded.

That year, China's economy was undergoing a period of anxiety and excitement. On one hand, a large number of people in collective-owned units and state-owned enterprises were laid off and the old "iron rice bowl" guarantee of lifetime security was broken. Many families faced a dense fog of uncertainty. At the same time, private enterprises were flourishing. Three places in China became the most dynamic business zones: Pearl River Delta, Zhejiang Province (represented by Wenzhou), and Zhongguancun in Beijing. Pearl River Delta and Wenzhou were noted for foreign trade and manufacturing businesses. Zhongguancun, sometimes called the Silicon Valley of Beijing, was regarded as the cradle of intellectual heroes working in the IT industry. From 1988 to 1998, Zhongguancun developed at a fast pace, with an average of one new company founded every day.

China's internet industry was on the rise, with Zhongguancun at its centre. Thanks to a new policy of openness after years of seclusion, the Chinese economy finally caught up with the latest global trends. Charles Zhang, an overseas returnee who founded Sohu, was ranked by Time Digital among the world's top 50 digital elite in 1998. Yahoo!, founded by Jerry Yang, was a star company. Highly sought after by Wall Street since its listing in 1996, its stock price peaked in 2000.

Google came into being that same year. Baidu made a late appearance in China in 2000. Jack Ma was still working on his Chinese yellow pages and Alibaba had yet to be founded. No one could have predicted that the Chinese internet would be dominated by three giants (Baidu, Tencent, and Alibaba) in the years to come. And no one could have predicted that JD would become China's fourth-largest internet company.

In 1998, JD Multimedia was engaged in a pedestrian offline business: stocking and selling goods at a rented counter in a large building, first at wholesale, then retail. China's retail industry developed in a short period of time after the arrival of the open market economy. In its early stages, the market was full of extravagant profits, confusion, chaos, fraud and corruption.

At stores in Zhongguancun, authorized goods and knock-offs were sold side by side. Whether consumers could buy products at the right price depended largely on how savvy they were and their ability to bargain. If buyers didn't pay close attention, sellers sometimes took advantage of them. JD Multimedia was born in this environment.

Liu's approach differed from many sellers in Zhongguancun. He had no set purchasing channel, no financial backing, no team. He did his business alone and insisted on selling his products with clearly marked prices. He refused to bargain. Many customers first turned to other counters for better prices, but eventually came back to Liu because they found his prices were more reasonable for genuine products. He made his first sale at 98 yuan. Slowly, through word of mouth, JD Multimedia accumulated a loyal group of customers. Three months after he started his business, Liu was too busy to handle everything alone and hired his first employee.

JD Multimedia originally focused on video-editing hardware and systems for wedding photo studios. With the expansion of the company, Liu moved his stall from Haikai Market to the PKU Resources Building, facing the Silicon Valley Computer City, where he rented three offices in succession. The company began to sell magneto-optical products, CD burners and videotape conversion systems, 70% of which were sold to retail counters – much like the one where he'd first set up his business, at Computer City in Zhongguancun – and 30% to individuals. In 2002, JD Multimedia opened its first counter on the third floor of Silicon Valley Computer City, selling CDs as well. The business turnover rate was as much as 80% higher here, because JD Multimedia employees sold the products and provided additional technical services.

During this period, Liu laid the foundation for the future JD Mall.

Authentic Products

Unlike most of the other sellers, Liu began issuing invoices when he first started his business in Haikai Market. Invoicing meant that proper taxes were being paid and that the transaction was entirely above board. It was a declaration: "I sell authorized goods." That gave customers full confidence in their purchases. The Administration for Industry and Commerce at one point audited JD Multimedia for three days and found no tax evasion, no smuggled goods, no fake discs. Copying CDs was a common and easy process; one just silk-screened a logo onto blank discs and created packaging identical to the genuine ones. By doing this, gross margins could be dozens of times higher than for authorized products.

But Liu refused to create or sell knock-offs. He sacrificed easy profits to sell only authentic goods at lower prices, which had no competitive advantage compared with the counterfeit CDs that were ubiquitous in Zhongguancun. One customer who worked in data backup for a bank sought 300 to 500 CDs at first, saying he would purchase in bulk if the quality was good. But the customer was dissatisfied after finding JD Multimedia's price much higher than the other counters'. Gang Jian, later the general manager of operations management for JD's Home Appliances Business, told the sceptical customer: "If you believe that what the others sell are authentic products, then go for them." He showed the customer proof that JD Multimedia's goods were valid and authorized, and pointed out that, if the CDs were to be used for data backup, then quality mattered and he should be wary of cheap discs that could fail after a few days. This struck a chord with the customer, who continued purchasing from JD. He felt the products had the best cost performance and that JD called a spade a spade, without cheating or swindling.

In 2011, Pacific Digital City in Zhongguancun closed down, causing a stir in the industry. At that time, China's e-commerce was the rising sun. The company that by then was called JD Mall exceeded 30 billion yuan in sales and became the leader of self-support B2C (business to consumer) e-commerce in China. In contrast, the computer cities in Zhongguancun were the setting sun. A large number of counters closed and the building emptied. Liu remembers an exchange he related to some colleagues after the market closed: "Last night I chatted with some friends. A classmate said, 'Congratulations, you've killed Pacific Digital City.' Astonishing! In fact, you were not beaten by JD, but by yourself! Ask yourself, how many times have you substituted the fake for the genuine? How many smuggled goods and fakes have you sold? How many customers have you cheated? What goes around comes around!"

Low Price

Liu believed in small profits but quick turnover, and he knew that the controlling force lay in scale. A company would never dominate if its sales volumes remained 2-3% of the total market. "You can't always count on windfall profits," he said. "From the start-up to now, there is no such phrase as 'windfall profits' in my dictionary. What is the biggest problem with many businesses in Zhongguancun? They had the idea of windfall profits. They wanted to earn 20 million yuan from an order of 50 million yuan. From the first day of our business to now, we have been planning on a long-term basis, and we have had small profits but fast turnover, with scale as our first priority."

At the peak of the magneto-optical products boom, JD had a 60% market share in China. This was achieved through low prices. Price wars had always been JD's most direct and productive means of competition. They often involved setting different prices in the morning and afternoon. JD beat other agents with this strategy and, as a result, became an exclusive agent.

JD employees called some of the difficult customers "hard nuts" and experienced salesmen told Sun Jiaming not to deal with them anymore. Sun discussed it with Liu, who told him to try anyway, that maybe they could be won over by another, more resourceful salesman. Just as newborn calves don't know enough to be afraid of tigers, Sun actually had the gall to knock on the doors of the toughest customers. But these big buyers remained indifferent to him. Every day, he told Liu about his unsuccessful encounters and Liu taught him to modify his approach.

Liu suggested lowering prices. A price near cost, sometimes even lower, was offered to the customers every day. Whether the customers bought or not, they'd be offered new quotes every day. Sooner or later, they'd find it would be their loss not to buy from JD Multimedia. They bargained with other sellers but were rebuffed. Then, they might place a trial order with Sun. Finally, once an agreement was reached, customers would place new orders with JD Multimedia and continue to do so as long as the price was no higher than elsewhere. In the long run, it was worth it if it secured a steady stream of repeat customers.

Good Service

When JD Multimedia sold wedding photography and video conversion systems in Haikai Market, it faced clients who knew little about IT hardware and technology. So, in addition to providing products, Liu also began offering technical training. Chen Shikuan, later director of planar image production at JD University, joined JD Multimedia in 1998 as a technical engineer. He spent 15 days training a client from northeast China in every aspect of computer use. The customer didn't even know how to use the mouse at first: he had tried holding it up and gesturing in the air with it. As part of his training, the customer learned how to burn a CD.

Once Chen incorrectly edited a customer's video, resulting in poor definition. Liu criticized him, saying he must redo the project to the customer's complete satisfaction.

JD's concept was simple: deliver better services to customers and they will return. More than 10 years later, JD had become an e-commerce giant with annual sales of 260 billion yuan. Looking back, it was fascinating to see that the "customer first" approach that remained central to this huge company's values had originated at a small sales counter in Zhongguancun in 1998.

Stepping into E-Commerce

While Liu worked like a horse, the Chinese retail industry was developing along the lines of professional chain stores, best represented by Suning and Gome, with home appliances as their primary products. In 1998, Gome closed its small stores in downtown Beijing and opened a large, 2,000m² location in a shopping centre near the Third Ring Road. This reflected the new criteria for appliance sales site selection: a business area of more than 1,000m² and a warehouse of 200m². Since 2000, Suning and Gome had expanded nationwide by rapidly opening new stores, with Gome opening more than 300 a year.

The retail format of offline chain stores reached a peak in 2004 after Gome and Suning each went public, using their IPO capital for acquisitions and rapid expansion. Huang Guangyu, the founder of Gome, topped the list of richest people in China in 2004 and 2005.

At the same time, a new retail business model, e-commerce, began its quiet ascent in China. Strangely, the country's retail industry all but ignored it. The internet industry showed great interest. There was excitement on one side and dead silence on the other. In 1999, Wang Juntao founded 8848, the pioneer – and ultimately the martyr – of Chinese e-commerce. The company relied on Lianbang, a software sales company, which offered relatively complete supply chain management. However, after two years of rapid development, 8848 suffered serious internal friction and missed the window for listing while it waited for its finances to improve.

In 1999, Li Guoqing and his wife Peggy Yu co-founded Dangdang. They began by selling books online, similar to what Amazon was doing so far away in Seattle. Shao Yibo also returned to China and started EachNet, a website similar to eBay. In the following year, Joyo.com, an e-commerce company also similar to Amazon, was founded. Back then, there were two e-commerce models: B2C, with Amazon as the template; and C2C, or consumer-to-consumer, the model that had eBay as its template for online auctions. Amazon was founded in 1994 by Jeff Bezos, an entrepreneur of great vision and quick temper. On 15 May 1997, when Amazon was listed, its stock price was $18. By April 2015, it had reached $370, with the company's market value topping $170 billion.

Amazon's business model was to purchase merchandise from brands and manufacturers and stock them in its own warehouses. Users ordered on Amazon's website and received their purchases via UPS, FedEx, and other carriers who completed "the last mile" transportation and delivery. When Liu was establishing JD Multimedia, Amazon had already hired Wal-Mart logistics executives and was spending $300 million a year on warehouse construction.

The internet surged to new heights. NASDAQ, dominated by internet companies, broke 2,000 points in 1998 and approached 5,000 in December 1999. In a rising stock market, Amazon's stock price climbed to $106.69. But in April 2000, the bubble burst. Market value of $8.5 trillion evaporated overnight and Amazon's value fell from $22.8 billion to $4.2 billion.

In 1999, another B2B e-commerce company called Alibaba was founded by Jack Ma in China. Alibaba gathered China's foreign trade businesses on its website and made a profit by providing paid services to merchants – TrustPass and the ranking of search engines for Adwords Advertising.

The rise of e-commerce and the complexities of doing business over the internet were far removed from Liu's JD Multimedia business. He buried himself in the retail world, researching inventory and procurement. It all seemed to be thriving until 6 March 2003. On that day public health authorities in Beijing reported the first cases of Severe Acute Respiratory Syndrome (SARS). The shadow of death loomed across the country. Streets from Beijing to Guangzhou were nearly empty. The retail industry, so dependent on foot traffic, suffered a heavy blow. All computers in Zhongguancun went on sale, with average price reductions of 30-40%. For IT products, the greater the backlog, the cheaper they become. In 21 days, JD lost more than 8 million yuan and the company's paper capital sunk to less than 30 million yuan. In those dark days many people thought it could take from six months to a year to get over SARS.

Liu was afraid that his employees could become infected, so he closed down all 12 of JD Multimedia's sales counters. Some of the staff left Beijing before the highways were closed. The rest stayed in the office and Liu cooked their meals. If losses continued like this, the company would wither and die in two or three months. Liu's staff met to look for a way out. One colleague said: "We can't meet customers for transactions face-to-face. Why don't we try to trade via the internet? We don't have to meet each other then."

The employees of JD Multimedia started marketing CDs using online postings. On a bulletin board called CDbest, a moderator wrote a message saying that JD Multimedia was the only company he knew that never sold fake discs. JD had built its reputation on five years of selling genuine goods and genuine goods only. And now these efforts would pay off. Thanks to the moderator's recognition, JD won the trust – and, more importantly, the purchase orders – of an initial 21 online buyers. This marked the first step into online retail for JD. The approach was simple: initiate group-buying activities on a bulletin board system, with published product descriptions, prices and sale deadlines. Li Mei, director of the JD Mall Administration Centre, was known as "the first person of JD e-commerce". She was the first JD Multimedia employee formally responsible for online sales. She recorded customer lists with pen and paper and, after receiving payment, she would find the goods and package them one by one, in accordance with the customer's requirements. After that, she'd mail the packages via regular postal channels and send the customers tracking numbers via text message. If the customers were near Zhongguancun, the goods were delivered to their doors by the company driver in a Jinbei van or by Richard Liu himself in his Hongqi sedan.

Liu adopted his usual low price tactic, even selling CD-burning devices below cost, which was well received by customers. JD Multimedia took the opportunity to clean up inventory and open up the market. Selling under-priced burners might be a money-loser in and of itself, but customers would buy more profitable CDs after they bought the burners.

Liu's interest in the internet began to grow. He began web-surfing day and night. He posted at midnight and might be found responding to comments at 5 am. The company had relocated to the Yinfeng Building on Suzhou Street, Zhongguancun. It was the first property Liu had ever bought, and served as both his office and his residence. He napped on the floor at night when he felt tired and worked normally during the day, but he was essentially working around the clock. Liu looked excited, like a changed man in the eyes of his employees.

After selling on other websites for six months, Liu decided to establish an independent site to sell products. Not only did he want to control the customer contacts himself, he was troubled by the ever-escalating commissions that the CDbest bulletin board charged. On 1 January 2004, *www.jdlaser.com* was formally launched online. It featured more than 100 items, but the website was rather rough. On the product page, none of the items had compelling product or brand descriptions, just basic text and dull product specifications, with two or three pictures.

JD Multimedia was technically so weak that I'd rank it among the internet companies with the lowest technological starting point. Liu knew programming, but he was a complete internet layman. Xin Bo, the company's most technically competent employee, had done video editing, but was by no means a professional technician. The simplest system patches and firewalls were left undone. As a result, the site was constantly breached by hackers who left messages like, "JD's webmaster is a big idiot". When he learned of this Xin hurried to the server centre and solved the problem in two hours. But before he returned to his office, hackers had left a follow-up message: "JD's webmaster is still an idiot." Luckily, the perpetrators did no damage beyond poking fun at the company. Subsequently, Liu recruited JD's first formal technician, Lv Ke, who later became senior director of operations and maintenance in JD's R&D department.

Focused Determination

In 2003, China's offline retail giants were still indifferent to e-commerce. But foreign players began to take notice of the opportunity. In 2003, eBay acquired Eachnet. In 2004, Amazon took over Joyo.com and entered the Chinese market.

In 2004, Liu gathered his team together to discuss dropping the company's offline businesses and becoming a purely online retail company. He'd concluded that the offline user experience was unsatisfactory. Online, consumers could just click and buy without bargaining. They could distinguish the authentic from the fake, and they could buy cheaper products and still get proper invoices. Moreover, JD's online growth was much higher than offline.

Liu's ideas did not gain much support. Employees argued that internet penetration was low and not many people had computers. Internet orders were not seen as reliable and the market was uncertain. Although online growth was rapid, that was attributable to the small base. Who knew whether the growth would continue?

In 2003, JD Multimedia had a sales volume of 80 to 90 million yuan and was the largest domestic seller of magneto-optical products. The company planned to open 500 stores in the future both to fuel and to fulfill the explosive offline growth they expected. Meanwhile, Suning and Gome were competing with each other by opening stores across the country. Taking Suning and Gome as references, Liu's employees believed their offline future would be brighter. There was a clear business model and better profit margins. Why take another path with an uncertain future?

Without Liu's stubbornness, today's JD wouldn't exist. In meetings he listened to everyone's opinions, chose the ones that conformed to his thinking and then guided the discussion in the direction he desired. The outcome would be, more or less, the notion he had formed before the meeting. He anticipated his employees' opposition, and overruled their objections. He had made up his mind to close the stores.

In the end, all of the company's retail sales counters were closed except one, kept solely for purchases. Due to its roots there, JD Multimedia had relationships from agents in various Zhongguancun stores and by maintaining a presence, JD could get wholesale prices that were impossible for individual customers to land. This sole counter was kept open until 2006.

Some employees left the company when Liu decided to close the stores, because they thought the boss was taking foolish chances and were afraid of what would happen if the transition went wrong.

If JD had not started e-commerce and had not closed its offline stores, then its path would have been to develop chain stores. It would have watched as e-commerce siphoned away its offline market share while still feeling reluctant to abandon the cumbersome stores after years of investment and expansion.

A small boat can make an easy turn. Liu's focus and determination helped him catch up with the newly rising Chinese e-commerce market. Having survived the internet bubble that burst between 2000 and 2002, China's internet was revived. In 2003, William Ding, the founder of NetEase, became China's new richest man. The country's digital elites brought a breath of fresh air to Chinese business: their rapid wealth accumulation stemmed from knowledge innovation, from the creativity of talented teams, from clear stock ownership incentives, from public and transparent capital promotion, and from modern enterprise systems. It was these people who would create the most exciting stories of success over the next decade, gradually replacing an older generation of entrepreneurs and becoming China's new business leaders.

Few e-commerce companies had survived the internet bubble, and it wasn't until 2005 that the real growth of Chinese e-commerce began. Liu was lucky enough to climb on board at precisely the right time.

Like JD Multimedia, many sellers in Zhongguancun eventually ran stores and websites at the same time. But most of these websites faded away. Newcomers to e-commerce, everyone had to explore and learn one step at a time. The companies doing both were not highly motivated to learn new ways of doing business because their physical stores took up too much of their time.

Liu's concentration and focus were key to JD's early traction in the marketplace. He had learned the importance of these qualities from his parents, who had run many businesses, including a small factory, a shipping operation and a wholesale store.

Various Chinese industries – foreign trade, real estate development and others – had made money over the preceding decade. But Liu didn't try any of them. He believed that he would succeed if he concentrated on one thing and did it well. He thought those who shifted from one trade to another, just because others made money here or there, would always end up with nothing done properly.

After more than a decade, Liu had the following views on the nature of business, and JD is an outcome of this philosophy:

First, business was made up of chains. One could not rely on intuition, but had to use sophisticated analyses to make business judgments. Every chain was linked with another. You'd know what you had to do next when you had a well-considered plan. Eventually, the financial products JD brought to market would be inseparable from e-commerce. Without e-commerce, JD's financing business would never have existed.

Second, the most basic tenet of doing business was quite simple: create value and gain profits. Profit was the curve, but value was the baseline, and it was constant. Income might be higher or lower than the value, but no matter how it fluctuated, it wouldn't deviate terribly far from value. The earnings trend and the value trend had to be convergent. You could create value and become rich by collecting waste paper.

JD's logistics expansion was based on value. Providing shopping platforms, improving logistics to ensure better consumer experiences, reducing costs, and improving inventory turnover rates all created value.

As public trust and confidence in JD grew, customers began to request more products from the company. They wanted to buy things like CPUs (central processing units), hard discs and CD players. They continued posting their demands on bulletin boards. Liu pushed his staff to stock certain categories. No one knew what might sell well and what might not. Purchasing was driven exclusively by customer demand. To meet that demand, the purchasing team would first get goods from Zhongguancun, then warehouse and shelve them.

Confident that JD Multimedia's merchandise was genuine and knowing it sold at lower prices, customers flocked to the company.

At the end of 2004, following JD's annual meeting, Liu felt for the first time that the business was on solid footing. When it had been acting simply as an agent for suppliers, the company faced great risk and could have faced ruin if suppliers no longer chose to authorize JD to sell their products. In other words, JD's fate rested in the hands of others. There certainly seemed to be lots of customers, but without supply, there would be nothing to offer them. At the end of each year, Liu worried about whether he could connect with the right kinds of suppliers the following year. On the internet, JD connected directly with its customers. It could buy products from Zhongguancun stores and sell them to consumers. Now the stranglehold that had been suffocating them finally loosened. By having direct relationships with enough customers, you could turn the tables and put the stranglehold on your competitors.

In Liu's words: "Success in retail, in its essence, is to understand consumers and deliver what they need into their hands. A retail business only needs to do two things: cut costs and improve efficiency. Traditional retail shares many similarities with e-commerce, such as procurement costs, marketing costs, inventory costs, and so on. Offline retail businesses have rental costs, and store location largely determines foot traffic. With commercial real estate becoming more and more expensive, rental costs will also be higher and higher. For online retail, the costs are in buying traffic, IT research and development, and logistics."

He continued: "You need to do nothing but understand the consumer's needs and reduce inventory costs by making precise predictions about future sales. Traditional retail operational efficiency is relatively difficult to control, and sales forecasting is nearly impossible. In 2001, when JD engaged in retail business, it tried to predict how many computer mice could be sold every year but those projections were inaccurate. Supply chain management for traditional retail and for the e-commerce marketplace is nearly identical. Purchasing and operating are essentially the same."

When offline retailing reached a certain scale, Liu said, it was difficult to avoid the three-tier management structure of headquarters, branches, and dealers. Likewise, it was hard to avoid conflicts between direct sales and franchisees. Online retailing, however, could establish a centralized management structure. All work could be done at headquarters, with logistics and customer service set up elsewhere.

Liu cited Southwest Airlines, a company that focused mainly on inter-city routes in the US and was famous for its low-cost operations. For decades, while the major US airlines were struggling, Southwest was profitable. "All successful innovation models over the last 10 or 20 years were related to transaction cost reduction and efficiency improvement," he said.

An Unpolished
Gem

Liu broadened his horizons at every step. He started his business from a humble sales counter and reached online sales of 10 million yuan by 2005, although with razor-thin profits. That year, the owner of Beareyes.com offered Liu 18 million yuan for his site and he nearly sold it. Had Liu agreed, the future of Chinese e-commerce very likely wouldn't have included him.

He discussed the offer with Sun Jiaming and Zhang Qi, later a senior director of operations at Paipai.com. Sun and Zhang were against the idea: this company was created with their collective efforts. What will we do if you sell it, they wondered. Liu thought that if he sold, he would probably turn around and create a new, very similar site. So instead he decided to carry on with JD.

In 2005, JD established its online purchasing department and Sun Jiaming became its head. Insular, and having little contact with the outside world, JD didn't know about Newegg.com. The people of JD know only how to work like plow-horses. Newegg, founded in 2001, entered the Chinese market before Amazon and by 2005 had sales of $1.3 billion. For a considerable period, Newegg was the first choice for many Chinese consumers purchasing IT products online.

In 2005, Newegg was a foreign enterprise with American blood. Its sales dwarfed those of JD, which was still a crude and unpolished start-up, rough in every way. JD deliveries took 10 to 15 days, and packages got lost on the way. Customers grew impatient. "Last mile" delivery service was terrible in China. Most distribution stations were franchised stores and service quality was unstable and hard to control.

JD Multimedia had no management system for warehousing, no shelf numbers, no barcodes. Packaging personnel located goods purely by memory. New warehouse management staff spent nearly a week identifying the more than 300 different products and memorizing their respective locations. It was not until 2006, when the company moved warehouses to Phoenix Mountain, in Beijing's northwest Haidian District, that they began shelf-number management of the warehouse. Even then, the concept wasn't supported by the older staff: "Why create shelf numbers? We can remember them. What a burden to add a number before shelving!" Fortunately, Liu understood the advantages of shelf management: quick retrieval based on a numerical system, not human memory, made for a more professionally efficient and scalable process.

Nor was there was any monitoring system in the warehouse. Some customers claimed that they had ordered two CDs but received only one. JD had no way to tell, and so – because customer satisfaction was primary – they would send off a second item. Later, as one interim solution, JD Multimedia weighed all the packages before shipping to the customers.

To save money, Liu asked employees to bring discarded cartons back to the office for reuse. Once, Liu saw a couple throwing a pile of household appliance cartons on the side of the road. He pulled over, picked up the cartons and stuffed them in his trunk. He heard the wife said to her husband, "Look, that rubbish collector must be better off than you. He's driving a better car!"

JD continued expanding categories based on consumer needs, from CDs and burners to mice, keyboards, memory sticks, hard discs – and then notebook computers. Notebooks were high-end products at the time, costing more than 10,000 yuan each. Liu hesitated. What if they didn't sell?

Moving warehouses became an integral part of JD's development history because each move meant its sales volume had doubled. In 2002, Liu bought Room 1202 in the Yinfeng Building, which served both as an office and his residence. This 160m² area also included the warehouse and other departments including purchasing, marketing, finance and after-sales. As it got into e-commerce, the company rented the 100m² room next door for warehousing. Six months later, the warehouse was relocated to a 200m² facility in the building across the street. In another six months, the warehouse was moved back to the Yinfeng Building, this time into the basement, where previously there had been a basketball court. Liu told his employees they would not have to move the warehouse for two years. Nonetheless, six months later the entire company pitched in and helped move the warehouse to Phoenix Mountain. It was a tough, tiring endeavor. Liu and his crew worked hard. They spread cartons on the floor to rest when they were tired and fortified themselves with box lunches and Laoganma chili sauce when they were hungry.

In 2005, the company's ERP (Enterprise Resource Planning) system collapsed. The system, programmed by Liu himself in 2000, was quite basic. At the time, each CD sold was recorded in the system and Liu could see the sales details daily. Most sellers in Zhongguancun were poor bookkeepers and didn't keep track of their transactions. But JD's system allowed them to reconcile their sales. After the ERP collapse, Liu and Lv Ke began to develop a new inventory management system, and the website was closed for three days while they checked the inventory. Liu designed the system modules by making notes and drawings on paper. He talked to Lv about the framework and ideas. Lv then wrote the code. Every evening, Liu went to the warehouse to run tests and called Lv from there to revise the system while they were on the phone together.

At times, Liu had a flash of inspiration. When he had a new idea, he would call Lv and they would work through it together, put it online immediately, and circle back to correct the inevitable mistakes. He didn't take the time to think through every last detail before taking action.

The later management system architecture was basically born out of this system developed between 2005 and 2006. That's one reason Liu has always been so keenly attuned to the company's management system and so willing and able to make quick decisions even about large, strategic moves.

A Lion
Shepherd

As of 2006, JD Multimedia's teams, though lacking in formal education and limited in professional knowledge, were enthusiastic and diligent. The lack of talent stemmed from the company's humbler roots at the sales counter in Zhongguancun. There were no exciting origin stories. Most staff were paid 800 to 1,000 yuan a month, simply not enough to attract high-level talent.

Later, an investor described Liu as a lion who went into battle with a flock of sheep, and in the process the sheep gradually turned into wolves.

At those early days, JD employees worked in very rough conditions from 8 am to 10 pm, with only one day off on the weekend. Even then they had to work overtime. They were young and supported each other when they couldn't make ends meet. To save money, some shared a flat in Liulangzhuang, a village in the city two kilometres to the west of Haidian Bridge, with a monthly rent of 300 yuan.

They worked furiously all day and drank together in the evening. They believed they were different from people working in other companies and felt a great sense of pride. If others criticized the company, they would rebut them. What did Liu do to sustain the team in these harsh working conditions, to keep it moving on and improving? He drew on the lessons of his youth.

Liu's mother Wang Shaoxia was warm-hearted, cheerful, caring, and always ready to help relatives and friends. Liu inherited some of her characteristics. From a young age he acted like an elder brother to Wu Jie, a younger cousin who grew up with him in his grandmother's home. When he was in first grade, Wu still couldn't count from one to ten. Liu, then in junior high school, wouldn't let Wu eat dinner until he learned how to count. In his last year of junior high, Wu skipped school to learn martial arts at the Shaolin Temple, returning home only when he ran out of money. Liu made a special trip back from Beijing to reprimand his cousin for not being more enterprising. Instead of agreeing to change his behaviour, Wu defiantly talked back and got a slap from Liu.

At the end of 2006, Wu graduated from university and returned to Suqian to take the Civil Servant Exam. Liu invited him to come to Beijing to work, and Wu chose the Suqian Bureau of State Administration of Taxation, as the work was traditional, stable and prestigious. But in less than six months, Wu told Liu he was bored, dissatisfied with his income, and had little meaningful work to do. He wanted to resign. Liu told him that he had chosen this profession and should carry on. Only after he truly understood the work could he decide whether or not to continue. Three years later, Liu asked Wu whether he was comfortable with his work. Wu said that, although the job was easy, the income was only enough to lead an ordinary life and he still wanted to change. Liu agreed that, since he had thought it through, it was time to leave.

In a similar way, Liu acted as an elder brother within JD, at times domineering and demanding. For example, without warning he would approach Zhang Qi and ask him the price of a display. If Zhang could not answer correctly, Liu would say: "How can you not know that? What are you doing all day?" As a result, Zhang studied all the product prices, every day, and would eventually come to remember the purchase and selling prices of each of the nearly 900 products they carried.

Zhang Qi, who had an unassuming look and an honest face, joined JD Multimedia at the age of 16. It wasn't easy for him to work in a bustling place like Zhongguancun. But every morning he came early to clean the office and prepare for the day's activities. At first, he was responsible for deliveries. He was asked to be quick. Some of the counter merchants would call three distribution agents in succession to order a single item, and would accept it from whichever agent arrived first, even if the price was 10 yuan more. To win over customers, Zhang had to be fleet of foot.

For a year and a half, Zhang delivered goods and settled accounts. He was then transferred to the post-sales department. The repair process for defective products was time-consuming. First, customers sent the product to JD Multimedia, where it was returned to the factory for repair before being sent back to the customer. As sales increased,

Sun began in deliveries at JD and later became a salesman. On one occasion, JD Multimedia planned to sell a new burner model at a price of some 600 yuan. None of the salesmen had customer accounts of their own; all were at the same starting line. The one who had the most sales would get a 1,000 yuan bonus. Sun pocketed the bonus and was promoted to supervisor six months later.

Sometimes, Liu knew his team made mistakes but said nothing so they could learn from the setbacks. Wang Na, later manager of food and oil in the general merchandise department, joined JD in 2005 and began by selling digital products. Prices fluctuated drastically, sometimes on the same day. Once, he purchased some digital cameras, but by the time the goods arrived two days later, the market price had already dropped, resulting in a loss of several hundred yuan per unit. Although he'd stocked only four or five cameras, he felt guilty and approached Liu to apologize. Liu did not scold him. Instead, he told him it was normal in business to win some and lose some. Liu told him that when the market was unfavourable, he had to get rid of the goods in a timely manner or he'd lose more. After that, Wang was especially sensitive to prices and would immediately clear the stock when there was slightest hint of price reductions.

Liu's concern for employees in their daily lives set a good example for Sun and others. One day it was raining heavily but they needed to go out to arrange merchandise. Zhang said to Yao Yanzhong: "You stay in. I am the older employee. I'll go." Even 10 years later, this incident deeply impresses Yao, who later became supervisor of the computer accessories group in the IT and digital department. Yao learned to drive and bought a car with the help of Sun and Zhang. Over dinner one night later, Sun proposed a way to help employees afford apartments. As a result, in 2012 JD launched interest-free loans and provided down payments for employees who wanted to buy a place of their own. Yao bought his that same year. "At JD, you just need to do a good job," he said. "Others will think about buying a car or a house for you."

Childhood
Adventure

L iu stressed to his employees that young people needed to follow their passion and work hard so they wouldn't have regrets in their older years. Every day, they had to maintain a positive attitude, set short- and medium-term objectives, and aim for higher goals. JD awarded salary raises twice a year for those who performed well. However, material incentives were always limited. There had to be deeper, personal things employees were passionate about. After they'd met assigned targets, they received not only the promised bonus, but also "spiritual" satisfaction: the pride of victory, the glory of leading a bigger team, the dignity of having dialogue with higher levels and ever-increasing social status.

A few years ago, when I first met Liu, I described him as domineering. "That was not what I wanted to be," he said. "I may appear like that, but we define ourselves as impactful, not domineering. We emphasize the impact of our team. We have strong impact when we compete with anyone and we can defeat any rival." These words reflected the slogan he posted on walls in the office, "Fighting! Fighting!" It was all consistent with the overriding goal he'd set: "To be the biggest e-commerce company in China and one of the top five in the world."

Liu had his feet on the ground but made no secret of his ambitions, even though at that time he was working in an office with cockroaches crawling across the floor. He had been ambitious since childhood.

Suqian near Lailong, where Liu was born and raised, is surrounded by poplar trees and rice paddies. His hometown in the countryside near the town of Lailong, was surrounded by fields and muddy roads. From primary school to senior high school, he lived in his grandmother's home: a single-story, three-room structure built of red bricks. The white walls were mottled and peeling, and a white mosquito net hung over the simple plank bed. It was a typical peasant home in northern Jiangsu. In the late 1990s, Liu built a home of his own less than a kilometre from his grandmother's, a two-story brick building with three rooms on each floor and a yard in front. The exterior walls are decorated with white tiles, and the gate with red tiles and arched eaves. Over the door was a horizontal scroll stating "Jia Xing Cai Yuan Wang" (a prosperous family generates good business). Set against the run-down, red-brick bungalows, Liu's house looks particularly new and distinctive.

Liu's father used to be an accountant in the production brigade. In 1979, a household contract responsibility system was implemented in rural areas. His family borrowed 2,500 yuan and bought a 10-ton freight boat. They earned shipping fees transporting sand from Xuzhou to Yangzhou, and porcelain from Yangzhou to Xuzhou. Local people usually bought a small boat with the family's savings, borrowed money, and in a few years paid off the debt and sold the small boat. Then they borrowed again to buy a bigger boat, and so on.

Lailong was home to sand factories. A two-day trip could earn 20 to 30 yuan. With 100 trips a year, gross income could reach 2,000 to 3,000 yuan. About 1,000 yuan or more would remain after deducting for diesel fuel and other operating costs. This was a fairly good income in rural areas in the early 1980s. Rice was only 10 cents per jin (about half-a-kilo) and pork was only 70 cents.

Three years later, the Liu family borrowed 10,000 yuan and bought a 40-ton concrete ship with two diesel engines. Their destinations now included Huai'an, Siyang and Huaiyin. The one-way distance was more than 100 kilometres and the round-trip usually took two weeks. On the way, there were three floodgates where they'd sometimes have to wait several days to pass. One could earn more in shipping than from farming, but it was much riskier. It was like skating on thin ice, filled with constant fear and anxiety. Accidents happened every year. Some boatmen Liu's parents knew had died this way. Some boats were sunk by waves or collided with other boats.

Liu's parents ran the ship year-round and lived on board. As noted, Liu and his sister were raised in their grandmother's home. In today's terms, they were "left-behind" children, as their parents worked elsewhere and the children rarely saw them. His grandmother was a typical Chinese rural woman, all skin and bones because of her harsh life. At the age of five, Liu began to take care of his three-year-old sister. When she said she was hungry, he would set up a primitive oven with several bricks on the ground and cook a pot of rice, usually charring it. As he grew older he would do all he could for the household, including collecting food and fetching water.

An important impetus for Liu's entrepreneurial drive was his desire to improve the family's situation. He wanted his grandmother and mother to lead better lives. He was deeply attached to his grandmother, staying with her until he went to college. Once, his grandmother went to visit a relative in Shanghai and came back with some fruit for her grandchildren, one pear for each. Liu was in high school in Suqian. His grandmother, with the biggest pear in hand, walked half a kilometre to Lailong, rode nearly 30 kilometres to Suqian by bus, and then walked another three kilometres to Suqian High School, where she handed the pear to Liu.

Liu worked part-time while away at university. Keeping just enough money for his own daily needs, he sent the rest to his grandmother to help with her expenses. In January 2000, during a heavy snow, his grandmother died. He cried over the phone when he heard. He flew to Xuzhou and grabbed a bus to Suqian – a five-hour trip. Reaching home at 11 pm, he threw himself to his knees in his grandmother's mourning hall and remained kneeling through the night. On each Chinese New Year and Tomb Sweeping Festival, when he goes to his grandmother's grave to worship, he cries. He still regrets that he hadn't been able to send her to the best hospital, with the best doctors, when she became ill. Now, the family's situation has improved, but his grandmother is gone.

Through these experiences, Liu understood the Chinese peasants' unspeakable bitterness and tears of blood. After building its own logistics network, JD employed a large number of rural workers. They enjoyed higher wages and stable benefits, as well as a working environment that was good by industry standards. All these benefits could be directly credited to Liu. After several years of working for the company, these employees could afford to buy a house and a car in their hometowns, and provide a decent life for their families. Liu had been particularly kind to the front-line deliverymen. Many were very grateful to him and excited to see him at the annual meeting in Beijing.

Liu has always been kind-hearted and he sympathized with Chinese peasants for their hard lives. Before Spring Festival in 2014, Liu saw the news that a left-behind child had killed himself, and he could not help crying. He immediately ordered that any staff who were on duty during the Spring Festival be given an allowance of 3,000 yuan for each child they had. This was to give a chance for the left-behind children in the villages to reunite with their parents during the Spring Festival. Before the 2015 Spring Festival, the company announced it was maintaining this welfare policy, even though the cost had now become tens of millions of yuan a year.

Liu thought that the way his family had run its shipping business had limited their success. They always sailed only one boat. Even when they traded up from 10 tons to 40, or from 80 to 120, it was still just one boat and could only make limited money. He once asked his parents why they didn't set up a shipping house, buying many ships and hiring others to sail.

His parents said they felt more confident sailing themselves. It occurred to Liu that if he were to start such a business, he would buy a fleet of boats, sail from the Yangtze River to the sea and ship cargo all over the world, with 100,000 tons on each boat. Many years later, sitting in his 200m² office, Liu said: "My dream was always to create a great enterprise from scratch."

Liu's childhood was marked by a turning-point experience: he left Suqian alone, for an adventure that left an indelible mark on his life. Everything that followed – his unwillingness to settle for the mediocre, his desire to create a great enterprise – was sparked by this adventure.

In the summer of 1989, after graduating from junior high school at the age of 15, Liu left home without informing his family and went to see relatives in Jiujiang, Jiangxi Province, and Huangmei County, Hubei Province. His father had promised to take him to Shanghai if he was admitted to Suqian High School, but that trip never materialized. Liu, deeply disappointed, left home with only 50 yuan, saved from pocket money his grandmother had given him.

Before then, Liu had never traveled far from home. He had never traveled by train, let alone by air, which was beyond his imagination.

But he found a tattered map in the village and noticed that a highway ran from Suqian to Xuzhou, and a railway from Xuzhou to Nanjing. He set out in the morning and arrived at Nanjing at 1 am the following day. Although he had little money, he walked to the Jinling Hotel from the train station. The 37-storey high-rise hotel, ablaze with lights, overwhelmed him. He'd never seen such a tall building.

He couldn't afford a Nanjing map, so he asked people how to get to Jiujiang, Jiangxi, and was advised to take a river steamer. So he walked to No. 10 Nanjing Wharf, asking directions along the way. He slept under a bridge, on a jute bag borrowed from a beggar.

On board the steamer, Liu tasted instant noodles for the first time in his life. Having only eaten homemade noodles, the machine-made variety was a new concept to him. He thought the instant noodles were the most delicious thing in the world.

Among the passengers on the boat was an old showman. He told Liu stories and taught him some magic, including more than 30 card tricks. When he disembarked in Jiujiang, the old man invited Liu to come with him to see the world. The man's confident, freewheeling style was such a great temptation to the teenager that Liu nearly agreed to become his apprentice. But, knowing that he wanted to attend college, he said goodbye to the old man instead. Many years later, Liu performed the showman's magic tricks over drinks with JD employees.

This travel experience left a deep impression on Liu. For the first time in any serious way he started to think about the meaning of life in general, and about his own life. In the classroom, teachers had tried to prompt him to think about life and ideals, but they hadn't got through to him.

Next, Liu boarded the ship *Jiangwu 129*, in Nanjing, and traveled upstream to Jiangxi. On the ship's top deck, as he watched the Yangtze River rolling east and the prow splitting the waves, lines from poems he'd learned in school came flooding back: "The spring water flows to the east;" "The lonely sail is lost in the boundless azure sky." He realized that life was like the river that would never return once it had flowed into the sea.

Later, Liu would occasionally mention these thoughts to his sub-ordinates. Life gives us only one opportunity, he suggested. Your children are not you. When you leave this world, you'll never return. You can't live a second life. If there is an after-life, it is a new and different one. You won't even remember how you lived in your previous life.

Liu pondered these universal questions during his long trip. He didn't want to grow up to be like the adults in the village, whose lives were little more than a daily struggle for food.

What was the most important characteristic for entrepreneurs? The spirit of adventure. Liu's adventures at the age of 15 were transformative. Ten years later, he began another adventure, seeking wealth and honour by taking risks. His restless, adventurous genes ignited his ambition and spread, like wildfire across the grasslands.

This childhood adventure also taught him a lesson: you had to go out and see the world. This concept stuck in Liu's mind ever since. He told his cousin Wu Jie: "If you don't attend school, you'll never walk out of Lailong, and your life's journey can be easily predicted from birth. You deserve a chance to see the world outside."

After one achievement in his career, he'd gathered the children of his middle-school classmates and taken them to a summer camp in Beijing, together with a group of poor students he'd sponsored. He also invited a team of JD management trainees to visit New York and stay with him there. The reason was simple: these trainees had been working at JD for two or three years and their lives had stagnated – they needed to go abroad to broaden their horizons.

On 20 March 2015, in his spacious office in Beijing's North Star Century Center, Liu spoke with fervour and assurance:

"I feel that global businesses are increasingly converging. In the past, China was curious about the world. At start-up time, I remember the common questions Chinese entrepreneurs asked when they met their foreign counterparts. How do you manage people? Why do you do this or that? We were curious and puzzled about business practices abroad. Chinese companies, including their professional manager system, processes, and systems, all have something to do with foreign enterprises. At the beginning of reform and opening up, there was large gap between China and the rest of the world. Chinese people were like peasants in the city. It was the same as when I first went to Nanjing, wondering how it could be so prosperous, with neon lights flashing everywhere, since this was rarely seen in rural areas. Today, however, if anyone goes to Beijing after 10 years in Nanjing, he might think Beijing is very big, but just that – not overwhelming."

He continued: "After exchanging experiences with foreign entrepreneurs over many years, now we feel there is no essential difference in various countries' management styles. Chinese entrepreneurs can understand what others are talking about, especially among the emerging internet companies. They use the same language in their dialogue with each other."

After visiting many enterprises abroad, Liu said, one came to understand that the pursuits and methodologies of each enterprise could be different. What he found amazing about European companies was their hundreds of years of heritage. Some families had been engaged in a certain business for eight or ten generations and the present boss was the seventh or eighth family heir. He cited a famous bakery in the United Kingdom, overseen by the 12th generation of a family. Every day, it baked hundreds of loaves of bread. When it sold out, even if there were people in line, they said, "Sorry, no more for today." With its reputation, sales and scale, the owners could have increased sales 10 times over by automating the process and baking more and more bread. But they focused on quality, and even went away on holiday together, as a family, for several months a year. In New York, too, he found a famous Japanese restaurant that closed down so its proprietors could take breaks for a few months each year. Making money was important, but recreation and personal happiness were more important.

"The Chinese people, instead, seize every opportunity to make money," Liu said. "If he can sell 10 loaves of bread today, a Chinese person won't sleep in peace if he sells only nine. He will strive to sell 11 tomorrow. So I think, if there is anything different in philosophy between Chinese entrepreneurs and their foreign counterparts, it would be the pursuit of success. Many foreign entrepreneurs want to be successful in order to have a better life, happiness and a better family life. For Chinese entrepreneurs, making more money is the most important measure of the enterprise's success. In China, as long as your company makes money and you are rich enough, even if you were despised and disdained by countless people in the past, you can become a hero. For example, some people made all kinds of fake health products, spent a great deal on TV ads, and made tens of billions. Everyone thinks these people are Godfathers, successful entrepreneurs. You are labeled a success if you have money."

To that extent, Liu said, there remain differences between Chinese and foreign entrepreneurs. "I am not saying that Chinese enterprises are wrong on this point. Money is an important factor driving the development of Chinese business and society in general. Likewise, if all Chinese entrepreneurs and Chinese people set goals like the Europeans – 'I don't want to work; I just want to enjoy life' – there will be big problems. When entire countries stop working, and the money doesn't fall from heaven, what then? The government does not create wealth, it spends it. You want to rely on the government? How? Cheating money out of other countries, issuing national debt and then defaulting on it like Greece?"

He went on: "I don't admire those Europeans who only want to enjoy leisure time. If everyone just spends money, and wants the government to provide higher benefits and look after the aged, and no one wants to create value to pay taxes for the state, then the country will end in bankruptcy. However, Chinese people are stretched, pursuing nothing but money."

Liu said he had greater respect for the American enterprise model. He views the US as a rich country with a basic welfare system to ensure people are able lead a dignified life. But at the same time, the country doesn't feed those who are simply lazy. If you didn't work hard in America, he said, you'd have a lower quality of life. If you work hard, your life could get better and better.

"I hope that one day Chinese entrepreneurs will aim for the pursuit of happiness when they do business," he said. "But you don't achieve that through indolence or a sense of entitlement. It comes through innovation and effort. When compared with Europe and China, I'm convinced the US has set up a better system. It inspires you and discourages laziness, so everyone can live with dignity and happiness."

PART II

2007-2010

I n 2007, with its first venture capital investment, JD was on the fast track. Venture capital had opened the door to a new world for Richard Liu. From its modest beginnings, this company began to remake itself from the guerrilla troops of Zhongguancun's computer city into a regular army.

That year, JD Multimedia officially became JD Mall, and changed its domain name to *www.360buy.com*. Liu's ambition had moved beyond an e-commerce website selling only IT products. With JD Mall, he'd hoped to meet the needs of all kinds of consumers.

From 2007 to 2010, the company persistently expanded its territory, adding product categories like home appliances, general merchandise and books. During this period, JD also established the logistics strategy of warehouse integration. It also expanded distribution and delivery beyond China's north and east regions, to the south, southwest, central and northeast regions. A truly national coverage model was developed.

In 1996, Jeff Bezos proposed the idea of "Get Big Fast" to Amazon employees. In his view, the bigger the company, the cheaper it could buy from wholesalers, and the stronger the channel capacity. The faster the company grew, the more areas it could expand into. And that would position it as a potent brand at the leading edge of e-commerce.

Like Bezos, Liu had a strong belief in economies of scale. For a long time, he was prepared to lose money in exchange for more product categories, better logistics management and greater scale. From 2007 to 2010, JD's annual sales grew roughly 200% year on year. But it still needed to fuel investments; it would have to work year after year at raising funds.

Financing

2007: Opening the New World

JD turned to e-commerce at just the right time, neither too early nor too late. SARS in 2003 provided a small spark for e-commerce, but what really brought it alive was the revival of China's internet sector after the bubble burst in the early 21st century. Contributing socio-economic factors were the sustained growth of China's internet user population and the overall consumer dividend brought by China's economic growth. After 2007, the country's e-commerce industry engaged in the "Great Leap Forward" with strong market and capital support. Even badly managed companies could grow 100% a year.

As JD grew faster and faster, Liu realized he had to raise funds. Observers suggested he reach out to the venture capital world. Late one October evening in 2006, Liu met with Xu Xin, the founder and president of Today Capital, at the Shangri-La Hotel in Beijing. Xu's first impression of Liu was that he dealt in good faith and was very ambitious, his sights set on achieving first place, never second. She felt she'd found a swift horse. Xu was also amazed to learn that JD, without spending a penny on advertising, was increasing its sales by more than 10% monthly. It was evidently a business model that worked.

Their conversation ended at 2 am, and Xu immediately booked flights for the next day. She and Liu would catch a 9 am plane from Beijing to Shanghai, where Today Capital was based. This meant Liu would not have a chance to meet other investors. Xu had wisely orchestrated it all; she didn't want to lose the swift horse.

The investment manager of Today Capital, Chang Bin (who later joined JD as vice president of JD Investment), began due diligence. He found that JD had its share of online critics. The perception was that white-collar consumers bought from Newegg, while students shopped on JD because of its low prices and because it was a way to avoid going to the crowded Zhongguancun counters, where they might be cheated. Today Capital concluded that most of the shortcomings cited by JD's critics could be fixed.

Chang Bin surveyed 30 JD customers and heard that the company was convenient, inexpensive and professional. At that time, there was a group online that was keen on DIY (do it yourself) computer projects and very loyal to JD. The company was known for special promotion sessions called "Liu's Dark Night" – midnight specials where CPUs, hard drives, motherboards and more were sold at rock-bottom prices. Chang also called 10 suppliers and was told that although JD wasn't a big buyer, the team was always spirited and a pleasure to deal with.

JD was a small company, and the team clearly needed to improve. It lacked standardized financial systems and other internal systems. Liu mainly focused on inventory, sales and cash flow. Today Capital spot-checked the stock and cash situation and found no mismatch. It also did due diligence on senior employees and found that they respected Liu and were loyal to him.

Recalling his days in JD, Zhang Qi felt he was most stressed during that 2007 financial due diligence review. He knew this financing was a matter of life and death to JD and feared he'd say the wrong thing and spoil the funding. He called Liu and unsuccessfully lobbied to be excused from the meeting. In the office, he faced four or five people from Today Capital and chatted for a few hours. He was asked: What was your experience after joining JD? What's your personal impression of Richard Liu? Do you have faith in the company? Are there any serious problems? He answered with discretion, but was so nervous that he broke into a sweat, not knowing if what he said was wrong or right.

During the internal discussions at Today Capital, one partner said the IT component business for DIY computer enthusiasts was out of date. Another wondered how they could make a valuation on a business that didn't make money. But their survey showed that consumers loved JD's services. They only criticized it because they cared about the company and wanted it to improve. With Today Capital's investment, JD could not only improve its service delivery but also expand its business. Xu Xin had the final say, and Today Capital invested the money.

Liu said he'd hoped to raise $2 million. But Xu Xin asked: "How can $2 million be enough? When the opportunity comes, you have to risk your life to charge forward and expand rapidly. To become number one you need $10 million." The valuations were set by Liu. Xu Xin agreed without hesitation or a counter offer.

There was a pause before they were to sign the agreement. Before turning to Today Capital, Liu had once raised 5 million yuan from a private enterprise. But, after the company invested an initial installment of 1 million yuan, it wanted to withdraw because JD was losing money. Today Capital feared a trap in that previous financing agreement and asked to review it. Liu showed his faithfulness and shrewdness by refusing the request on the grounds that he had signed a confidentiality agreement.

"He was particularly stubborn," said Xu. "The other party had already breached the contract. How could the confidentiality agreement still be enforced?" Today Capital suspected that the terms between Liu and the private enterprise must have been very strict because they were never able to see the agreement. Xu Xin took a step back. If Today Capital could not look at it, perhaps a lawyer could. The lawyer only needed to determine whether the agreement posed a threat to Today Capital. That approach was agreed, the lawyer found no such problem, and the two sides signed the funding agreement.

JD was badly in need of the infusion. The company was stretched thin and could barely afford to pay its employees. Today Capital immediately provided a bridge loan of 2 million yuan, half to return to the previous investor and half to pay salaries.

Liu and Xu agreed that, in the coming few years, they would not seek profits. They would risk everything in a sprint to grab market share, and take out 18% in options to reward the team. In the agreement between JD and Today Capital, there was a target incentive clause. In order to set the targets, Chang Bin asked Liu to make a business forecast for the next three years. Liu sent a fax projecting sales of 350 million yuan in 2007 and 1 billion yuan in 2008. In 2006, JD's sales were 80 million yuan. Chang looked at the numbers and thought: "Four times yearly growth in 2007 and three times in 2008? Are you kidding?"

Today Capital also worried that the target was too high and that, if it wasn't achieved, it would impact employee morale. After further discussion, they set a more reasonable four-year business objective: sales would grow 100% per year, and in the fourth year JD would make a profit. If the company could achieve that goal, then Today Capital would reward the team. This clause was written into the agreement.

As it turned out, JD's 2007 turnover was about 360 million yuan and its 2008 sales were about 1.3 billion. JD surpassed Liu's target predictions that had seemed so impossible at the time. He'd had a keen grasp of the business and even factored in a safety margin. Later, I asked Liu about this. He said that the target they set was "a piece of cake; why wouldn't I agree?"

On 28 August 2007, JD and Today Capital held a press conference in the China World Hotel in Beijing to unveil Today Capital's $10 million investment. This was the only press conference about financing in JD's history. With capital in hand, and Xu's desire to quickly start brand promotion, JD began its first marketing activity. There was no marketing department, and Xu recommended that the company retain marketing consultant Xu Lei (later senior vice president of JD). JD placed advertisements in metro and bus stations that had heavy commuter traffic, and produced radio ads that ran in Beijing and Shanghai. The company's visibility – and its popularity – jumped overnight.

In the past, JD's only means of promotion had been to give users a discount, which earned today's money. Advertising was about earning tomorrow's money. Liu was not used to that line of thinking. He was excited about the growth in users, but thinking about the large amount of money spent on ads caused him stress.

In January 2007, JD had 100,000 registered users, and 10,000 active customers that month. It was an insignificant player in China's internet industry. Most JD employees in those days came from simple backgrounds. They had a different temperament from the overseas returnees and the talent from famous schools that other companies recruited. JD was a stranger in China's internet circles. Unlike companies that, from the beginning, harboured dreams of changing the world and changing human history, JD followed a traditional approach to business. Venture capital opened the door to a new world and broadened his vision. It pulled him from storefront retailing into the world of the internet. In 2007, Liu had only a vague idea of what the internet was all about. He was curious and eager to learn, and, once he found something valuable, he made careful note of it.

2008: A Winter Chill

In 2008, the cold winter of the capital markets settled in.

JD started pursuing its second round of funding when its valuation dropped significantly, from $150 million to $120 million, down to $100 million, and then $80 million. At the strategic tipping point of $60 million, a well-known fund promised to invest. Then Lehman Brothers declared bankruptcy and, suddenly, the market dried up. A fund met with Liu and cut JD's valuation to $30 million, but was rejected.

This financing stage was one of the toughest times in Liu's business life. He contacted 30 or 40 funds, sometimes two or three a day, but no one wanted to invest. Each investor had the same question: "How can your company make money? What are your advantages compared with Taobao's model? What are your advantages compared with the cost structure of Gome and Suning?"

Many investors seemed more willing to believe stories told by those who were already successful. They had little time for those who weren't.

In his most difficult hours, Liu sat alone in the New Island Coffee shop, next to the Yinfeng Building, sipping wine to relieve his stress. Later, when this period in the company's history was recalled, Miao Xiaohong, Richard Liu's assistant, asked Liu why he hadn't told her of these difficulties. He said simply that he'd feared employees would lose confidence and leave the company if they knew.

Liu kept the financing challenges from everyone except Miao and Chen Shengqiang (later CEO of JD Finance Group). He set up a virtual firewall that kept employees from knowing how difficult the financial situation had become, allowing them to concentrate on their work.

Soon, the company's funds were nearly depleted. On one occasion, Wang Xiaosong, vice president of JD Group and GM of the communications business division, came to Chen Shengqiang with a payment order. He said a supplier would not ship them an order of goods before receiving payment. Previously, whenever he went to Chen for money, the two would argue and Chen would offer many reasons why he couldn't approve the payment. This time, Chen was unusually calm. He looked at Wang and said: "Xiaosong, tomorrow is pay day. If I give you the money, then there won't be enough to pay the salaries." Wang said nothing more and walked away with the payment order.

Recalling this time, Wang said: "Liu liked to share JD's planning to motivate us. We believed him, but also felt that perhaps he was too aggressive. When there was difficulty with payments, we'd wonder whether our boss was exaggerating because, miraculously, money would always roll in at the most difficult time. I really admired his ability in fund raising." Liu had never exposed his anxiety in front of employees. He was always full of confidence, always telling them the money was coming. When things got particularly tough and employees appeared disconsolate, he would motivate them through his speeches and they would cheer up at once, ready to rejoin the fight.

Today Capital had made four or five bridge loans to JD during hard times; now the investment firm also began to worry. In November 2008, Today Capital invited Liu to its annual meeting. Liu introduced his company on stage and caught the attention of Francis Leung, a well-known Asian-investment banker and founder of Peregrine in Hong Kong. Xu Xin also recommended Liu to Francis Leung, and deliberately arranged for them to sit together at dinner. Leung felt that Liu was a man of dedication and trustworthiness. He could tell that Liu knew both retail and the internet. They shared the strategic view that Chinese retail efficiency was too low, with middlemen taking up too big a chunk of the profits. They both en-visioned the elimination of intermediaries, which would allow profit sharing with the end-users.

Leung had already planned to invest, but he wanted to find a part-ner to do due diligence and co-invest with him. He thought about Li Xufu of Bull Capital Partners, who used to be his apprentice at Peregrine. (Xu Xin had also been Leung's subordinate at Peregrine.) Since its inception in October 2007, Bull Capital Partners had made no investments.

Chang Bin took Li Xufu to see Liu. Li asked: "Why is it that such a good company doesn't make money? Do you think major appli-ances will be a good business?"

After spending time with Liu, Li sent a short message to Chang Bin, saying he had decided to invest in the company. JD requested the money within 21 days, because it was nearly the end of year and Liu had to repay the earlier loan to Today Capital.

Chang and Li had an interesting conversation. Li said he thought this company could earn him an eightfold return. Chang agreed that such a thing was possible. A year later, Chang confessed to Li that, at that time, he did think Today Capital could earn an eightfold return, but Bull Capital Partners could only profit fourfold. He had just echoed Li's view. Li laughed and said: "Look, you were wrong."

Francis Leung said: "I trusted Li Xufu's judgment and he trusted me. I was optimistic about this industry and this man. The man is more important than the business model. No one can be sure about a start-up model. To many investors, making money is more impor-tant than cash flow for a company. In fact, the most important thing is the cash flow. If cash flow is positive, the company will survive. If not, it will die. Loss is like bleeding; when it can produce cash flow to staunch the bleeding, then it can still survive."

During the financing process, there were ongoing negotiations between JD and investors. Miao Xiaohong noticed that successful agreements were closed with investors who'd met Liu only once or twice, while those who met and negotiated multiple times usually didn't work out. In 2008, Leung personally invested $1 million in JD.

His investment went on to return a 100-fold profit. "I lent a hand when JD was in its hardest time," he said. "I deserve it."

The financing experience in 2008 offered a profound lesson for both Today Capital and JD. One must seize financing opportunities when they materialize. Employee turnover, sabotage by rivals or deteriorating performance may not kill a company, but lack of money certainly will.

After raising $27 million in 2006, e-commerce rival Dangdang received no investment in 2007 and 2008. Another competitor, Joyo Amazon, had to trim its budgets after its US headquarters was impacted by the 2008 financial crisis. At the time, Liu treated Dangdang and Joyo Amazon with respect. They were like the big brothers in e-business and he was a new player. However, this new player chose to use his cash to expand his offerings and build a logistics system. Compared to everything else that had come before, this was the real turning point in JD's evolution.

When contemplating Chinese internet companies, many investors looked to successful US startups for parallels. With JD, for example, the proposition was never that you invest this year and reap profits the next. Investors who studied Amazon thought that a "Chinese Amazon" would appear at some point. They asked themselves where it would come from. JD stood out as the company most similar to Amazon. Without Amazon's success, how could JD have persuaded investors that it needed to burn cash for five more years, even losing significant money as part of its long-term goal to succeed by building a new business model?

Investors literally bought into Liu's ideas; they gave him a lot of money. When the market was good, investors were optimistic and would invest in more companies. But when the market was bad, they became cautious and would not consider any but the top three companies in the market. At this point JD's attitude became: I'm the big boss. I have money and you don't. Let's get on with the game. When the market is bad, you'll disappear because you have no money.

"This model required heavy investment," said Liu. "I could not be restrained when the market was irrational. But for many industries, the one who first comes to his senses is the first to die. When everyone was irrational, I was too. And that required a lot of money. Luckily, before anyone came to their senses, JD had already gotten the money to sustain itself for long enough. When everyone came back to their senses, many were wiped out."

Funding firmly in hand, JD began its massive brand expansion, determined to quickly seize the market and crush its rivals. The company inundated news sites with ads, and for a time Baidu users couldn't avoid seeing JD banners prominently featured on the right side of their screens. During the financial crisis, portal ads sold at a discount. This allowed JD and Vancl to capture a lot of user traffic with little expenditure. With this surge in traffic, low product prices and ever-quicker delivery, the two websites grew quickly. In the following four years, JD and Vancl would become the most dynamic e-commerce companies in B2C.

2009: The E-Commerce Opportunity

In 2003, sparked by the SARS crisis, Liu made his foray into e-commerce. That same year, Jack Ma created Taobao. Its rival was eBay, which entered China by merging with Eachnet. Ma, knowing China well, overran eBay with an aggressive, cost-free-for-sellers model. Taobao doubled its growth year-on-year. It had strong operational ability and was particularly good at cooperating with offline businesses. After defeating eBay, Taobao had no rivals in the C2C market and marched confidently forward.

Finding that China had suffered little from the 2008 financial crisis and that the consumer market was still hot, the venture capital community began considering its next prime investment area. VC firms thought that China's domestic consumption meant great potential for e-commerce.

It was hardly possible to create another Taobao. But JD's model held promise and funds poured into Chinese e-commerce.

E-commerce needed to address three issues for consumers: price, convenience and guaranteed quality. Taobao had solved the first two, but not the third. JD stressed that it sold only authentic and licensed goods. It scaled up in size by losing money, won over more users with its speed, and also did quite well on brand-building. But its costs for maintenance were also growing as it constantly built new warehouses and improved its delivery systems.

Nonetheless, JD's image at the time was still comparatively weak. Its home page seemed dry and lifeless, unlike Taobao's, which had launched a variety of activities and promotions such as Valentine's Day and Singles' Day, and had leveraged them to the max.

In 2007, JD began to expand its categories, from IT products, mobile phones, small appliances, and general merchandise, to books and more. And it was successfully turning new visitors into customers. So while JD spent to expand its scale, it was learning how to simultaneously attract new customers and retain them for the long term. Other B2C companies were spending heavily to buy traffic, but found that users were like locusts in search of food; they'd move on to wherever there were discounts. Investments could not be aimed only at acquiring traffic and one-off sales, they had to be oriented toward winning customers. If the conversion rate was too low and unsustainable, an e-commerce company would not prosper. Some users shopped only once on certain e-commerce sites, placing orders only when they found a specific bargain.

To attract customers, certain e-commerce sites offered incentives such as a free 6 yuan towel to those who bought a product, even if they purchased an item costing less than 30 yuan. Some companies had excessively high packaging costs as they sought to impress customers. Further, the cost of "buying" website traffic rose higher and higher. So, while websites could spend 50 yuan acquiring a user, this money didn't even buy them 100 yuan of sales. Effective marketing had to focus on fostering loyal users and rewarding them, not drawing in those who were looking only to get a free towel for buying a cheap cellphone case.

Throughout 2008 and 2009, an advisor tried hard to convince Liu to part ways with Today Capital, lower JD's valuations and issue himself shares. "Today Capital helped me when I was in my most difficult time. I can't do that," Liu responded. "I need to honour the contract I signed." Liu never told Today Capital about those conversations, but the firm's principals heard about them from others and realized they'd made the right choice.

As an old saying goes, a gentleman's promise is heavier than mountains.

Xu Xin once told Miao Xiaohong: "It will be good enough if I can earn 10 times my investment." Miao related this to Liu, who said: "No, I am determined to have her earn at least 100 times." In 2014, when JD was listed, Today Capital realized a 150-fold return on its investment. Why should investors have faith in Liu? Because he fulfilled his promises, year after year.

2010: A Game of Billions

In 2010, Mecox Lane Inc., the first Chinese B2C e-commerce company to be listed in the US, opened the floodgates for venture capital investment. The period from 2010 to 2012 was the golden age of e-commerce in China, and billions of US dollars poured into the industry. In December 2010, Dangdang went public in the US and its shares immediately soared.

From 2010 on, many vertical e-commerce companies easily garnered tens of millions in US investment dollars. Funds such as Tiger invested capital globally and across many industries. They invested in Dangdang, JD, Vancl and Letao. They bought not only the teams, but the whole stadium.

Looking back, this was also a dark time for venture capital funds. Some companies believed they could simply spend to acquire users, markets, shares and core competencies. That didn't end well for many of them. Consumers received the benefits of low-cost products and services while venture capital funds paid the ever-mounting bills.

China's e-commerce industry was awash in hundreds of billions of US dollars. The entrepreneurs were the players, as were the venture capital funds. The nature of venture capital is to advance social and technological development. It had made great contributions to e-commerce, but VCs could not win the game of e-commerce at this scale. They had to quietly retreat after they'd completed their mission, so to speak. Like the countless e-commerce companies that disappeared over time, VCs played supporting roles and were easily forgotten, even though their contributions were indelible. Chinese society lacks respect and compassion for losers, no matter what they'd done along the way.

In April 2010, Hillhouse Capital invested $265 million in JD, based on a valuation of $1 billion, marking the biggest investment in China's internet. Later, it added another $50 million. Most companies could hope to raise a maximum of $200 million or $300 million with their IPOs. Zhang Lei, chairman and CEO of Hillhouse Capital, lived by this philosophy: If you decide to gamble, go big.

Unlike other investors, Zhang demanded that the founders retain a certain level of control. Without such provisions, he would not invest. After studying the history of many companies, he'd concluded that a business was not necessarily successful if the founder controlled it. But if the founder didn't control it, he believed, the company was doomed to fail. He also worried that some shareholders were easily tempted and would be eager to sell their small stakes. He called this "neighbour risk".

Zhang asked Liu how much he needed for financing. Liu quoted $50 million to $75 million. Zhang said he would either invest $300 million or nothing. Liu turned him down because $300 million could easily make Zhang JD's largest shareholder. They eventually agreed on $265 million. Liu retained control of the board and special voting rights.

Zhang and Liu hit it off from the start. Both had graduated from Renmin University, and they were open and honest with one another. When Zhang had asked Liu if he needed financing, Liu admitted he did but said he preferred not to approach venture capitalists because they didn't understand him. Zhang and Liu talked for hours in Hillhouse's office before reaching an agreement. Many internet entrepreneurs, to please potential investors, would say their companies were asset-light. But Liu said that JD was asset-heavy and that only by owning substantial assets could it guarantee the customer experience. His frankness impressed Zhang.

In 2007, JD hired PricewaterhouseCoopers to conduct an audit despite the fact than annual sales were only several hundred million yuan and the audit would cost several million yuan. Still, Liu thought it was critical to have all financial data truthfully presented to investors. "Many problems stem from not talking straight to investors up front," he said. "A lot of information is kept back which should not be. Some companies want to fool people, and after they get funding they hide their actions from the investors. Problems arise as a result."

Chen Shengqiang, former chief financial officer of JD (later CEO of JD Financial Group) said he realized early on that if they discussed operations at the first meeting with a group of investors, they could then talk about everything else. But if they began by talking about finances, then there would be no second meeting. What JD needed were investors who really understood the business, not those just fixated on columns of figures. Some investors worried about false data because there were no audit reports at that time. Chen would summarize the previous week's data in a report to Liu every Monday morning. Liu would forward a rolled up weekly report to investors, giving them a complete, unvarnished picture of the company's operations and a clear idea about what to expect.

Strategy

Real leaders often thought from a macro perspective and had an overall grasp of the market, technology, and industry trends. Why was everyone optimistic about Amazon? Because Amazon had established large-scale storage systems, IT systems and other infrastructure that became its core competencies. If Bezos had remained focused only on selling books, why would he bother doing those things? His strategic vision, of course, was never limited to the current business.

JD's biggest strategic moves were ideas that Liu clung to and promoted, despite strong opposition from investors and his own management team.

In the business world, some people would always see further than others. As a boy, Liu was an introvert. Upon graduation from junior high school, most farmers' children chose to go to technical secondary schools or secondary normal schools because they then could begin working for the state right after graduation. Liu had his own ideas. "I didn't want to go to a technical secondary school," he said. "I wanted to go to high school, then college. I wanted to go to the largest cities in China, either Beijing or Shanghai." Later, when he applied to colleges, the schools he chose were in those two cities.

In 1992, when Liu graduated from high school, he proposed that his father buy a pond in Suqian, fill it in, and then either sell the land or keep it to build a house on in the future. The property would definitely appreciate in value over a decade. Liu had a profound understanding of rural areas, even as a junior high school student, predicting that they would decline and most of the population would move to urban areas. He also knew that everything in the urban areas would be more expensive, including accommodations, food and clothing.

For years JD faced pressing questions from investors, the media and its competitors. Why was it not making money? How could it make money? "If JD had not transformed to full-category e-commerce in 2007, it might have achieved meager profits," said Liu. "The 3C space has a high degree of standardization and can be profitable by controlling operating costs. If we only did 3C, we would not have needed to invest so much in developing JD's delivery service. But transformation can lead to substantial investment as well as prolonged losses." His theory was that the profit should not be stowed away in a bag. There were more territories that needed to be explored. The harvested capital and fertile resources had to be reinvested, as a farmer would sow his seeds.

The specific category a new e-commerce player chose to enter greatly influenced its future development. Why was the veteran e-commerce company Dangdang overtaken by JD, the latecomer? A key reason was that Dangdang started its business selling books, but that market was too small and was characterized by widespread discounting. The income from it was insufficient to support an e-commerce platform that needed to expand.

In contrast, JD chose the 3C category, where the market size was far greater than books and featured higher unit prices, frequent product upgrade cycles, and stronger brand name penetration. In the 3C category, JD focused on IT, while Coo8.com concentrated on home appliances. The word-of-mouth effect could be particularly influential on mobile phone and computer purchases. When JD discounted prices to the lowest level, the information would spread virally as users took it upon themselves to share the news, effectively lowering JD's user acquisition and marketing costs. The supply chain for major appliances also had more components, and that brought opportunities to offer services such as in-home installation in addition to delivery.

Accidental factors led JD to focus in on 3C in e-commerce. And it got the pace of category expansion right, beginning with IT products, then digital communications, on to small appliances, followed by major appliances, then general merchandise and books. Yet again, Liu's strategy proved correct.

Participating in the major appliance business required sizeable investment. You had to build separate warehouses and delivery was more difficult. For example, JD needed to hire people to haul air conditioners and refrigerators upstairs to customers' flats. It needed people who could also handle installation, after-sales and other services. Management urged Liu to think twice before starting down this path, but he was determined. Users came to JD to buy mobile phones, so why not home appliances too? Appliance manufacturers also needed JD. Gome and Suning were taking too great a share of the offline business. The manufacturers faced a threat to their profitability. Indeed, some feared for their long-term survival. New categories had to be added if JD wanted to continue growing and profiting.

Liu also met with fierce opposition as he chose to add books, but he insisted it was necessary if JD was going to be the seller that truly met all of its customers' buying needs. None of the investors initially supported category expansion. Only half of JD department managers supported it. But Liu's strategic vision had panned out, again and again, and the dissenting voices gradually diminished. However, Chinese e-commerce remained a risky proposition.

At JD board meetings, one member either convinced the others or ended up being convinced. If neither side was won over, the matter was taken to a vote. Among the nine board seats, Liu controlled five. When I asked why some large investors didn't have voting rights, Liu explained: "If everyone has the right to vote, then the company wouldn't be able to make decisions. If what you propose is denied by others and what others propose is denied by you and we can't reach an agreement, then the company will sink into an utter mess."

He strongly felt that venture capitalists needed to understand this about the industry. "If they don't understand, they won't give you controlling interest. They won't know the right way to go and whether your future direction is in line with their expectations," he said. "JD's investors dared to give me the controlling interest because they knew the industry and knew JD's strategy was on the right track."

When JD executives vote, they follow the majority rule. "My vote is only a single vote. I once suggested adding rice to our offerings and then expanding to soy beans and mung beans," said Liu. "Most teams thought the probability of success was low and turned me down. If the founder of a company is always right and never wrong, then the company is doomed. I am not God. It's impossible for me to be right all the time, on everything. I have to subject myself to the collective intelligence."

Most of the time, he was an absolute dictator on strategic decisions. JD was not created by Liu alone, but its strategies originated with him. That might, at first, sound dangerous. However, everyone but Liu had heavy, all-consuming responsibilities in their day-to-day jobs, and the more time that people spent immersed in the necessary daily business operations, the less time they had to ponder loftier strategic matters. An executive once complained to his superior: "Don't press me too hard. I am fully occupied by the routine all day long and can't even think properly." Only one who jumps outside the box of routine has the mental capacity to think about longer-term strategy.

Liu dominated management deliberations. He thought everything through thoroughly and told his subordinates to execute accordingly. He was the source and he motivated others from top to bottom. This style of top-down enforcement was not uncommon in Chinese enterprises, which operated in the context of a rigidly patriarchal society. This was especially true among the pioneering entrepreneurs of the 1980s and 1990s, who were in effect the parents of their companies. Those businesses stood or fell on the word of their leaders, whose authority could not be challenged.

Liu believed that, in a rapidly developing company, there had to be a strong leader with absolute control to guarantee orderly growth. Private companies had to be autocratic. Democratic companies were doomed to fail. The founder needed to be in charge at the strategic level to ensure no one made mistakes on the core matters – such as the user experience, in JD's case – that differentiated the company. At the same time, top-line corporate strategies had to be specific and clear, and everyone had to proceed in accordance with the strategic objectives.

Game

Winning with Scale

JD began getting smarter about dealing with its suppliers in 2005. The company had originally sourced goods from the stalls in the Zhongguancun market, later turning to provincial agencies or national distributors as they grew. In 2005, JD's sales were no more than 30 million yuan, reaching 80 million yuan the following year. Although growing rapidly, the volumes were not yet large enough to entice many distributors. When the buying team went seeking 10 units of a product and special payment terms, distributors often told them it wasn't worth their time.

In 2007, Yao Yanzhong was the buyer in charge of notebook computers. Through acquaintances, he managed to get an appointment at Acer, but when he arrived on time at Acer's office with his superior, Sun Jiaming, they were kept waiting for an hour. They were finally shown into the conference room, where they told their hosts that JD wished to buy customized Acer products. The Acer representative agreed they could do business together, but told them the minimum customized order would have to be 1,024 units per month. At the time, those volumes would have exceeded monthly sales of JD's entire notebook product line. The two left the meeting in humiliation.

Yao and his colleagues went out every day to meet agents and manufacturers. In order to persuade suppliers, the buying team prepared lengthy presentations concerning the global economy, worldwide e-commerce, China's e-commerce landscape, and JD's development, as well as details on their fast-growing business and the future of certain product categories. The JD team was enamoured by the comprehensive presentations it had created. The buyers had convinced themselves that the scores of charts and graphs were exciting and compelling. However, when they caught members of their audiences dozing off, they realized the need to dramatically tighten up their pitches.

Liu told them the time would come when they would not have to run around so much. They would just need to call suppliers, he predicted, and the goods would be delivered. Yao remembered wondering whether this could be even remotely possible. Yet, by 2011, Acer had dispatched an employee to work three days a week in JD's offices.

Liu put it this way: "In the early stages, we wanted to partner directly with manufacturers, but they weren't interested. Some brand distributors were reluctant to cooperate with us, so we had to go to agents. I always wanted to focus on expanding scale. If a retail business had no scale, then it has nothing. Scale may not mean everything, but without it there would be nothing. We could start doing it bit by bit. For example, when our volume doubled, we went to them again. If that was still not enough for them, we'd double again. When our volume approached 10-20% of their total, they'd have to talk with us. At that point, if I did not reach out to you, you had to reach out to me."

Liu was smart, straightforward, and resolute. When you spoke with him, you couldn't beat around the bush; you had to stick to the point or risk being cut off. His team was enthusiastic and persistent. They stuck with a task until they got it done. When they first tried to cut deals with agents, they were denied entry time and again. But they persisted until they got a foot in the door.

Liu always stayed close to the buying and merchandising team, often spending time with the staff so he could understand sales and related problems. Sometimes he would lead a small competitive battle in person. He would lower the price for a certain product, even when told it was close to cost and would not generate a profit.

For example, computer displays that cost JD 600 yuan each sold at a rate of 30 to 50 units a day, priced of 649 yuan. Liu asked the buying team to order 500 units at a time, which reduced the cost per unit to 550 yuan. They then sold the displays at 599 yuan each and sales volume grew. This was a typical tactic in JD's early years. Why did the company grow so fast? It had something to do with Liu's courage and a lot to do with JD's procurement volume. Sometimes, if his team wanted to purchase 200 units of a certain high-quality product, Liu would tell them to stock 10,000 instead. If you took a small quantity, the cost would be higher. But if you stocked more, the cost would drop. Consumers could buy at a much lower price, and they'd want to spend more. And buy more from JD.

In 2008, during the company's "18 June" anniversary sale promotion, Liu took hundreds of thousands of yuan from his own pocket and asked his team to launch a "Liu's Special" promotion. "Buddies, spend this money on customers," he said. He personally arranged the products and models for the anniversary promotions. The aim was to find new ways to delight customers and acquire new ones, regardless of the profits, costs and sacrifices. For example, at its 11th anniversary, JD released CPU memory-bar units at 11 yuan, digital cameras at 111 yuan, and laptop computers at 1,111 yuan. The move was risky, but it helped Liu make a name for himself in the market.

In the early years, at JD's annual meetings, Liu would hold up a wine glass and toast one table after another. He asked the merchandising team members one by one: "What's your scheduled target next year?" Some of JD's new employees did not know Liu's way of operating and would answer honestly: "10 million yuan." "If you try harder, how much can you achieve?" Liu asked. "Maybe 13 million yuan." Liu would raise his glass and say: "If you can make it 13 million yuan, you know how much bonus you will get; if you can make it 15 million yuan, your bonus will be higher still." It was unbelievable for new employees. But this was the JD way. If you could do it, then you would get what you were promised.

The Retail Sprint

In April 2007, when Cui Linwei joined JD as employee number 166, the buying and merchandising team of 40 people focused only on IT products. Its office was in the Yinfeng Building. A spacious room held eight rows of desks, each with 10 seats. The first two rows were for customer service, the two rows at the back were for post-sales, and the four rows in the middle were for merchandising. There was a ringing din of loud, overlapping telephone conversations. The supervisor had to stand up from time to time and remind the merchandisers to lower their voices in deference to customers on the phone with staff in the front rows.

Back then, JD could only connect with suppliers through difficult, time-consuming footwork. The team would go to market stall counters and offices in Zhongguancun to collect business cards. Cui Linwei was responsible for the PC display product line. He collected display suppliers' cards and filed them by brand, model and price. He called these suppliers to place orders. At that time, JD's low price policy had stung many offline manufacturers, so they didn't want to supply to JD. Some of the smaller agents hoped to offload inventory to JD, to book easy sales, but they didn't want to offend the manufacturers for fear of losing agent authorization. Cui and others devised a solution, which was to place an order with one agent this month, and then another the following month, to diffuse the pressure on them. As a result, they had four or five agents for each brand. In order to pursue the lowest purchase price, JD had developed suppliers in Beijing, Shanghai, Guangzhou, Qingdao, Chengdu and elsewhere.

In 2008, JD started to lift the bar for their suppliers. Previously, the company had made deals with suppliers from the market stalls, but not all those products were fully guaranteed. Since JD chose to sell only genuine goods, some suppliers who were found offering smuggled or counterfeit products were kicked out of the supply chain. In accordance with company policy, buyers had to negotiate with the general agents. Cui Linwei talked with a general agent of PC displays in Beijing about an order of 2,000-3,000 units per month. The general agent thought this was not enough and specified a higher minimum quantity for each order. In addition, he also demanded shipping freight and cash settlement.

In order to bring this distributor's terms down to more reasonable levels, Cui Linwei proposed selling the distributor's unsold goods, such as a large number of high-end displays that JD had stockpiled. Cui told him that while demand for these items might be limited in Beijing, JD could reach consumers nationwide. In fact, JD sold out. Seeing that JD could in fact, help them, the distributor agreed to supply more products. Occasionally, JD would be given some best-selling models and rebates. One display was about 1,500 yuan per unit and the rebate was 20 yuan. JD made little money at that selling price, sometimes even bearing a loss on the rebate, but saw it as a way to grow volume. Only bigger scale could win more support. The target for the Beijing distributor was 40,000 display sales a month. In good times, JD could move 10,000 units a month.

After completing the first round of financing, JD introduced its first batch of professional managers. Wang Xiaosong joined JD at this stage. Liu interviewed him and after 20 minutes told him that he was hired. Wang felt that Liu was sincere and straightforward, although he was quite surprised to be offered the job on the spot. The HR manager, it so happened, was less pleased about having had no influence on the decision.

In January 2008, Wang Xiaosong had resigned from Wal-Mart and left Shenzhen for Beijing. Many of his friends thought he had lost his mind to leave Wal-Mart for a little-known Chinese e-commerce company, but Wang felt Liu was a man of integrity, courage and clear thinking. He saw in Liu a strong leader who was willing to share his wealth with others. At the end of that year, he received a year-end bonus far exceeding his expectations. "When I first arrived, we did not discuss salary and benefits," said Wang. "But I found I got far more than I'd anticipated."

On his first day at JD, Wang got a taste of the company's unique way of operating. While he was going through his own new-employee orientation, he was called to help the recruiting team interview new candidates. And the next day, since the company was so short-staffed, he found himself joining others in one of the periodic waves of what they called "warehouse blasting". This was a process that was necessary whenever there was an unexpected surge of orders. Everyone was recruited to rush to the warehouse to work overnight. No one thought about whether there was payment for overtime, or whether warehouse work was in their job description.

This experience made a deep impression. Product information and orders could be transmitted online, but the goods themselves had to be delivered to customers through a process of manual labour. This was a company where online and offline activities went hand-in-hand.

In JD's office in the Yinfeng Building, the pillars were pasted with the "Fighting! Fighting!" slogan. It was like a battlefield. The merchandising sector was booming, and phones rang incessantly. The space was tightly packed. At times suppliers had to stand while talking to JD's staff.

The retail functions of that era were poorly organized. The merchandising team usually took care of everything. In the morning, it would negotiate prices, place orders and submit account statements to suppliers, either in face-to-face meetings or over the phone. In the afternoon, the team would receive goods, check and package them, then wrap plastic film over the boxes to protect merchandise from damage. Carriers were reluctant to deliver the goods to JD's suburban warehouses due to the high transportation costs. They just dropped everything off at the front entrance of the Yinfeng Building and the retail team had to retrieve the stacks of goods from there. JD would dispatch these commodities to the warehouse twice a day. Each day the retail team had to plan what new orders should be placed the following day and how to carry out related promotions. In the evening, they had to answer user questions, respond to reviews and maintain online product pages.

By any measure, JD was still small-scale. It was not easy for this upstart to negotiate favourable payment terms with suppliers, the way the larger players could. At first the deals were all cash-on-delivery, and later they were allowed to pay once a week. Some suppliers worried about JD's creditworthiness. One afternoon, a salesman who apparently had had too much to drink at lunch came to JD demanding immediate payment. He acted rudely at the reception desk, claiming that JD could not afford the payment and that he would stop dealing with the company. Wang Xiaosong took him into the office and calmed him down. Still, the scene was repeated again and again.

In the early years the retail team had to work particularly hard to find and win over good, reliable suppliers. This could even be detrimental to team members' health. Wang Xiaosong, for example, often had to dine with agents and share rounds of drinks with them, despite his low tolerance for alcohol. More than once he got sick and couldn't remember how he got home.

I heard similar stories from JD's retail staff. Some passed out after drinking sessions with suppliers. Others would show up for work on mornings after these sessions with severe hangovers, their eyes red and swollen. Their sacrifices and their abilities were recognized in the end, when suppliers gradually began to see the promise of online sales and the benefits of working with JD. In this way retail team members were a bit like the guerrilla fighters who had strong individual combat abilities and were good at setting up an ambush.

Advancing Upstream

At first, JD's retail team had only the most superficial understanding of procurement. Employees approached it as if they were still working the stalls of the Zhongguancun market. For instance, the team would call each of its seven suppliers, one by one, to ask the price, then simply choose the cheapest. Next they would compare the selling prices on other websites and set a lower price. This resulted in a fundamentally unstable supply chain and a lack of strategic cooperation with suppliers. Price was only one factor in sales; follow-on services should also have been taken into consideration. Retail teams need to consider overall strategy and an integrated solution, not just focus on price. After joining the company, Wang Xiaosong educated himself about category management, pricing strategies, inventory management, negotiation skills and other related business processes.

Small dealers might list a product for 100 yuan, while a larger general agent in Beijing unapologetically asked 103 yuan for the same item and wouldn't compromise. But the small dealers' supply could not meet JD's demand. To secure reliable supply channels and the best prices, JD's retail team had to bend over backward to establish relations with large suppliers. Otherwise, the company's future would be in jeopardy.

Nokia was then a top-selling mobile phone brand on JD's site. The largest supplier JD dealt with was Nokia's provincial agent. Wang Xiaosong was invited to attend the supplier's 2008 annual meeting and was seated between the sales promoters of two large Chinese brands, Gionee on his left and BBK on his right. This indicated JD's position among the dealers.

Nokia was the leader among mobile phone manufacturers. To avoid alienating its offline channels, Nokia wanted to control fast-growing online channels like JD. Chen Ting, director of Nokia (Microsoft) Mobile Phone Marketing in China, recalled that JD was just one of Nokia's many online customers. By the end of 2008, although JD's Nokia sales amounted to only 2 to 3 million yuan a month, he thought they had professional integrity and high standards. It impressed Chen that after Nokia sent sample telephones to JD's marketing department for evaluation, the phones were always returned in accordance with procedures.

Once, JD sold Nokia phones nationwide that had been stocked from Beijing, which violated the sales agreement and brought a fine of several million yuan from Nokia. JD's overall profits were no more than several million yuan a month at the time. Wang appealed to Nokia, explaining that JD had acted in good faith. Subsequently Nokia's general managers for the Beijing and Tianjin regions reversed most of the fines. They even gave JD a permit to sell nationwide, the first such arrangement in China. Unfortunately for Nokia, it was entering its twilight due to the rise of smartphones. JD was improbably becoming the rising sun. "Even as Nokia's market share continued to slip, JD treated it equally," Chen Ting said. In 2014, JD allotted 20-25% of its phone sales space to Microsoft Mobile, Nokia's parent company.

Those sellers who won the channels won the world. Take Lenovo and other manufacturers as an example. They excelled in the layout of offline channels. They spread their goods layer by layer through the delivery system, and reached their brand tentacles deep into the cities, counties, towns, and villages across the country. As prices increased, all distributors got a share. JD bucked this trend and eliminated redundancies by reducing circulation links to a minimum. They sold products to consumers at the lowest prices and shook up not only the delivery system but also the manufacturers' fixed pricing system.

The delivery system built in the 1980s gradually matured. But an urgent need for change was just around the corner, and in 2010 the situation changed drastically. One general agent for IT brands complained to manufacturers that JD had upended the market by launching a price war, although that agent continued supplying to JD. The IT industry as a whole was declining in volume, so he had no choice but to supply JD or he would be unable to meet his volume targets.

JD pushed relentlessly forward with its upstream channels tactics and approached manufacturers directly for supply. Cui Linwei went to BenQ first and was given a batch of slow-selling products. JD priced them at 1,200 yuan each, 200 yuan lower than the market price, selling out 1,500 units in two days and demonstrating its sales capability. He negotiated with BenQ again, saying, "I'll help you maintain a pricing system and help you deal with the slow sellers. In return, you give me better resources."

In early 2011, Cui could see that the balance of power had shifted. Originally, the marketing team would have to go to suppliers again and again, almost begging for product. Now, manufacturers came to JD's door, asking: "How about doing a promotion on our brands? How can we support you?"

Fighting!

Kicking Newegg Out

In the first quarter of 2009, in the IResearch B2C e-commerce enter-prises survey, Dangdang ranked first, Amazon second, JD third, and Newegg fourth. JD management discussed when their company would become number one in the industry. Based on sales and growth, they predicted they would reach that position as soon as the end of 2009. That shocked everyone because it was downright unbelievable.

JD, once mocked as a small-time "township enterprise", began by learning from Newegg in 2005, and then fighting with Newegg in 2006 when, at its annual meeting, it set a goal of surpassing its rival. Newegg China's volume was then 1.5 times JD's. The resulting price war between the two was fierce. If Newegg sold a headset at 39 yuan, JD immediately dropped it to 38. When Newegg cut to 37 yuan, JD would drop to 36. JD's cost was 35.5 yuan. When the price fell to 36 yuan, Newegg had no further move because its cost was higher than JD's and it simply could not afford to go lower.

JD could make decisions and implement them quickly, and was willing to make almost any competitive move. Once Newegg began to sell something, JD would begin a price war. JD tried to win by los-ing less, while forcing Newegg to suffer greater losses. Since Newegg had a larger sales volume, if each product sold generated 10 yuan of loss, then JD would lose 100 yuan on 10 units, but Newegg would lose 1,000 yuan on 100 units. JD employees were always attuned to Newegg's prices. They updated the JD website around the clock and made price changes frequently. Newegg had a longer decision-mak-ing chain and couldn't respond as quickly.

By mid-2009, the competing websites had significant overlap in both categories and users. JD had clear strategic judgment and worked hard to follow user demand. It rapidly expanded catego-ries to meet user demand for a one-stop shop. The idea was to get a much lower cost and sell to consumers at a lower price. Once again, JD demonstrated that it was seeking scale ahead of profits. But Newegg was not active in certain categories. Its leaders were professional managers who focused on the company's short-term, overall indicators, rather than market share and reputation among the customers. The head of Newegg's China Region was replaced every year or two, and many of its corporate policies could not be fully implemented. Continuity could not be guaranteed, either. The American boss didn't quite understand China, disliked price wars and was unwilling to spend on advertising. After 2009, JD no longer worried about Newegg.

Book Wars

In 2010, JD introduced its book category, directly targeting Dangdang.

Liu aggressively pursued his full-category strategy. Over the course of JD's history, the board of directors had consistently opposed expansion into just two categories: major appliances and books. The opposition to major appliances was due to the complex supply chain. What was more, Suning and Gome were companies the JD team greatly admired. For books, Dangdang and Amazon each accounted for half of online sales in China. Both the board and management thought it was not a space JD should enter. They believed that marching into a duopoly market was unnecessary and unwise.

But Liu wouldn't be deterred. At a board meeting in early 2010, he said he would only invest 10 million yuan in the book space. If that was lost, he asserted, he would give up. The truth was, he knew, that once it got rolling, how could it be stopped?

In May 2010, Shi Tao joined JD and became the vice president of the book category. He asked Liu how determined he was to compete in books. He pointed out that Dangdang and Amazon had been in the business for 10 years in China, amassing a large pool of users and significant brand awareness. JD faced great challenges and would need to invest significant resources. Liu promised to provide Shi with the resources and support he would need.

Shi had little time to prepare. The book category was scheduled to go live on 1 November 2010. That gave Shi just six months to build a team, complete development of a back-end system, and arrange warehousing and delivery systems. Beyond that, he still had to sign purchase agreements with suppliers because JD had no book inventory.

Amazon.cn was a mature company. It followed strict procedures, and decisions needed to be approved through multiple management levels. In 2010, JD was transitioning from guerrilla warfare to becoming a regular army. Its processes were far from perfect. On the other hand, JD had enough open space to sprint when it needed to, especially in the fields that most interested Liu. His company's execution force was formidable.

Liu received weekly reports from the books sector. Books were commodities with hundreds of thousands of varieties and the company knew it would need to upload a monumental number of web pages into its back-end system. That would be no easy task. It was not that the R&D team didn't lend support, but R&D was also running at full capacity and had multiple priorities. When Liu called R&D directly to ask why the requirements from the book-marketing sector hadn't been met, he received weak explanations. "No matter what the problem is, get it done immediately," Liu responded.

When Shi Tao had joined Amazon.cn in 2006, the company was working to sign with all publishers in the market. By 2007, it had signed more than 200 of them. Shi thought it was a miracle. No one had ever signed so many publishers so quickly. At JD, in just three months, he signed 500 publishers. The purchasing team had eight members. Every day, on average, each member visited four or five publishers.

In August 2010, Gao Yan came to JD from Amazon China. To keep the unannounced book venture secret, JD rented a small space in the offices of an advertising agency. Most people in JD didn't know their company was entering the books category. Gao worked together with two or three staff members from R&D to build the back-end system. They sat together to discuss what was needed. They did spot checks as the system was being developed and made quick fixes when there were problems. Every day, they rushed through supper, then rolled up their sleeves and worked overnight. When Gao arrived, she talked quite often about Dangdang and Amazon.cn, to the point where it began to grate on members of the R&D team so much that one told her, "Why don't you use their systems? You are in JD now. Do as JD does." Later they came to accept that they had room for improvement and began to add fresh elements inspired by what they thought other companies were doing efficiently. In just three months, the storage and back-end systems were set up and 200,000 book titles were loaded online.

On 1 November 2010, JD's books category went live, as scheduled.

Raiding Dangdang

Books represented the strategic category JD felt it needed before it could say it offered a full range of services to consumers. The 3C space was seeing good sales, but consumers seeking books naturally turned to Amazon.cn, which also sold 3C products. Liu wanted consumers to know they could buy everything they needed from JD. With Dangdang and Amazon.cn as its chief rivals, JD's book section had to be a full-range store, not a specialized boutique.

Books were highly standardized products that enjoyed much greater search and browse efficiency than other products. The search optimization in Google and Baidu produced good results and attracted new users. First-time registered users and book buyers typically would soon buy cell phones, and three to six months later they'd return to purchase computers. They would then buy peripheral equipment for computers, followed by general merchandise and clothing.

When JD put books online, the Chinese book market as a whole totalled about 32 billion yuan. Dangdang took up about 2 billion yuan and Amazon.cn about 1.5 billion. Adding in scattered businesses such as Taobao, online sales totalled no more than 6 billion yuan. The rest was taken by the offline market.

JD played a smart price war with new tricks. Even Yang Haifeng, a seasoned executive in the publishing industry, learned a few things from the e-commerce company. When JD's books first went online, many people did not know the company had begun offering them and traffic was limited. Liu told his team to give some away for free. To Yang, this was unthinkable. As an experiment, they chose several best-selling titles and told diamond-level users – those who spent more than 30,000 yuan a year with JD – they could choose one book for free and it would be shipped to them at no charge. Almost instantly, book traffic grew by a factor of 10.

Liu also asked his team to develop a membership system. Members designated bronze level or above would enjoy an additional discount on books. But this system had to be introduced before Dangdang's public offering. The job was completed in two days and two nights, and it had a great impact. Those who were not yet bronze level users sought to attain that distinction.

In early 2011, JD started a book price war. Dangdang's daily book orders were in the 120,000 to 140,000 range, while JD's numbered just 3,000 to 5,000. Huang Ruo, then chief operations officer of Dangdang, was not in favour of head-on confrontation. He asked his employees to pick 50 3C products that were best sellers on JD and sell them at 100 yuan less.

The price war became increasingly vicious. Huang took the book category provocation as an opportunity to threaten JD in other high-impact product spaces, like laptops. "For a book of 20 yuan, you give a 5% discount, just 1 yuan," Huang said at the time. "However, for a laptop, I can cut by 100 yuan, and we'll see who can afford the loss. JD will withdraw in three days."

JD held that if a minimal sacrifice could lead to bigger gains down the road, it was worth the short-term loss. It had undercut its rivals with lower prices, but the overall loss was insignificant.

In May 2011, JD began a sales promotion on children's books, with a maximum discount of 60%. This, from JD's point of view, was courageous, but not foolhardy. Children's books suffered losses, but sales across the entire book category increased five times over. And it represented a sharp poke at Dangdang's core interests.

Dangdang responded by forging alliances with 24 children's publishing houses to resist JD's advances. Dangdang's children's book sales accounted for half of its market share, and one-third of its book sales. Children's publishing houses at the top level supplied Dang-dang exclusively. JD and Amazon.cn could only get supplies through distributors. While these children's publishing houses worked exclusively with Dangdang online, they were not as strict offline. JD intended to point out to these publishers that their practice violated industry rules and they were obligated to supply JD directly.

After this price war, JD suffered a setback in the book market. Its competitors complained that JD had disrupted the market. As a result, Chinese regulatory agencies such as the SAIC (State Administration of Industry and Commerce), the Beijing Administration for Industry and Commerce, and others began frequent audits of JD's purchase discounts. JD employees were summoned to official inquiries every day or two. The publishers also held meetings and collectively denounced JD through the media.

JD explained to the government that it was not receiving goods directly from the publishers, that it was just running a short-term promotion. Further, JD argued that the price war was the result of monopolistic conduct. People in the book sector found it hard to continue their resistance. Later, many children's publishers would end up working directly with JD.

Dangdang insisted on monopolizing upstream product resources by locking in long-term cooperation agreements, to maintain advantages with product selection. Amazon's approach was to immediately follow whomever sold at a lower price. Its long-term strategy was to give users the impression that it offered low-priced goods every day. It would not take the initiative to launch large-scale discounting promotions. JD, on the other hand, believed that pricing power in the competitive market relied on resources and strength. As a newcomer, it had to make boldly radical moves. If its rivals offered discounts of up to 50%, JD went straight to 52%.

The publishing industry was divided into two factions. One rooted for JD, claiming that the number of readers had declined and publishing houses were having difficulty surviving. If someone could expand the market with a flexible, competitive strategy, this faction believed, they should naturally be supported and encouraged.

On the other side were the major publishing houses. They claimed that market order and their fat profit margins should be maintained and price wars should not be tolerated. JD sought their support while complying with their demands. For example, there was a rigid demand not to cut prices on technology books, but for literature more flexible strategies were possible.

The triple confrontation actually helped the industry. Previously, the only e-commerce channels were Amazon.cn and Dangdang, so book companies had to pick one or the other. With JD in the game, it would be OK to give up Amazon.cn or Dangdang. But if one gave up JD and Amazon.cn, would Dangdang be able to fill the gap?

JD put its book category online and started a series of price wars just as Dangdang went public. After that, Dangdang began to expand toward mother and baby products, 3C and other categories. This old e-commerce company had begun by selling books, which still represented its core business. With JD's entry into the space, Dangdang was forced to pull employees from other activities to deal with the book price war. If Dangdang lost in books, then it could lose the entire war.

In June 2011, Dangdang's share price was $19 and it had a gross profit margin of 20% and an expense ratio of 17.5%. Later, when Dangdang scaled up and confronted JD head-on, its gross profit margin dropped to 14%, the expense ratio rose to 24.2%, and its share price once dropped to a low of $5.

Books greatly increased JD's base of new users. Book buyers made up about 30–40% of the company's new customers. The price war with Dangdang and Amazon.cn also gave JD valuable insight into the two older e-commerce companies' user bases. They had been among China's first wave of online buyers, and over a decade had grown up with the two websites. They were people in their thirties with solid finances. The book price war made them aware of JD and many became customers of the newer company's 3C category. Thus e-commerce competition is nothing but competition between supply chains and consumer purchasing taking place on another playing field.

After JD expanded into books, its competition policy changed and it focused more attention on the user experience. While JD formerly had considered Dangdang its major competitor, by 2012 the running battles were no longer necessary. Books only needed to maintain optimal prices while achieving the gross profit margin indicators. In June 2014, JD's book sales had surpassed those of Amazon.cn. JD had become the number two online bookseller in China.

Logistics

A $1 Billion Bet

JD and Amazon share many similarities in their development. Both companies provided full-category and one-stop consumer shopping platforms. Both purchased and marketed on their own, controlling the supply chain, and both opened their platforms to third-party sellers. JD used to be China's Newegg, when it sold only IT products. In 2008, it overtook Newegg. JD used to be the online Suning, when it sold only 3C products, and before it expanded its categories to books and general merchandise. JD will likely be seen as China's Amazon for a long time to come.

Needless to say, Amazon's Bezos and Liu had similar thinking. Or, perhaps Liu had been inspired by Bezos, who also scaled up big through significant investment and left little opportunity for mid-sized e-commerce companies. Their logic was to expand through financing, seeking rapid growth rather than profits, as long as cash flow was positive.

When did JD make the transformation to something unique and not just an imitation? In 2007, Liu considered building logistics, and integrating warehousing and delivery into one, something Amazon had not done. Amazon's logistics efforts focused on warehousing and it passed the "last mile" delivery to FedEx, UPS and others. Unlike the US, where a standardized and efficient logistics system already existed, express companies in China were disorganized. The express market was a mess, with different companies dominating different regions, and only one – EMS – having a nationwide network. Express companies usually expanded their territory by franchising outlets, which led to extremely uneven service quality and sloppy management. Products were frequently damaged or even lost, with inside theft thought to be a frequent cause.

Liu proposed at a board meeting that JD build its own logistics infrastructure, including delivery service. The investors were reluctant to refuse him directly, so they asked for a budget. Liu came up with a figure of $1 billion. Some investors were horrified, pointing out that it seemed insane to propose spending $1 billion when the company had so far raised less than $20 million.

Xu Xin did the calculations. If JD built the logistics, integrating warehousing and delivery, and there were only 20 orders a day in a given city, the company would be sure to lose money. It would take 2,000 orders a day to break even. But it would take a long time to go from 20 orders to 2,000. Some cities might need nine months, and some two years. Could JD withstand such losses?

Liu insisted on forging ahead. Although the investors weren't sure his decision was correct, they believed in his keen business sense.

In August 2007, Liu began pilots in Beijing and recruited shipping department heads. In May 2008, the Beijing Shipping Department set up five stations, each covering a large delivery area. For instance, the Asian Games Village station covered most of north Beijing, ranging from Tiantongyuan in the north and the North Second Ring in the south, to Badaling Highway in the east and Wangjing in the east. Five deliverymen took care of an area of about 100 km^2, delivering 300 to 400 orders a day. In the first half of 2009, the Asian Games Village station was divided into three sites. The company also fast-tracked the establishment of new delivery stations. By 2010, JD's delivery service had covered the massive area within Bejing's Fifth Ring.

As Liu saw it, there were two reasons for JD to build its own logistics system. First, more than half of customer complaints were about slow delivery or product damage, which were both directly related to logistics. Rough loading and unloading was common. Packages were tossed into the truck or onto the ground. Hard drives, for example, couldn't withstand this treatment. They might look fine on the outside but could be severely damaged internally. Second, most third-party courier companies could not collect customer payment on delivery. The ones that did always delayed payment to JD – 15 days was considered fast. Besides, it was a high-risk proposition, as there were many franchised outlets for express companies. Some of the franchise owners took the money and disappeared, and the logistics companies could do nothing about it.

If you could not expect the logistics industry to change itself, then you had to force the change. At that time, JD did not have detailed cost estimates and did not know how to calculate them properly. The company was prepared to do what it had to in order to reduce customer complaints and win new users.

During the Spring Festival of 2008, Liu returned to his hometown of Suqian. Speaking about his business with former classmates at a party, he confessed to some of them that logistics was "JD's development bottleneck." He told one, who was in the motorcycle accessories trade: "If you want to expand, you'll have to do a really good job on logistics in this region."

JD took on the most painful and difficult supply chain management work. In 2009, the CEO of Newegg China had mocked JD, saying: "We'll never do logistics. We shall cooperate with third parties." Before long, however, Newegg had all but disappeared in China, while logistics had become JD's core competency.

Taking Over Yunda Delivery Station

In April 2007, JD established an office in South China, covering the six provinces of Fujian, Jiangxi, Hunan, Guangxi, Guangdong and Hainan. Yi Wenjie served as the first general manager of the South China Region, before later becoming general manager of Central China. Liu came to Guangzhou for the launch of the new regional office. When he said goodbye to Yi at the Baiyun Airport, he held his hand and said: "Yi, the business in Guangzhou is up to you now."

The office in South China started with 13 employees. Its headquarters was temporarily located in a rented apartment with three bedrooms and a living room in a residential quarter on Shipai Street, Tianhe District, Guangzhou. Employees would be seen working at their computers in pyjamas. Observers might have thought this was a company involved in some shady sort of business. In just a month, these 13 employees had completed the office renovation at No. 48 Hailian Road, Haizhu District, built more than 2,000m^2 of warehouses, and processed shipments of more than 2,000 orders, all by third-party delivery.

Soon after the establishment of the South China office, Kang-wang Station, the region's first delivery station, was built in Liwan District, Guangzhou. The station also began assembling its own delivery team, with six deliverymen covering shipping in Liwan and Yuexiu districts. In 2008, the second station in South China was set up in Shenzhen, covering Luohu, Nanshan, Shekou and Yantian Port. Three months later, to meet increased demand, a station was set up outside the customs office in Bao'an District, an area notorious for its lack of security and thieves who, it was said, wouldn't hesitate to cut off a hand.

With a wide delivery area and inefficient system in Shenzhen, more stations were needed to strengthen the network, but that would take time. Yi Wenjie told the Shenzhen Region manager to approach the supervisor and deliverymen at the region's Yunda Express facility. The manager invited the Yunda workers for drinks after work and described JD's ambitions and the salaries and benefits it offered. The supervisor said, "Sounds good. I will come over tomorrow." He then went home and told his landlord, "I have found a new boss. You'll have to sign a new contract with him." The Yunda supervisor and deliverymen started work immediately after their initial training. Practically overnight, the entrance sign was replaced and it was reborn as a JD delivery station.

JD set about hiring the Yunda delivery team because the drivers were locals who'd grown up together. Wherever they worked, they'd share private chatter about their employers and discuss how they were treated and what company management was like. JD respected its deliverymen and paid them on time, and the company didn't mind if employees wanted to tell others about that.

It was hot and humid in South China. When the first station was set up in the south, some deliverymen lived in the facility. Liu went to the station and decided at once that all stations must have air conditioners and water heaters. When he dined with Yi Wenjie, he asked: "Yi, when can you have it done? Give me a date."

The deliverymen were understandably happy. Under its previous ownership, the building didn't even have an electric fan.

At JD, if someone could not finish the day's deliveries, his colleagues pitched in. At other express companies, the couriers were just in it for the day's 100 yuan pay. They cared little about whether others had finished their tasks, let alone offering to help. It was the same hard job, but with JD, the income was higher and the team atmosphere was better. And so, other express delivery workers soon came knocking.

Nearly a decade later, 10 of the 13 original employees in South China still worked for JD. There were four reasons for that: their faith in the company; the good working conditions and room for promotion; a desirable income; and a caring and considerate boss who gave off positive energy and made them feel valued.

Warehouse Overloading

In November 2008, JD's orders exceeded capacity, and the company encountered the most serious warehouse overloading in its history. It took the drastic step of discouraging new orders. It literally encouraged buyers to spend their money elsewhere. If people continued ordering and deliveries backed up, JD's loss in customer reputation would be much more serious than the sales volume temporarily lost due to an interruption in orders.

At 6 pm nightly, employees at the Yinfeng Building drove to the warehouse, where they would receive goods, pack, and shelve, with only enough time to grab a boxed meal. The food wasn't good; they sprinkled it liberally with Laoganma chilli sauce to make it more palatable. They usually worked until 1 or 2 am, returned home, and showed up at the office early the next morning. They truly experienced the hardship of the warehouse worker. Those responsible for packaging had blades strapped to their hands for cutting adhesive tape, and some people's hands were covered with scars and even frostbite, because in winter, the warehouse could be colder than it was outside. The shelvers perspired heavily as they ran around; some found that their jackets were soaked when they left in the early hours. The employees who printed out the express orders had to stand nearly motionless, and despite the electric heating fans, their feet would still feel numb after long, hot soaks at home.

This warehouse overloading problem prompted Liu to invest more in logistics. In 2009, he decided to build JD's first proprietary warehouse, instead of renting the facilties as before. Chen Shengqiang estimated that an automated warehouse would cost $100 million to $150 million. He asked Liu: "Are you sure you want to do this?" Liu replied, "Yes." He asked again: "Seriously?" Liu replied, "Seriously. It must be done."

JD had not yet created departments for government relations or marketing. When Chen tried to negotiate property deals with various government agencies, he got bleary-eyed in the first round of the required drinking sessions and didn't get very far. In Jiading District, Shanghai, a government official told Chen: "We already have Newegg. It's an international company." He turned a cold shoulder to JD. Around that time, a high-ranking official of the Administration Committee of Jiading had just returned from a US business trip. He asked his staff to contact Chen because, when he'd visited Newegg in the US, he had heard JD badmouthed. He firmly believed that only losers spoke badly about their competitors.

JD's business had expanded rapidly since 2010, and it added warehouses for food products and books. But in many cases, building storage networks alone couldn't keep up with the pace of growth. Due to the healthy level of funding from its investors, JD was on solid financial ground. In those years, JD's biggest problem was that it could not find an individual warehouse with enough space. E-commerce saw a huge growth spurt in 2010. The government was relatively backward in logistics facilities planning, so property for that purpose was in short supply. At JD, 40% of the warehouse operations were relocated every year as they outgrew their surroundings.

In addition to the warehouse space shortage, there was a shortfall of logistics management talent. There weren't many experienced e-commerce workers anywhere in China, so JD had to promote from within or recruit from the logistics industry. Junior staffing was also in short supply. In order to recruit employees, HR tried everything: participating in job fairs, working with local labour authorities; running ads; encouraging student internship programmes; and more. A few hundred secondary school students and 18- to 19-year-old college students would show up. But when they saw the warehouse working conditions the next day, 10 or 20 of them would leave immediately.

From 2008 to 2009, the workforce situation became increasingly dire. JD needed people, but its brand appeal was limited and its warehouses were in remote areas. As few people liked such work, a large number of contract workers were hired. JD's own employees enjoyed great employment packages, with benefits, wages and insurance. Temporary third-party workers, however, received significantly fewer benefits. And that caused discontent in the workplace. As a result, internal divisions appeared between regular employees and contractors. By the end of 2010 Liu decided to eliminate temporary contract workers, and hire only full-time employees so benefits could be homogenized. Equal pay for equal work. That would make management and training easier as well.

Dangdang had warehouses in seven cities and JD in only five. And the two were no longer of the same order of magnitude. In March and September 2014, I visited North West Freight Market and Prologis Logistics Park in Pixian County, Chengdu. In 2012, JD, Dangdang, Amazon.cn and Vancl worked out of the same park. Two years later, Vancl, Dangdang and Amazon.cn had exited their warehouses, with Dangdang and Amazon.cn relocating to Meishan, about 100 kilometres away. Most of the warehouses in this logistics park became JD's stock houses. MI, another rising company in 2013 and 2014, had a warehouse adjacent to JD's.

Relocating warehouses was enough to make people sigh about the cruelty of business competition. Some JD staff felt they'd run hard and fast, and had seen one competitor after another fall at their feet. It was frightening for them to recognize that if you were but one step slower than your competitors, you'd fall behind.

Dangdang slowed its category expansion and financing, while JD continued to raise funds and to invest and expand. It expanded scale with investment and the investment in turn drove the growth of scale. Not many companies could sustain 10 years of rapid growth and continue growing for four successive years after its scale had reached billions – but JD did.

"2 11" Delivery Guarantee – A New Benchmark

In 2010, JD launched a delivery guarantee dubbed "2 11," because it introduced two daily 11:00 cut-off times for rapid deliveries: If customers placed orders before 11 pm, they would receive their shipments before 3 pm the next afternoon. If a user placed an order before 11 am, he or she would receive the goods that same day. This scheme was proposed and implemented by VP Zhang Limin, who was then in charge of the shipping department. Zhang had joined JD in February 2010, after 16 years with the China Post and stints with S.F. Express and ZJS Express. His first proposal after joining JD was to improve delivery service dramatically, guaranteeing deliveries twice a day in at least eight cities.

Living up to this commitment was challenging, as it hinged on warehouse inventory and positioning to reach a given consumer within the delivery time targets. A new operating model was required. Even though total orders hadn't changed, inventory had to be conducted daily at 11 am and again at 11 pm. This affected operations and required the staff to understand and accept the new methodology.

JD was a company that made decisions quickly. When Zhang wanted to launch a project, he would develop a draft for comments and consultation with other departments. After a meeting lasting no more than 20 minutes, a decision would be made to carry out the regional pilot. If the pilot succeeded, it would be officially rolled out on a wider scale. Zhang had the authority to implement his ideas. If he met with any difficulty, he spoke to Liu directly, without holding anything back, and usually got the support he needed. Because Liu was so familiar with the company and immediately knew how to approach virtually any problem, these conversations often took less than 10 minutes.

Still, swift decisions often lack detailed consideration. Who was sure to make no mistakes when faced with new and unfamiliar areas? What kind of hard, cold data could prove something would be possible or impossible? The only answer was to try. JD was tolerant of mistakes and encouraged trial and error. In the long flow of history, there was no place for hesitation. Quick decision-making was at times more valuable than debating too long over whether a decision was right or wrong.

Someone in management suggested that implementing the delivery guarantee was impossible, that it would increase costs and perhaps stir up more consumer complaints. But Liu supported the scheme. He believed that in order to prevail against others in the industry and build a stellar reputation, JD had to set the best-in-class benchmark.

JD made the delivery guarantee apply even to huge parcels weighing hundreds of kilograms.

For all the risk and effort, JD's delivery guarantee raised the threshold of the e-commerce user experience to new heights. Now others would have to pay a higher price to compete.

Teamwork

For a long time, Liu's life seemed endlessly repetitive, working and talking business with his team members. He focused on JD's development and wanted no distractions. He was quick-tempered and sparing with his words. If others could not follow his thinking, he lost his temper. He'd been known to ask: "Why can't you understand such a simple thing?"

Liu insisted that discount coupons should not remain valid for longer than 15 days, but the team that issued coupons often rejected this. Liu would become angry without bothering to explain why. Later, he told Miao Xiaohong: "If a user purchases from JD once a month on average, and there is no expiration date for the coupon, then he'll be in no rush to use it. With a deadline, he'll be motivated to use the coupon quickly, boosting his average purchase to twice a month." Unfortunately, his rookie team often couldn't keep up with Liu's thinking. He got irritated and Miao had to remind him not to show it.

Execution is the Key to Success

In 2007, JD introduced its first professional managers and began to upgrade its image.

After the company had completed its first round of financing, Xu Xin recommended Xu Lei as JD's marketing consultant. Xu Lei recommended renaming JD's web domain and the two racked their brains for hours. Liu suggested www.360buy.com and the decision was made. A week later, Liu called Xu Lei to say the new domain name was ready and could be put online. Xu Lei, who'd thought it impossible to launch a new domain name in less than a month, suddenly realized how impressive his new company's execution actually was.

From 1996 to 1998, Liu had worked for a Japanese company, doing computer maintenance, warehouse management, and managing distributors. He was outgoing, down-to-earth and detail-oriented at work. When he organized training meetings for the distributors, he supervised all the details, down to where to position banners and slogans. He spared no effort. The experience he gained in storage management and reseller management proved helpful to his later start-up. The Japanese company held meetings every day at 8:30 am, when they would discuss the day's work priorities. Liu borrowed this system for JD.

JD's morning meeting focused on business, such as the company's operations and management details. It might last only five or 10 minutes, or more than an hour if necessary. If there was a problem in business operations, it could be passed to company managers right away. Clear instructions could be issued in the meeting and passed down to front-line workers that same morning. The fast pace of the morning meeting kept everyone alert, knowing they had to pay attention to execution. It had to become second nature to them. The meeting was really the starting point of JD's execution culture. When employees retreated to the smoking room to relax, they'd discuss work issues with their colleagues. They seldom joked or gossiped. They'd say that eight hours at JD was different from eight hours at any other company.

Xiao Jun, senior director of JD's operation and maintenance division, joined the company in 2007, when there were only five people in R&D. He spent two months on systems planning, presented the results to Liu, and received Liu's reply the same afternoon: "Go ahead with it. I'll give you a year and some people to work with."

In the first half of 2009, to retrieve a particular product from the warehouse took three or four hours because the system didn't work well and staff had to search through piles of goods. Liu spent six months sitting next to Xiao. In the morning, he'd tell Xiao what the system needed, and Xiao would develop it that afternoon. The next day it would be tested online. After the prototype was done, they looked for a team to enlarge it. Liu was intimately familiar with the system, because he had built the early systems architecture himself. The logic of the company's four core systems – purchasing and marketing, warehousing, delivery, and post-sales – was fresh in his mind. Liu became impatient when Xiao became confused with his coding, telling him: "I'll write it for you."

In 2008, Li Daxue was hired as JD vice president responsible for all of R&D. Before his arrival, R&D was divided into two major functions: research and development, and operations and maintenance.

Li began the overall revision of JD Mall. With 10 engineers, he rented a villa in suburban Beijing and worked on it for three months. He rose at 5 am or 6 am every day to write code and worked until after midnight. The company hired a housekeeper to take care of their daily lives. They went home on Sundays for a rest, returning to the villa in the evening.

This was the first major revision of JD Mall, setting the website's current overall look and category-layered architecture, and expanding back-end capacity to 100,000 orders. Since JD's sales at that time were 5,000 orders a day, 100,000 was an ambitious number that seemed to allow for much growth. On 1 November 2008, the new system was put online, and sales immediately exceeded 10,000.

Liu was very sharp about raising questions and he was also very strict. If performance continued to be poor for two or three quarters, he would replace a unit head. Once, when he asked for 200% growth, the head of the business argued, saying the goal was too difficult. Liu immediately interrupted him: "Sorry, you did not understand my question. My question is how to grow, not why it can't grow." Xu Xin never saw this man again at management meetings.

Entrepreneurs needed the spirit to fight to the end. Some would argue that execution was more important than strategy. Stick to what you are doing, be persistent, work harder, and eventually you will go farther than the others.

From Amateur to Professional

In 2008, JD had more than 1,000 employees, and Liu had a growing sense of unease. He believed that JD needed someone to look at the outside world, future industry trends, and the competitive landscape with one eye while monitoring problems within the company with the other. In 2009, after the Spring Festival, Liu Shuang joined the company. He had an uncanny ability to see the big picture.

JD was a pragmatic company. Managers advocated hard work and competed with each other. Since Liu Shuang's position was more theoretical than operational, other executives were dismissive of him. If he was really so capable, they suggested, he should sell things and fight alongside us. When Liu Shuang issued a report, they accused him of throwing his weight around. He said nothing to Liu, but the boss was aware of it. At the morning meeting the next day, he said to the more than 20 executives present: "This position is very important. We'll set up a special department in the future. You should keep your opinions to yourself and cooperate with his work." Liu Shuang had been with JD less than a month at that time. He was shocked. Afterward, he emailed Liu: "You've asked me to help you solve problems, not to make more problems for you. I am very grateful to you. But please don't do that again. I will get along with them in time."

Richard Liu did not like AdSense, a program that helped direct traffic to the website, believing that it would intercept users. He also hated spending money on the marketing department and wanted to close it down. This was Liu acting impulsively, and it could be risky to act based solely on one's personal feelings. If you didn't spend money to drive traffic while others did, you'd lose your users. Liu was hard to convince, but he took a step back and agreed to a one-month suspension of the program to let the data talk. In that month, JD's new user growth rate fell behind its rivals. Convinced by the data, Liu agreed to resume using AdSense. Many people thought Liu was stubborn, but that was never entirely accurate. He just needed to be convinced with facts and reason. He made mistakes, but admitted if that was so and corrected them quickly.

JD's earliest employees came without prominent backgrounds or professional credentials. But they were capable and smart, they listened to Liu's direction and could execute to his precise specifications. In the process of JD's expansion, all types of professional managers came onboard. It was crucial for Liu, who worked his way up from humble beginnings, to be able to build up his management capacity during JD's development. A regular army was slowly developed from a band of guerrillas. The test for Liu was whether he could lead the regular army into big battles.

In 2007, the first batch of professional managers joined JD in senior management positions. The guerrillas began to take on the rudimentary shape of a regular army.

The new blood brought proven methodologies and badly needed standardization to the management process. These new managers made decisive upgrades and bold reforms to JD's various functions, core management, and information systems. Previously, for example, JD did not have a supplier reservation system; managers just copied the rules and processes their former employers had used and implemented them in JD.

It was clear that JD had to recruit professional managers. Its scale, management style, and marketplace challenges tested the company's ability to sustain operations over the long run if it merely relied on the self-education of JD's original talent. During this period, JD saw a collision between old employees and professional managers. Some left, not because they weren't capable, but because they could not adapt. In the old days, any employee could call or email Liu. Now, with a more regimented hierarchy, all employees had to report to a manager, and for many this was hard to accept. The handicraft workshop had turned into a mechanized assembly line. Some sense of pain and loss was to be expected.

Xu Xin of Today Capital presented Chen Shengqiang to Liu as a candidate to run finance and Liu agreed that Chen would be an asset. But Liu had stubbornly insisted that new employees should not earn more than older workers. Liu himself was paid only 10,000 yuan a month, so Chen should be paid less than that. "How about making it 20,000 yuan?" Xu Xin suggested. "Today Capital will share the other half for a trial period." Three months later, Liu asked Xu Xin to help him find more professional talent like Chen. And, in the end, JD agreed to pay Chen a competitive salary.

Many companies would counter an executive's initial salary demands by offering 30% less. But Liu would suggest just 50% and then offer a block of stock options. Many walked away. Those who accepted the offer identified with the company's philosophy and believed in its potential.

When Chen joined JD as finance chief in April 2007, JD had not been an eye-catching choice. But Chen was optimistic about the industry, having been among the first users of Chinese e-commerce. By 2000 he was already a VIP customer of Joyo.com. He also had faith in Liu and believed he was capable of doing great things. Over the years, Chen wore many hats at JD, from acquiring land for warehousing to raising funds. After JD was listed, he said: "Liu trusted me and I returned his trust."

JD instituted monthly business analysis meetings, focused solely on data analysis. Decisions made at one meeting were reviewed at the next to identify which policies were implemented and to find reasons why others weren't. In some cases these reviews led to employee dismissals.

Chen believed that his greatest contribution to JD came at the October 2010 business analysis session, where he shared a review he had done of the workforce, sparked by constant warehouse overloading. Looking at the company's development trends, Chen realized that just adding manpower would ruin JD. There had to be room to optimize operational efficiency, but this required data analysis, not just instinct. In the past, JD's data was manually recorded. Chen and his team built the analysis framework from an operations standpoint, sorting out the analysis framework, trimming out more than 1,000 indicators and setting up the system. In this way, the company was able to compare differences in operational efficiency from horizontal and vertical perspectives. For example, for packaging personnel, human efficiency could range from 30 orders daily in one region to 50 in another. There had to be reasons for such differences, and the system was able to pinpoint them.

In June 2007, Yan Xiaoqing joined JD as a director. At that time, JD had no vice president, but six directors, all under Liu's direct supervision. JD's processes were not yet standardized. For example, there was no specific process regarding business trips. Yan Xiaoqing wrote a detailed request for a trip after he came onboard, explaining the purpose and agenda. Appreciative of Yan's discipline, Liu described it to all employees in an email, asking them to follow the process before taking future business trips.

In January 2008, Yan was promoted to vice president, JD's first, with responsibility for customer service, warehousing and other areas. In April, Li Daxue came on board and became JD's second vice president, responsible for R&D. And in January 2009, Xu Lei became the company's third vice president, in charge of marketing.

During those years of rapid development, there were not many rules and regulations in management. This disoriented employees who came from more structured, traditional enterprises. E-commerce itself was an emerging field that changed with each passing day. The company was still able to run faster in the designated general direction without too many petty restrictions.

During 2009, new business requirements popped up from time to time. Managers often had to take over a new department with little notice. Without notice, new business functions would suddenly land in a division. For example, Xu was responsible for marketing. Then, in a morning meeting in March, Liu said, "I'm simply too busy. You're going to take care of group sales." All of a sudden, responsibility for 10% of JD's total sales was thrown to Xu. In April, JD found that the company also needed to deal with the government in a more formal manner, so Xu had to take on the task of government relations as well. But since no one was hired for government relations for another two years, Xu arranged for the public relations staff to cover that work.

JD had not yet received much attention from the government. In 2009, China's e-commerce was gaining strong momentum and Liu Qi, Communist Party Secretary of Beijing, visited Alibaba with his delegation. On his return, he asked the director of the Beijing Commerce Committee whether there were any good e-commerce companies in Beijing, and the official pointed him to JD and Vancl. During Liu Qi's November visit to JD, he said: "Your business is good. Warehouses are rented. Goods are supplied. Everything is supplied by others." As Liu once said, "JD's warehouses are rented and goods are supplied. What does JD rely on? People!"

Brotherhood

On 12 May 2008, the Wenchuan earthquake shocked all of China. The editor of ChinaCar.com.cn learned that the Red Cross needed vehicles with off-road capabilities and made a public appeal. Liu had a Hummer SUV. Without hesitation he signed up to drive to the disaster area without consulting anyone in the company, although he did mention it briefly to investors. Xu Xin could not deter him. She said to Liu: "You are very brave, and we are deeply moved. But I should warn you that while you are looking after people in the disaster areas, you still have responsibility for your employees and shareholders. Promise me to come back safe and sound. So many people count on you."

Miao Xiaohong also tried to dissuade him. But Liu said: "There are three requirements for participating in this mission: an off-road vehicle; free time; and being able to pay your expenses for the trip. I meet all those conditions. How can I not help?"

Liu sent an email to all JD employees before he departed. "If anything happens in the course of my mission," he wrote, "I expect all of you to continue to operate the company as usual." Without telling him in advance, Liu deputized VP Yan Xiaoqing to handle all corporate affairs during his absence. Photographer Kong Yi of JD's corporate culture group volunteered to go with Liu. He left his wife a note and rushed off.

On 14 May, a relief mission motorcade gathered in Beijing. After driving two days and one night, they arrived in Mianyang, where something unpleasant happened. The editor of ChinaCar.com.cn abandoned the group; apparently he had come along just for publicity. Because of his managerial reputation, Liu was elected captain of the team. Shortly thereafter, they entered Nanba Town, Pingwu County, where they stayed for half a month. They transported the injured, shipped materials and traveled with medical teams working to control the outbreak of epidemics. They ate half-cooked rice and didn't have a place to wash their feet. Liu was exhausted and napped anywhere he could, rising to action whenever needed. They were in the greatest danger when Liu and Kong Yi's car was stuck on a precarious road, with mountains on one side and cliffs on the other. Fearing the start of another earthquake, they could only watch helplessly as stones rolled down the hillside around them.

When they returned to Beijing, the SUV was covered with mud and dirt. Liu emerged from the car, thin and dirty, unshaven, and warmly embraced Sun Jiaming.

Liu was unceasingly honest. When the editor who had deserted the mission half-way bragged in an interview that he had covered the whole distance, Liu and his teammates were furious. They invited the editor to a reunion dinner in Beijing, and Liu said: "A primary school in Nanba Town collapsed in the earthquake. Sorry, but you and your website have to set it up again with your own funds." Everyone applauded as the editor hung his head.

Liu was a natural, charismatic leader. In a strategy meeting once, when everyone was talking about the company's difficulties and morale was low, Liu suddenly cut in. "There is nothing we can't do," he said. "And there is nothing others can do better than we can. JD must chart its own path to success. We only need to find our own way. The difficulties you discuss are nothing. It's no big deal." His plain-spoken message, enlightening and inspiring, once again boosted employee morale.

Many founders of excellent companies are not necessarily "good men" in a traditional sense. They can be strict, even cruel, when expectations are not met. Some people aren't comfortable working with leaders like this. Many professional managers were infinitely easier to work with. The paradox was that these founders, some of whom shared characteristics with ruthless dictators, were also brimming with charisma. Many people were willing to follow them and were attracted by their spirit.

The reason was that they were visionaries. They could perceive business trends and respond quickly, making good decisions one right after another. They could command teams to victory and unite them in the battles for success. Lesser men, no matter how nicely they treat the employees, couldn't succeed, because their people were not motivated and did not feel fulfilled. The best leaders could provide employees with bigger and better stages upon which to meet their own potential.

The best leaders shared company victories with their employees. Liu once said: "To work with me, employees should, first, trust me; second, have confidence in the prospects of the company; and third, believe the company will share the achievements after its success. This is essential." In 2007, before Today Capital came in for the first round of financing, Liu distributed 13% of his shares to employees. At that time, the company had only 100 people.

As Liu often said, in the early years he focused on two things. First and foremost, there was the user experience. Every day he spent time probing users' thoughts and JD's shortcomings. His second focus was on his employees. He paid attention to their thoughts and their working conditions. "What you need to do is to treat your employees with integrity. For more than 10 years, JD's employees have known I've been honest with them. And they were honest with me too. If you don't fool people, they will not deceive you."

At the 2010 annual meeting, Liu stopped at each of the 200 tables to share a toast. Wang Xiaosong was afraid Liu was drinking too much, and asked him to slow down, even offering to substitute water for the wine. "Take it easy," Liu said. "I'll never drink water when I am drinking with my brothers." At another dinner, Wang said, "President Liu, you are a real drinker. But I've never seen you drunk." Liu smiled. "There is something you don't know," he said. "I am like two men. I can't allow myself to be drunk in front of you. I have to hold myself. But after you've gone, you have no idea how wasted I get."

Each time, no matter how late the feast lasted, Liu was always the one who drank the most. The next day, he would show up at the morning meeting on time. He was in fact usually among the first employees to arrive at work. This was the invisible pressure. Older employees said they felt terrible after drinking too much and wanted to stay in bed in the morning. But they remembered that the boss had drunk more than they had, and knew there was no way they could show up late.

Back when he was a student, there were periods of a few months when Liu had almost no money. On one Spring Festival Day, a friend in Beijing invited him to have dumplings. Having only 1.4 yuan in his pocket and unable to afford bus fare, Liu walked from Renmin University to Sport University in heavy snow and returned on foot. Although he was completely broke, he didn't ask his parents for money. He'd made up his mind before going to college that he would support himself during his education. "Once you've made a decision like that, you should stick with it. If you give in once, you'll always find excuses for asking for money from your parents for food, and then for books, and so on."

Later in his career, Liu became a fan of desert racing. To him, crossing the desert was a fun challenge and a way to relieve stress. It was quiet there, with no phone signals, no internet, no noise. The sky was blue and the sand dunes golden. It was a time to enjoy some peace of mind. Investors often worried about his safety during these excursions. "I hold the steering wheel, and I am the master of the risks," he would tell them.

During one 10-day desert crossing, he could not receive calls from his executives. "The company has clear lines of delegation," he'd said. "As long as they have adequate authorization for HR and finance, they can manage the business at their sole discretion."

He first went desert racing on 1 May 2008. His car got stuck in the sand, but his teammates joined together and pulled it out immediately. Everyone was tired, but no one said a word. No one needed to. Liu realized that mutual support was vital; without it, it would be difficult for anyone to move a single step forward.

Once, as JD negotiated with a small home-appliance manufacturer, the company asked for 5 million yuan as advance payment. If the goods were not supplied on time, it would mean a loss for JD. Wang Xiaosong, nervous, thought it prudent to ask permission, so he went to Liu's office. Liu glanced at him with a puzzled look and said: "Why do you ask me to sign the payment order?" Wang explained it was because the amount was large. "Have I told you there is any limit when you sign an order?" asked Liu. Wang said

Management
Trainees

Learn to Walk before Running

In 2007, after the first round of financing, JD recruited its first batch of management trainees. Since training costs were high, Liu was prudent, recruiting just two trainees that year, and only eight the following year. He thought they would spend the first two years in training. Later, he rued his decision to save costs on training, because it led to a talent shortage during JD's feverish expansion. For middle-level management, 70% were external hires and 30% came through internal promotion. In 2013, Liu had to propose that, in the future, 70% should come from inside the company. He didn't want 100% internal promotion, though, believing that a homogenous team could be problematic.

The second round of management trainees, in 2008, met with the most demanding job rotation. They worked in the warehouse for three months in winter. Wang Shan, later senior manager of HR, had to get up at 5 am each day to catch the first bus to Playwell Warehouse in Fengtai. The commute took more than two hours. Every evening she ate in the warehouse, worked until 11 pm or midnight, then took the warehouse truck to Suzhou Street. By the time she reached home and threw herself into bed it could be close to 2 am. It was an exceptionally cold in winter in Beijing, dipping to 10 degrees below zero. In the warehouse, the cold air rose from the concrete floor, permeated shoes and moved up to the knees. Even several pairs of socks and a pair of thick snow boots couldn't stop the cold. Someone came up with the idea of spreading insulating foam on the ground to help keep employees' feet from freezing.

There is a company saying: "In JD, there are only brothers, no sisters." In other words, in many cases people simply pay no attention to gender. Wang Shan is a woman. Before she came to JD, she never thought she would be able pull a manual pallet jack and haul goods to shelves. She had never thought that she would be jumping up and down like a monkey as she loaded goods. But in fact, she found that when she had to, she could do these things and more.

There were goals for each position. Once, Wang Shan was shifted to the invoice printing post. At that time, invoices were filled out and printed manually. The goal was to finish 1,000 a day. From 8 am until midnight Wang kept typing and checking for errors. The type floated before her eyes and her mind went blank, only her hands kept moving mechanically. Executive Wang Xiaosong, who was helping in the warehouse that day, kept encouraging her. "I don't even have the strength to breathe," she remembers thinking.

There were no preconceptions about management trainees, either among the seasoned managers or the trainees themselves. Warehouse managers viewed them as temporary labour and tried to make the best use of them. They did not treat them differently and often just asked them to do whatever was needed. The challenge for the trainees was how to complete the tasks assigned to them. "What do you do?" many asked. They had to explain, over and over, that they were management trainees. They got responses like: "So you immediately become managers?" In fact, they had no privileges. At times they might work harder than ordinary employees.

Warehousing often made the biggest impression on the trainees. By the end of the job rotation, these young graduates were numb and worn out, but knew they couldn't give up. If you decide to give up when you've climbed to 3,000 metres, you'll never see the rest of the landscape.

In April 2009, in order to prepare for the call centre in Suqian, Wang Shan, who was assigned to the HR department, went to Wuhan for recruitment with Director Zhuo Jie. There she tasted the style of a JD business trip. They arrived in Wuhan at daybreak but didn't eat their first proper meal until that evening. In between, they stuffed themselves with cookies. After the recruitment trip, Wang was sent to Suqian, where she was responsible for setting up the call center interior.

This was her first independent project. Every morning, upon opening her eyes, she found there were 100 things that demanded her attention. Sometimes she was so stressed that she wanted to cry. She understood nothing about blueprints or floor plans, but she had to learn quickly. And she needed to make on-the-spot decisions. What type of toilet, European style or the traditional Chinese squat style?

How do we install the windows? She studied all the price quotations and did all the implementation work. She also took care of hosting government receptions. The local people drank directly from the wine decanters, one after another. She was utterly overwhelmed. In order not to lose face for the company, she persevered, but she was so stressed that she would throw up when she got home in the evening.

When Wang Shan first came to JD, she asked Liu what she should learn first. Liu said: "Landing. You have to land instead of staying high in the sky. You'll do a better job when you are down to earth."

The 2008 management trainee programme turned out to be the most successful because the job rotation was the most solid, said Liu. Trainees rotated onto the front lines of the operations posts. Yu Rui, who later became vice president of JD Group and general manager of the East China Region, recalled that when he worked on rotation in the warehouse, every day after work he would swear: "What is this fucking place? Kill me if I come back here again." But then he would steel himself by thinking, "Come on. Just bear with it."

Rocket-like Promotion

Yu Rui, a rotund young man, looked polite and reserved with his black-framed glasses, but actually had a bold working style and his speech was like the staccato rattle of a machine gun. You would never imagine that he was a post-graduate from a middle-class Hong Kong family. In December 2010, at age 28, he was promoted to general manager of the Central China Region, only two years after joining JD. He went on to become general manager of the East China Region, holding the highest position any management trainee had yet achieved. Some said he was the model for all management trainees.

After he survived the job rotation, many departments extended overtures to Yu in private, trying to get him to join their teams. But not the logistics team. They dismissed him because he was a college graduate, and a law major at that, from Hong Kong. There was no way he'd fit into their department. But Yu asked Liu to assign him to logistics.

In truth, Yu didn't even know why he wanted this department so much. Six months later he realized this was the only job in JD that would give him an opportunity to lead a large team. His biggest sense of accomplishment didn't come from position or income, but from hard work, and a determination to change the team's living conditions.

Around the time of the Spring Festival in 2009, the Shanghai sorting centre was a mess. Liu sent Yu there to solve the problem. The discussion went like this:

Liu: Can you go on a business trip? Yu: Yes. Where to? Liu: Shanghai. When can you leave? Yu: Tomorrow. Liu: So be it. Go tomorrow morning.

The dialogue was typical of the JD style: get straight to the point and don't beat around the bush. Get moving and get things done.

Yu went to Shanghai with Liang Man, senior manager of the operations and purchasing department in the JD Administrative Management Center. A few days later, Liang asked Liu to let her return to Beijing because Yu had everything in control. Yu had stepped in at the most critical moment, working seven days a week, more than 14 hours a day, over several months. At times, he worked around the clock, not stopping for more than 30 hours.

Yu had experienced the job rotation. He understood what employees thought. He ate every meal with them, to create opportunities to talk. He treated employees on an equal footing and didn't discriminate against anyone because of their educational backgrounds. In a month or two, he straightened out the team and began to rearrange work shifts into well-delineated day shifts and night shifts. He gradually reorganized the sorting centre. Yu did not want employees to work overtime. When a shift was finished, he would send them home for a good rest.

One day, a woman who was responsible for invoicing worked the day shift and was off duty at 5 pm. After going through the security check and out the warehouse door, she ran back in and said to Yu: "Thank you. I've been at JD for six months. Today is the first time I've been able to see the sun after work." At that moment, Yu felt that what he was doing was meaningful and couldn't be exchanged for money.

In June 2009, the Beijing warehouse was in chaos. Four managers had been replaced in the space of a month, but the work was still not in order. The "18 June" anniversary sale was around the corner, but the warehouse was backlogged with goods. On 3 June, Yu was transferred to Beijing from Shanghai to act as the manager, and the original manager became a deputy manager. Zhuo Jie, the HR manager, took Yu to the warehouse. Before Yu had finished introducing himself on the podium, half of the employees had walked out, thinking: "How could a trainee like him lead us?" A small number of hard cases persisted in making trouble. The superiors also had concerns. If they immediately transferred the former manager out, the team might fall apart. If Yu could not handle the situation, the warehouse would be paralyzed.

After the company anniversary sale passed smoothly, Yu Rui spoke with those who he thought had growth potential and who seemed willing to do the job. He assigned them new tasks. Then he held a meeting to announce a big shake-up, and stripped the titles from the disgruntled employees. "You must not force the company to make choices," he told them. "If so, between you and me, your odds of winning are less than 1%." After the shake-up, the team stabilized. "If you want to win, you have to have the key, which is the team," he said. "For a team of 200 people, managers at all levels perform their respective duties. The team must have cohesion and be willing to work together. That's the most important thing."

Yu believed he'd put the shoe on the right foot. He also worked to improve employee benefits. Liu had asked Yu what support he needed to execute the "18 June" anniversary sale smoothly. Liu agreed to his request to invite everyone to dinner, and also said he would fund an incentive payment of 500 yuan per person. Yu would have the final say over giving bonuses individually or using them for team building.

JD's bonus process was not so rigorous in those days. Yu Rui took the list of names, went directly to Chen Shengqiang, and came back with a bag of cash. He granted bonuses on three levels, based on employee workload. The best workers could get 500 yuan and the lesser performers 100 yuan. He gave the money in three stages, saying: "As long as you work hard, I will fight for your interests and guarantee you daily support."

Yu asked the owner of a snack stall that appeared each morning near the warehouse to bring his kitchen to the warehouse at 11 pm and cook *jianbing* and other snacks in the canteen, so the night shift could have hot food. If this sort of thing happened more frequently, why wouldn't the staff work with you?

In early 2010, when the warehouse in Shanghai tested an automation system, it crashed and not a single order could be sent out. The East China Region accounted for 40% of all orders in the country. Yu was asked to handle Shanghai's orders in Beijing. "I'll do it. That's a promise," he replied. He then told the warehouse team: "Hey, guys. It's our time to stand out. Do the best you can." In the following week, more than 75% of JD orders shipped from Yu's warehouse. Every night, goods shipped from the warehouse in Beijing arrived at various delivery stations in Shanghai the next day. Even though JD's total volume at the time wasn't huge, the East China Region would have been totally disabled if the goods were not shipped in a week. Consumer complaints would have gone through the roof. If goods were not delivered in seven days, JD's reputation would suffer at a time when the company faced intense competition in the region from rival Yixun.com.

In December 2010, JD's Central China Region was established. "What if you manage the Central China Region?" Liu asked Yu. "If you believe in me, I'll do the best I can," Yu said. "Can you live permanently in Wuhan?" Liu asked. Yu's response: "Definitely."

JD's Central China Region integrated Henan and Hubei from the North China Region, and Jiangxi and Hunan from South China, into one area. Yu joked that it was a hard nut to crack: three out of four provinces had seen revolutions in the past. The biggest problem in the Central China Region was a management shortage. The best prospects usually chose to work in Beijing, Shanghai, Guangzhou and the coastal areas. Those who stayed in the local areas wanted easier jobs, which JD really didn't offer. When the company established a new sorting centre in Zhengzhou, Yu was at the gate at 4 am. The first truck was supposed to arrive at 4:30 am, and he had come to confirm that it did. The managers of the sorting centre seemed to take their time. The first one arrived at 6 am and the second at 8 am.

Learning to Endure the Highs and Lows

The first three groups of management trainees were lucky. JD's scale was smaller then, and Liu personally invested his energy in these people. He talked with them, recalled his early start-up failures, and shared his thoughts about the current management process. These young people had no managerial experience and probably only understood a fraction of what Liu said. Only later, when they had more experience, did the value of what he had shared with them sink in.

They had to write weekly and annual reports for Liu, and sometimes they received feedback. A saying at JD went like this: "One should guard against fire, theft and management trainees." That was because the trainees who had the right to communicate directly with Liu would report any problem they found. Liu would discuss these problems in the morning meetings and investigate. Department heads were upset and offended, and the management trainees also felt uneasy. Some department managers were resistant to the trainees, as they thought they would rat on them and make their jobs harder.

This also had something to do with the psychology of the trainees: some of them let their position go to their heads. They walked with their noses in the air, thinking they were special. Some learned their lesson, and became more modest and down to earth. But some stayed arrogant and made little progress for years.

Since 2010, JD's management trainee system has become increasingly regulated and standardized. The elimination system was not in place for the first three groups, but became part of the system in 2010. The trainees took exams and were assessed. About 80 were recruited at that time. They were divided into 10 groups, had military-like training for 18 days, and then worked in the warehouse for 14 days as a part of the job rotation. Each group stayed together from beginning to end, and grew to know each other well. If they were eliminated from the fast-track trainee system, they could choose to join the general staff or quit.

The company also formulated a three-year management training programme that rotated prospects through the stages of supervisor, assistant manager and manager – one stage per year. This gave them more training opportunities and more room for promotion than ordinary employees. If trainees didn't achieve stated objectives, specially assigned people would talk to them and point out the issues they saw. Later, capable managers from the executive ranks would be assigned to mentor the trainees. Each one took care of one to three trainees, joining them for meals and guiding them on a regular basis.

Liu Pei, who was later senior manager of the personal care products department in the general merchandise business division, was one of the management trainees in 2010. He joined IT buying and merchandising, known as JD's 38th Army. (The People's Liberation Army's 38th Army was famous for its bravery.) He won praise just a month after he entered the company.

From May 2010 to the end of 2011, Liu Pei had worked as an assistant, and was the last among the department's seven trainees to be promoted to product manager. He was introverted, and in his first meeting with brand companies, was too nervous to utter a word during the conversation, which was dominated by his boss and the brand people. After the meeting, his boss asked: "Why didn't you say anything? Who was supposed to control the situation? You or me?" Over the next six months, Liu Pei tried hard to overcome his shyness, going out of his way to speak to different people and to socialize with others. By 2012, he had broken out of his shell so completely that colleagues teased him, calling him "shameless".

Liu Pei had strong execution abilities and drive. Sometimes a brand company proposed a promotional activity and wanted JD to coordinate it. Others had turned down similar proposals because they required too much internal coordination between marketing and warehousing to pull off easily, but if Liu Pei believed the activity was worthwhile he spared no effort to see that it got done. At these times, his status as a management trainee also helped. The brand company liked JD's quick response, and so was more willing to cooperate and offer better resources.

In 2012, Liu Pei was in charge of the digital camera product line. When he handled the Casio Exilim programme, he stocked a third of all their products in China and earned JD 50 million yuan of net profit. At the end of the year, he was promoted to team leader.

In November 2013, Liu Pei was transferred to the general merchandise department. The category was not performing well at the time. The health & beauty group had a monthly sales volume of 40 million yuan, ranking fourth in the industry (excluding Tmall), after Yhd.com, Jumei.com and Lefeng.com. He had only five people on his team. Knowing he had to double sales, he asked his boss for more people and got 11.

Based on his analysis, the sales threshold for the health & beauty category was quite low. Why was JD behind? It was attributable to low exposure. JD had 40 million monthly active users who purchased from the company three times a month. If 1% of those users bought products from the group, that would be 400,000 people. If each of the orders was 80 yuan, sales would be 30 million yuan. Sales would rise immediately as long as there was enough exposure. Liu Pei began to visit the big brands. First, he convinced Procter and Gamble (P&G) to spend 100,000 yuan on ads. This proved effective, so P&G increased its ad spend to one million yaun. Then, in 2014, P&G spent 20 million yuan on advertising on JD. Liu launched the "JD Star of Campus (Head & Shoulders)" promotion, with P&G sponsoring 6 million yuan. As long as the advertising value the brands received exceeded what they got from traditional media, the brands agreed to invest in JD campaigns.

In June 2014, the monthly sales volume of the health & beauty category was first in the industry, and Liu Pei was promoted to senior manager.

Over the course of four years, Liu Pei always kept in mind what Sun Jiaming had told him: "In JD, you have to learn to endure the highs and lows. There is a time to stay high profile and a time to keep low key. Sometimes you need to forget your own identity. I always forget who I am."

Values

In his book *The Great Transformation*, Qin Shuo asked questions such as: "How many enterprises in China have truly established and practised their core values? How many enterprises can motivate employees to maintain their passion to fight? Why does passion disappear so fast? Why is dedication so hard to foster? Why are sloth and whining as contagious as the flu? Why are big enterprises always bureaucratic and small enterprises so easily content and accustomed to empirical thinking? Why is there always internal political and personal strife between headquarters and branches, resulting in internal communication costs higher than the external level?"

The book was published in 2002. After more than 10 years, enterprise management in China had advanced. But many companies either remained indifferent to the significance of corporate culture, or they just talked about it, rather than doing anything. I know a start-up that encouraged its employees to complete their tasks by any means, fair or foul. The founder believed that performance came first and the corporate culture could wait until after the company developed.

However, this company ignored the fact that corporate culture is the root of the company, not something to be grafted on later. Was it easy to introduce a new system, to absorb new technology, and to establish a new management system? No. But that was nothing compared with correcting a sick culture. It was extremely hard to reset those accustomed to doing whatever it took to achieve results. It was also impossible for a company that never had the instincts of a wolf to develop them. Corporate culture could be upgraded and expanded, but it would never be separated from the company's origins, the soul injected by the founders at the beginning.

Values were the result of cultivation, not regulation. The values of many companies might remain written on paper or on wall posters but they never really take root because the leaders say one thing and do the opposite. And the executives, middle-level management and lower-level employees just followed the example set by their superiors. Company values instilled through brainwashing would remain on the surface; they would never be absorbed into the hearts of the employees. If the values in a company were consistent, that was because the employees had similar values. The company just needed to create an environment where the employees and the company could resonate with each other.

Values were the foundation for team building. Shared values could make team discussions easier. With values as the yardstick, the team could understand its strategic direction. And, in the context of limited resources, they knew where to speed up and where to slow down.

When corporate values got distorted, team expansion could spin out of control.

JD's earliest corporate culture was based on Liu's original ideas, including integrity, cooperation and making friends. The years 2007 to 2010 saw JD's rapid growth. In 2007, there were just over 200 employees, but in time that number was multiplied dozens of times over. From the start, Liu knew this: "Nothing is more important than these two things: to build a good team and nurture the corporate culture; and to set up a management system regardless of the number of people. To manage 3,000 people, you need a management system, and it is the same case when it comes to 30,000 people. Once you have a management system, there will be no big problem, even if volumes reach 50 billion yuan."

At the 2009 annual meeting, Liu laid out his management touchstones: endeavour, values, desire, integrity, gratitude and persistence. It was Liu's philosophy for success, and it became JD's. When he started in business, he had no privileged background, no social connections. How did he make it? Through self-discipline, self-improvement, and by attracting a team with common ideals.

Prior to 2009, JD's performance assessment was primarily based on achievement. Liu realized that this was one-sided and that a values appraisal should be introduced. He set up a framework based on GE's personnel evaluation model. The vertical axis was performance capacity and the horizontal axis values. People with excellent values and performance were gold; those with good capacity and values were steel (the place where most employees resided); individuals with good values and relatively poor capacity were iron; people with strong capacity but lower values were rust; people with both lower capacity and values were scrap metal.

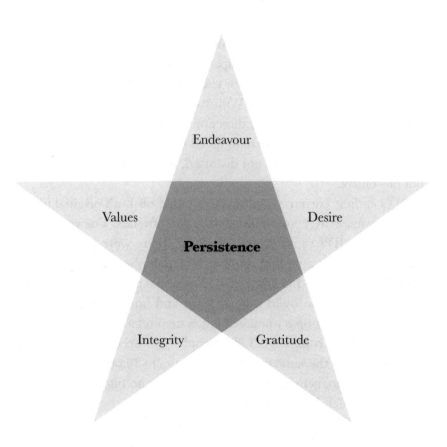

User Experience Matters

Liu was always obsessive about two things: user experience and integrity. The core value of JD is putting the customer first. In the early days, customers mainly referred to end-consumers – the ones who bought the products. Later, suppliers were considered JD customers as well.

In contrast with pure internet companies, JD's user experience chain was long. It included factors like page-access speed, order-process flow, storage and shipment speed, and after-sales response to problems. Liu had always been particularly strict about the importance of these links. JD's well-developed information system could capture comments from JD.com, public microblogs and bulletin boards. Staff could analyse this data, discover problems and refer them directly to the relevant directors and vice presidents, cutting to the heart of the problem.

Business opportunities were always there, but customers always demanded changes. In the 1990s, they watched videotapes; in 2000, video compact discs were popular; later, DVD and Blu-ray trended. And on the internet, people turned from downloading to streaming content online. Each change meant the birth of a new business and the decline of an old one. Companies that didn't keep up with the market risked elimination. Whether a company could keep up depended on whether it could turn customer demand into a force to drive development. Companies always hustled to keep up with changes in customer needs. They had to stay a step ahead in improving the customer experience. JD overtook Newegg, Dangdang, and Amazon. cn. It battled with Suning and Gome, and competed with Tmall. Yet what JD always concerned itself with was, above all, its customers.

Although JD became the leader in B2C e-commerce, the organization never grew complacent. For long-term development, an enterprise had to stay competitive. This was not accomplished through talking, but by sticking to the principle of "customer experience first" on each and every order. Meeting customer expectations and reducing operating costs complemented each other, and neither was dispensable.

Take the manufacturer's warranty on a cell phone as an example. During a store purchase, validating the warranty was as easy as stamping the warranty card. Online, it was more complicated. Customers wanted to have validated warranties on their purchases and JD was not then in a position to ask manufacturers to solve the problem for them. JD also could not ask deliverymen to carry a warranty seal with them. So the operating sector came up with a solution: it created a special warranty sticker that was attached to the warranty card when a customer received the goods. This approach became an industry trend a year after JD launched it.

Once when I was waiting for Liu in his office, he arrived wearing the red deliveryman uniform and said he'd been doing delivery work. Every year, he would spend a day making deliveries in person to understand first-hand the equipment, information system and entire process to test whether it was efficient and was as good as it could be for both the customers and for the company. It also reminded him not to take for granted the staff's hard work. A deliveryman had to ride an electric scooter loaded with at least three parcels, each weighing more than five kilograms. To prevent theft of goods from an unattended scooter, they had to climb stairs, delivering door-to-door, with one package on their backs and the others in each hand. Most of the time, Liu usually read user feedback online and rarely communicated directly with customers. On his delivery day, he asked customers directly how they felt about the shipping speed and packaging and the whole buying experience.

Liu had to put company values into daily practice and show right from wrong with personal commitment. If he could do that, employees felt that the values were not empty sloganeering, but the anchor that held them steady in the roughest of seas.

Most customers paid online at the time they placed their orders. But sometimes, before the goods could be delivered to their door, the price would drop. JD promised price protection. Users could submit the price difference online before they received the goods, or call customer service for a refund once they received their order. Once, JD was caught in a wave of falling iPad prices. The company discussed compensation with Apple, but failed to reach an agreement. If JD chose to make up the price difference on its own, it would suffer a three million yuan loss. At the time, JD's annual profit on Apple products was only in the millions of yuan. Management voted to make up for the price difference anyway, with only one participant objecting. State law had no specific mandate for price protection, so JD could legally have refused. But it didn't.

In its early years, JD invited 20 key users to visit its headquarters and its warehouse in Fengtai. These were some of JD's most loyal customers, and they were skilled in DIY computer projects. They were active buyers and were influential among the consumer community. Liu personally showed them around the office and announced that a particular laptop computer would be sold at an 80% discount on the spot. The visitors were quite excited, and placed orders right there, on the office computer.

Liu also showed these customers JD's operating system, and asked for their opinions on how to improve the company's homepage. And he also talked about JD's investment in servers, and how the team tried to improve access speed and user experience.

The values of a company often show the distinctive colours of its founder from its earlier stage of development. In truth, Liu's values remain the values of JD.

When Yang Qikun, later the senior manager of the wireless business unit in the communication business division, came to JD, he first served in the product management department. JD previously believed just putting products online would be enough for e-commerce. It later realized there had to be sufficient interaction between e-commerce companies and customers before they would buy products they could neither see nor touch. To this end, JD set up the product management department. Yang's direct superior asked him to register for JD membership and buy a product to compare the experience with other mainstream Chinese web sites. He was tasked with identifying areas in need of improvement.

Yang found JD's product information lacking. With only a name, and some simple and boring description, customers couldn't get sufficient product information, so they would hesitate to buy. In the next few months, Yang focused on optimizing product information, and was responsible for the photographic presentation of the goods. The most complete product introduction could be found on the website of the manufacturer. In order to transfer the information from the official websites as quickly as possible, Yang took screenshots and pasted them onto JD's site. Liu noticed and asked who did it. When Yang said he had, Liu said: "You didn't take one thing into consideration. The content of the screenshot is too large. The users will spend too much time opening the page. Many users will see many red crosses on the page when they open it, which will result in a bad user experience. JD's bandwidth and server will be under tremendous pressure due to users opening product pages hundreds of millions of times."

This kind of thing could have been finalized through communication with the technical department and vice president. But Liu's close attention to such details was a lesson to employees to understand what "user experience first" really meant. Liu would directly forward to his team online complaints he saw and inquire about the details. He often emailed after-sales personnel at midnight, telling them how to address problems. The post-sales staff grew nervous and began searching for complaints online so they could spot and fix problems before Liu saw them. Even if a customer was making trouble out of nothing, the team was asked to deal with it on the principle that the customer was always right. Through daily practice, the core values began to penetrate into the employees' bloodstream.

Wang Danghui, senior manager of the post-sales service department in the North China Region, was quick-tempered. When he was assigned to the job, he said he was not suitable for after-sales service, but Liu insisted. Once, a customer made an unreasonable request to return an item. Wang was so irritated that he threw down the phone. "What could enrage you to that degree?" Liu asked. Later he comforted Wang, advising him: "Next time, if you can't continue with the phone call, just politely hang up and have somebody else call the customer back."

In 2007, JD held the first "Users Meeting" and all executives were present. Only two employees were on duty in the post-sales area when a customer came to the reception desk asking to return a product. His case did not comply with the return policy of the company, so Wang tried to reason with him, but the customer started smashing things. Wang was so angry that he swore, then instantly regretted it. The customer refused to leave and demanded Wang apologize. In the end, Wang refunded him his 300 yuan purchase price.

Wang eventually smoothed out his rough edges. Later, when a customer came to make trouble and even tried to tear his suit, Wang just calmly took pictures and called the police. The customer abandoned his claim and left. "The days are much happier in JD now than in the past," said Wang. "The problems we have now are nothing compared to then."

Customers First

For e-commerce, in-person customer contact really only takes place at the delivery and customer service stages. For those e-commerce companies without their own logistics, then, customer service represented the only opportunity for customer contact.

In 2007, JD already had three regions: North China, East China and South China. There were small customer service teams in Beijing, Shanghai and Guangzhou. In Beijing, the team was no larger than a dozen people. It shared space with buying and merchandising, under very poor working conditions. The phones rang constantly and the office was quite noisy. To handle rapid growth, a call centre was set up in Suqian and all customer service teams were transferred there from Beijing, Shanghai and Guangzhou.

The Suqian Call Centre was officially established on November 20, 2009. Li Xuyong was the first director there. A few weeks before the opening, a team of 80 arrived in Suqian after a month of training in Shanghai. In the beginning, the call centre was in the office building of the Administrative Committee of the Economic Development Zone of Suqian. Some employees wanted to leave as soon as they arrived. There were no restaurants near the call centre, and conditions were tough. During the first winter there, Li got frostbite on his feet. The employee dorm consisted of six bunk beds with bare planks and nothing else. The managers and supervisors lived under the same roof and ate at the same tables with the employees, constantly appeasing these young people so that they would stay.

Previously, the overall rate of incoming calls answered was only about 50%. After the call centre was set up, Liu promised Li that all the employees there would get a raise if the answer rate reached 96%. Soon, the nearly 100 employees in the call centre could be seen running to answer the phones, even rushing to and from meals in order not to miss a call. In December, the answer rate reached 98%. The following year, a new goal was set: before the "18 June" company anniversary sale, they had to reduce the proportion of incoming calls to 28% of total orders. Incoming calls were 56% at the peak, meaning that for every 100 orders, they would receive 56 calls covering a variety of problems. If a call didn't go through, customers would redial, and this would also be counted. In the end, the call centre reduced the proportion to 27% before the deadline.

At the first training class for new call centre employees, attendees had to close their eyes and listen as the trainer spoke in different tones of voice. "Hello, JD is very glad to be at your service." The trainer would ask: "Did you hear the smile?"

I met Ding Kang, a young man born in 1990 who worked in the Suqian sub-centre of the JD National Customer Service Centre. His job was to answer calls from diamond-level customers. These are customers whose spending exceeded 30,000 yuan a year and who rarely made calls unless a problem was truly complicated.

A customer in the Suqian area had bought imported milk powder. A third-party seller shipped the goods through Yunda Express, but after seven days, it still hadn't arrived, and the baby had had no milk for two days. Learning that JD was not responsible for the courier's delay, the customer hung up after registering the complaint. Ding reached Yunda customer service through the tracking number. The delivery was indeed backlogged with the courier. It turned out that after the customer had complained directly to Yunda's headquarters, a vindictive deliveryman, knowing he was already in trouble, refused to make the delivery a priority. He told Ding it would take at least three days but that JD was welcome to come and collect it themselves if they wanted. Ding called the customer and said: "If you bear with me, I'll help get your package to you." The customer agreed but was sceptical.

The Yunda delivery station was 15 kilometres from the Suqian call centre, which closed at 6 pm. Racing on his electric scooter, Ding reached Yunda at 7:10 pm, and it took him 20 minutes to find the customer's parcel of milk powder. At 8 pm, he arrived at the customer's home, where the entire family was waiting at the gate. On his way back in the rain, his electric scooter ran out of power, and Ding had to push it all the way home. At midnight, just as he got in the door, he received a message from the customer: "Thank you, 38794." That was Ding's customer service number.

It's difficult to envision a stronger illustration of what it means to put the customer first. In the call centre, such stories abounded.

Zhuang Jingjing, who worked in online customer service at the Chengdu sub-centre of JD's National Customer Service Centre, got the job when she was 20, soon after she graduated from high school. After she began work, she was also admitted to college. Zhuang went to university and stayed for a month, but found that school life was quite different from what she had imagined. So, she returned to the call centre. She knew how stressful the work could be, but her supervisors and managers were good to her and treated her as a younger sister. Customers might make her cry, but her supervisors made her feel warm.

A loyal fan of Amazon.cn was eager to buy a set of books, but Amazon didn't stock them. A Baidu search showed that it was sold by JD East China, but the customer was in Wuhan, in Central China. The warehouse mode that JD used at the time wasn't set up to ship goods across regions. The customer, desperate to get this set of books, called JD customer service. In accordance with company procedures, customer service listened closely and asked the caller to be patient until Central China replenished its stock. But the customer wouldn't be put off, and insisted customer service fix the problem. Finally, the call was put through to the customer care department, which was the last stage, the place where the toughest customer complaints and unsettled issues were finalized.

Zhuang took the call. She told the customer: "I'm a book lover myself. I can tell how upset you are and I'll try my best to help you." When the customer hung up, Zhuang ordered the books using her own account. Although she was off the next day, Zhuang showed up at 8 am, picked up the books from the self-collection spot, and personally mailed them to the customer. Every day, she texted the books' location to the customer. On the fourth day, at noon, the customer received the books and texted Zhuang: "Maybe JD's sales system is not perfect, but your perfect service has made up for the flaw. I don't see why I shall not be a faithful user of JD."

Zhuang's service had gone well above and beyond the normal process. Although JD did not support cross-regional goods transfer, she had resolved the customer's problem in her own way. While many customer service workers would simply assume that they couldn't resolve this kind of problem on their own, Zhuang's story showed that, through proactive service, there was a way to solve problems, whatever they might be.

Call centres encountered all kinds of incredible demands. One caller told Zhuang: "My child is four months old. We've bought everything from JD. Now my baby is crying. If you don't solve this problem, I'll file a complaint." It was the end of the world if a complaint was not resolved by her group and landed with customer care, and Zhuang felt terrible.

She realized this was an outrageous and unreasonable request, but she could also tell that the customer was desperate. It turned out that he was the father of a newborn and his wife normally cared for the baby. But it was the weekend and wife and his mother were out. He was left alone with the baby and didn't know what to do. Zhuang guessed that the baby might be hungry, and suggested the father give him some milk.

Zhuang told him to read the instructions on the milk powder can and make sure the water he added wasn't too hot or too cold. He was scared to take the baby in his arms, but Zhuang soothed him: "Take it easy. You're the father. You love him." The baby stopped crying after drinking the milk, but started again when he was returned to the cradle. Zhuang thought perhaps the baby was sleepy, so she told the father to gently coax him to sleep, but that didn't work. Finally, she told him to change the child's diaper. But the father didn't know where to find a fresh one. Zhuang told him to look near the cradle, then taught him, over the phone, how to change a diaper. The call lasted for more than two hours.

Many people in customer service didn't have this much patience. Zhuang said: "I taught an inexperienced father to take care of his baby. This was customer service's biggest achievement." She clearly understood the difference between run-of-the-mill customer service and excellent customer service.

No Pain, No Gain

Du Shuang, a smart and stylish woman, is JD Group vice president and the general manager of the IT digital business division. She joined JD in October 2008 as a saleswoman, purchasing and selling electronics, including flash drives, mice, keyboards, routers and the like. Mice and keyboards were low-price items, perhaps 60 yuan or less per customer transaction. But Du regularly lowered the prices by 50 cents at a time. She was also a persuasive negotiator. Once, she purchased some mice from the Zhongguancun market, but the boss refused to deliver them because the order total was too small. Du did not give up: "Come on. This is business. Forget about the limits. Zhongguancun is so close to Suzhou Street. Please just send them to us." The supplier relented and delivered the goods by tricycle.

When the category she was responsible for saw sales increase from two million to 20 million yuan in eight months, she was promoted to department manager. Knowing Du used to work in a supermarket and knew how to negotiate display arrangements and collect the fees, her superior, Sun Jiaming, asked her to take care of brand management and negotiate with manufacturers on advertising cooperation. She became the first person in the IT department to negotiate a manufacturer ad investment that wasn't linked to sales volume. The investment was 50,000 yuan per year, regardless of product sales. JD's annual sales volume with this manufacturer was 2 million yuan.

Du had never asked for annual leave or sick leave, and she could drink with suppliers until the whites of her eyes turned red. Then, in October 2010, Du left JD. She didn't accept a competitive offer, send out her résumé or apply for other positions. She stayed home, contemplating how to be a better person. She had been working too hard and had neglected too many things in her personal life. Among other things, she'd long felt that she had problems socializing with the people around her. A manufacturer tried to hire her during this time, but she turned down the offer. She was sure she would go back to work at JD at some point. Those who'd known her at JD also believed she would return some day. Indeed, after a year's sabbatical she came back.

When she'd worked at the supermarket, Du was like a blank page; she didn't know the ways of the world. Her workplace was competitive. No one was there to help her or teach her, she had to learn on her own and she dared not ask questions. Soon after she came to JD, Du received a consumer complaint on product quality, and asked the manufacturer to contact the customer directly. A colleague who overheard the call warned her that was against company rules, and suggested that she should first contact the manufacturer herself and then the user. When she erred, her JD colleagues didn't set her up – they helped her out.

Zhang Qi, her superior, recommended her to Sun Jiaming. Du was later promoted above him, but he still worked hard to help her manage the team. "Your performance can directly demonstrate your skills," said Sun. "You will have the opportunity to rise up alongside your supervisor or even higher as long as you are good enough. I am deeply touched by such an open mind." When she returned to JD, Du was responsible for peripheral equipment. For six months running, this department had failed to achieve its targets, and the team was demoralized. After observing for three days, Du publicly declared that her team would earn the incentive package, which was as much as 2 million yuan for teams whose sales volumes exceeded the targets. At that time the peripheral equipment team's performance didn't even come close to target. How could it possibly qualify for the incentives? But for Du, nothing was impossible. One just needed to find the path. With a fulcrum, the earth could be moved. The trick was to find the fulcrum.

Within the peripheral equipment team there were groups that did well, and others that didn't. The good ones griped that they were being dragged down by the laggards, but Du would not allow the spread of negativity. She said: "Our team is a whole. Every member should have the same goal. If you are more capable, then you can do more, and earn more bonuses. Those having difficulties shouldn't give up. I see your hard work and you will get what you deserve." After trying to lift team morale, she began plotting out a plan for success. Du's high spirits and ambition energized them all.

Once Liu was strolling through the buying and merchandising department's area. When he met Du, he asked, "What are you doing? How is the business these days?" "I found a product model with a good price, but I don't know if I should stock 2,000 units or more," Du said. "Make it 10,000 units; I'll support you," said Liu. He recognized that Du's ability was reflected in the department's performance, and directly linked to actual returns.

In the traditional supermarket where she'd worked, there had been no objective performance evaluation, which was most unfair to her. Her value was solely decided by her boss. Although Du was dedicated to her work and had created more and more income for the company, her boss was not satisfied. Later, she realized she'd offended some people and was suffering the consequences. JD was completely different. She deeply identified with the passion and integrity in the company's values. Du was a fighter, energetic and persistent. If her team won under her command, she felt fulfilled.

In her former job, her ambition was buried because there was no stimulation from the external environment. If she had shown her ambition, she would have been considered strange and incompatible in that setting. At JD, finding herself in a job she was seemingly born to do, she became increasingly confident. Liu was never satisfied with current achievements. If Du told him sales were 2 million yuan, he would challenge: "Why not make it 4 million?" He always raised the bar and Du always tried to jump over it. She challenged herself to move forward.

Tang Yishen, director of JD's mobile, digital, and communications department, joined the company in April 2008. Previously, he'd worked for a large retail chain store where no one taught him anything. He sat around waiting to be assigned work. He wanted to learn how to place purchase orders and settle bills, but instead he'd be sent to run errands: "Tang, go to the finance office and see whether the money was paid." By the time he returned, the operation he wanted to learn had been completed. But at JD, his colleagues supported him; they would set their own work aside to teach him how to use the system, and encourage him to ask again if he didn't understand.

Tang's former employer did not like working during the day and preferred to have meetings at night. The meetings were not serious, but full of joking, chatting and playing games. Many people asked others to punch the clock for them the next day. There were frequent meetings, most of which seemed to serve no business purpose. As a marketing person, Tang was out of the office most of the day, negotiating with suppliers. He also had a lot of paperwork.

In his former company, he earned a little over 3,000 yuan a month, yet had to work until midnight every day. The company provided no training, and he felt neither appreciated nor recognized. He wanted to increase his income through advancement, but he observed that the only ways to boost his income seemed to involve bribery.

As soon as he joined JD, Tang felt he had come to the right place. The phone kept ringing, everyone was busy and the atmosphere was pleasantly hectic. A company would go nowhere if everyone is listless. At that time, people in buying and merchandising worked daily from 8:30 am until midnight. Because of the underdeveloped storage system, the materials management process was not proceeding smoothly and people were dispatched to the warehouses to help with inventory each week. Four or five people would manually count hundreds of thousands of memory cards, for example. But these young people were full of passion and energy.

Tang asked himself: "Why was JD so efficient as a start-up? Why did employees cooperate with each other so well, even without strict supervision?" He concluded that it was because they identified with JD, viewed it as their own business. Even after the company expanded, and the work was standardized with highly effective automated systems, employees who'd come through that early period kept their original dedication – to both themselves and the company. If you couldn't create value for the company, if you were easily replaceable, then you weren't worth much to the business.

What kind of enterprises are respected by society? Those that create value and create values for society. Throughout its history, JD never skirted the edges of the law or used loopholes to evade taxes. E-commerce had higher operating efficiencies than traditional channels. A purchase transaction that used to involve dozens of people could be fulfilled by a single deliveryman. Improving operating efficiency could create value for society and provide more employment opportunities. JD had offered 70,000 people jobs, as well as opportunities to improve themselves through various training programmes.

"I've devoted the best part of my youth to JD, from when I was a boy of 22 to nearly 30 this year," said Tang Yishen. "I think I am loyal to the company, with my every action and every thought dedicated to its interests. And JD returned this loyalty to me, through income, stock returns and the work environment. Many people I know also started as management trainees in other companies. They are in their thirties and have contributed for nearly 10 years, but they earn average incomes, have unremarkable work experience, and no stock shares. They feel sorry for themselves."

The best thing about JD's culture is that it recognizes people who are persistent and serious in their work. Yang Haifeng worked diligently in a publishing house for seven years without a promotion. Over four years at JD, he rose steadily. He brought his industry experience to JD and at the same time learned a lot about, for example, operations and e-books. Beginning as a marketing manager in the books division, he went on to head the books and audio-video products business division. At JD, he realized, you really do reap what you sow.

The people of JD work hard, sometimes to the point of exhaustion. They've been known to work until midnight, although no one insisted they do so. This was the essence of JD management: the company fully trusted its employees and the employees were responsible for results. If you had the ability and were prepared to excel, JD offered you a platform. When you achieved results, JD would reward you.

JD had a young team throughout this period whose members shared the same goals and wanted to achieve something big. In this energetic team, enthusiasm was contagious. Anyone who dawdled or sought personal gain at the expense of the team would be weeded out. JD's rapid growth and constant challenges helped sustain employee passion. As JD developed, these young people also knew that they'd sharpened their professional skills and broadened their horizons, which gave them a sense of achievement.

It is human nature that people want to improve their situations. The question is whether a company can offer them opportunities to fulfill that need. Often, if people are given a good platform from which to operate, they take positive action. But if a company's culture is unsound and a person's performance is not recognized, there is the risk of bad money driving out the good.

Zero Tolerance for Corruption

In one of JD's product divisions, a story has been told again and again over the years. Once, a JD employee was meeting with a supplier in JD's office. A bottle of water, bought by the supplier, was at their side. Wang Xiaosong deliberately passed by the employee to see whether he would drink the supplier's water. Passing for the third time, he saw the employee open the bottle and take a drink. Afterward, Wang brought this matter to the table and criticized the employee.

When I first heard this, I thought it was unnecessarily harsh. But as I learned more about the company, I realized that JD's efforts to combat corruption had gone beyond obsession and could almost be called paranoid. This comes from Liu's hatred of corruption, traceable back to the evils he witnessed in his boyhood village.

Liu's first major life transformation occurred in junior high school. In elementary school, he was skinny and small for his class; in junior high, he suddenly grew taller than his peers. He received his junior school education in the town, away from home, and during that period he lodged in the office of an accountant named Zhou. The office had copies of *People's Daily*, *Xinhua Daily* and *China Youth News*.

He was fond of reading *China Youth News*, a newspaper that depicted the pioneers of Chinese thought before 1989. It had wide coverage of life in foreign countries. For the first time, Liu learned that foreign parents, unlike in China, had no obligations to buy houses for or support their children until they got married, if even then. After the age of 18, many foreign children lived on their own and had to earn their own school tuition. The newspaper also reported stories about great inventors and individual successes in other countries. He could sense a spirit of respect for knowledge and self-reliance. Back in the village, Liu had been taught that American people lived in extreme misery and needed to be rescued. Reading the newspaper stories, he glimpsed a different world and felt that until then his view had been as narrow as that of a frog in a well.

But what he saw in the government compound was a different situation. The local officials were openly corrupt. And the law did not seem to apply to them. At the mid-Autumn Festival, all the village heads brought gifts to the town government officials: tractors appeared loaded with pigs, ducks, chickens, geese, eggs, crabs, eels, turtles and more. The officials and all their family members could simply grab all they wanted from this bounty. At every Spring Festival, an abundance of preserved meat hung under the eaves of the town government building. "While the rich wine and dine, the poor die of cold by the roadside." The young Liu understood this old verse for the first time. The villagers could barely feed themselves, subsisting on rice. They had no electricity and couldn't afford clothes. At that time, if children received clothes sent from Shanghai, they would be too excited to sleep because it was said the clothes from there were the very best.

But in the eyes of some government officials, as he recalled, villagers were inferior to animals. When veterans from the Korean War came back to the village, some had lost a leg. They were supposed to get a five yuan pension every month, but even this pittance was denied them. When these disabled veterans petitioned for their pension at the government gates, an official yelled and even kicked some of them. The official was an alcoholic who often looked for trouble after he'd been drinking. If you played mah jongg at home and there was even a penny on the table, he would accuse you of organized gambling. He asked local guards to arrest people, and he beat them in his room until they cried and begged for mercy.

In his youth, Liu was also greatly influenced by his high school teacher, Mr Qi. According to some of Liu's classmates, Qi's outlook on life had influenced them as well. Qi was outspoken, called a tough nut and marginalized in a society where it was common to establish relationships through bribery. Qi believed that, though he could not fight against this practice, he could refuse to participate in it. Although his father-in-law once worked in the Education Ministry, and Qi was also quite eligible for a similar government post, he rebuffed that easy path because he saw teaching as a more meaningful job. In the eyes of his students, Qi was free and noble. He treated all students alike regardless of their marks. Later, when they were in their thirties, they gathered together and reminisced about Qi. All of them felt grateful to have met such a decent and excellent teacher at such an important phase of their lives, when their world outlook had begun to take shape. He told the students that all men were created equal, that teachers and students were equal, and all the students were equal.

Qi also encouraged them to go to college and later to enter politics. This was one reason Liu chose the sociology department when he enrolled in China's Renmin University. In his three years of junior high school, he got a further glimpse into the undisguised corruption in the village. In order to be appointed a village head, some villagers bribed town officials with cash, and the officials could be seen counting out the money in public view. When the provincial government gave the village warm clothing to distribute to residents, local officials sold them instead.

It wasn't easy for sociology majors to find jobs, When Liu's eldest roommate proposed to a girl she turned him down, saying: "Students from your department can't find jobs, let alone afford to buy a house. Why should I marry you?" Liu, shocked, realized that if he had no money, he might never have a girlfriend. He decided to learn about technology. He bought some books published by China Industry Press and Tsinghua University Press and began teaching himself about computers. After he had learned programming, he began to make money by writing systems software. During college, he earned more than 200,000 yuan this way. He wanted to invest in his future and start his own business. A Sichuan restaurant in Beijing, located in the middle of Haidian Book Market near the west gate of Renmin University, was for sale at that time. This restaurant was popular. It was known for its good food and it turned a good profit. Liu cut a deal with the boss in three minutes, and the next day, he and his girlfriend brought enough cash to close the deal. He had no idea about title certificates or other requirements, nor did he consult a lawyer. He thought that finally he had a place to settle down in Beijing.

He was dumbfounded when the landlord came to ask for the rent four months later. No wonder the price was so affordable. He had been scammed.

Clinging to the idea of treating others as you wished to be treated, Liu tried to improve working conditions at the restaurant. He doubled the salaries of each of the 20 employees who stayed and gave each one a watch worth 100 yuan. The former boss had asked the employees to eat leftovers, but Liu insisted that leftovers be thrown away. The standard employee meal consisted of four dishes – two meat and two vegetable – and a couple of beers a week. After two months, Liu felt something was wrong. At first, the restaurant's daily receipts averaged 30,000 yuan, and was never less than 10,000 yuan. Now it was 10,000 yuan at most and on same days was as low as 2,000 yuan. The man responsible for the kitchen purchases began to ask for more and more money. Liu funded him with all the money he had earned and even had to borrow money from his parents and his aunt. One worker finally revealed to Liu what some of the others already knew: that the cashier was in love with the chef and they had embezzled the money.

The beef that cost 6 yuan was reported to Liu as a 12 yuan cost and bean sprouts at 0.2 yuan were reported as 0.8. Liu had specified that any meat not used up in three days would not be served. Perhaps 8 jin (4 kilos, or almost 9 pounds) of beef was enough for the restaurant over a day, but the embezzlers would buy 12 jin so they could steal a third of it in a few days. It was like a bottomless pit. In the end, Liu had to dismiss all of the employees, pay them an extra month's salary and close the restaurant. He had lost hundreds of thousands of yuan and was in debt for nearly 200,000. He was very hurt. "Did I not treat you well? Did I not respect you?" he thought. "What have I done wrong? I provided you with food and accommodations. I've never checked the accounts and never brought in a single relative to oversee you. Why would you do this to me? You are migrant workers and I am also a son of peasants. I'd earned that money doing months of coding, sleeping only two or three hours a day."

Frustrated, Liu began to question human nature. Of course others have always wondered whether people were inherently good or evil. Some people thought human nature was evil and that people became good only under the restrictions of society and its laws. Others argued that human nature was fundamentally good but became corrupted by a decadent society.

In 1996, still harbouring these doubts, Liu joined a Japanese company. In this foreign company, he was first asked to manage the information system, but he went on to study the management structure. Slowly, he began to understand how money corresponded to the materials, how spending was controlled, and how dealers were organized. Later, he was transferred to manage the warehouse, which was a necessary step for promotion and came with a salary raise. He spent one-third of his time in the warehouse, frequently working until after midnight. Dealers often came to pick up or deliver goods at night. He checked the goods, carried them to the truck, and recorded them on the computer. There was no overtime payment and the temporary workers refused to help out, so he worked alone and did the work of six men.

It was during this period that he got an in-depth understanding of the management attitude of a foreign company. The business had a complicated system of adding many thousands of detailed product flyers to shipments and they had to be checked to ensure there were no errors. The Japanese employees said: "Only the Chinese call it an error. We call it a mistake. A mistake is a mistake. There is no error at all."

Liu fully realized that the failure of his first business, the restaurant, was his own fault. With a better management system in place and appropriate processes, his employees' corruption could have been caught or prevented in the first place. The restaurant had not been well managed. For example, invoices were not numbered; if they had been, the thefts would have been much more difficult to pull off.

In the beginning, when he introduced a similar idea to JD's management, his employees suffered. Usually, when a company's CEO has some idea for corporate management, he'd incorporate it into the regulations, announce it to everyone, then execute it. But this was not the case with Liu. When he had an idea, he would go directly to the technology department and ask it to immediately make it part of the process and embed it in the system. Employees had to follow the rules in the system. In 2007, JD employed more than 200 people. Many companies of this size still had no system, relying purely on human management and implementation. Liu always built his thinking into the system and passed his ideas down through it.

Although this step had to be taken sooner or later, at the time it meant high costs – and Liu's subordinates were not happy about it. The system would not be suitable for every type of complex environment. Often, key factors hadn't been taken into consideration. Sometimes, a certain process was added into the system ad hoc in order to solve a problem.

"If the company suspects someone of embezzling 100,000 yuan," Liu said, "we will investigate and dismiss the guilty employee, even it costs us 10 million yuan to do it. Some people say that this is a vengeful mentality. It is not that I am merciless, it is that what you've done is completely contrary to my values and has subverted my dreams. As a kid, I was shocked by corruption's disrespect for human nature and human equality. I cannot tolerate corruption in my life. I won't accept it and nor shall you, unless you choose to leave the company."

The purchasing and marketing departments were always the ones that could be most susceptible to corruption. These employees had pricing power, procurement power and settlement rights. It would have been easy for someone so inclined to change the data in the system and hand over to the company just two indicators, sales and gross margins. It didn't seem like a serious exposure back then, but seemed scary in retrospect. Thanks to JD's corporate culture, no really big problem occurred. In every monthly meeting, Liu would expound his ideas. And his employees believed in JD. They didn't need to cheat to get ahead; they would have a better tomorrow by creating value through hard work.

Liu liked to share. All JD veterans held the company's performance shares. At first they didn't know what they were, and thought they were just pieces of paper. But they believed in Liu. It was this belief that supported them during JD's early development. Who could tell what would happen to the company in the future?

Later the purchase and marketing processes become more rigorous, with numerous checks and balances in the system and more oversight. Purchase prices were reviewed, for example, and required an official letter from the manufacturer. The sales price was reviewed. Profit margins were transparent and public. If there was any price adjustment, the department had to maintain detailed records.

Previously, everything was checked through reconciliation, when the purchasing and marketing staff submitted orders directly for settlement. These weren't recorded or filed, and couldn't be traced if there were any questions after settlement. Once the reconciliation process was reorganized, manufacturers had to send confirmation letters stamped with official seals before JD issued the settlement. Contracts had also been put into the settlement and approval system.

If process improvements and monitoring mechanisms were like the skin, then cultural development was the skeleton. Liu believed the first task was to establish common values with the aim of achieving success honestly. The second task was to establish mechanisms to share the wealth with employees. Liu believed that, after working for JD for five years, employees should be able to buy a house in their hometowns. Power could lead to corruption, so the third task was to ensure that systems and technologies were in place to solve and prevent such problems. Most importantly, if a leader set a bad example, his subordinates would follow it, so management had to set good examples and keep its noses clean.

The team had to always stay alert. After more than a decade of experience in purchasing and marketing, the managerial staff could tell whether there was a problem by observing the state of the employees. The company also had to establish a training system. Many core members of the buying and merchandising team joined JD soon after graduation. The company gave them the opportunity to buy houses and cars, and to live honestly. If the marketing staff took money from suppliers, they'd no longer be able to fairly and honestly judge the quality and prices of the products. How much money could suppliers give them? Tens of thousands of yuan? Hundreds of thousands? To ruin their careers and personal reputations for this sum would be a shame. People who began at JD developed the right values. But it might be different for someone who began in a company that turned a blind eye to corruption.

At JD, corruption represented a red line. However small the amount, once you crossed the line, your days there were over. JD once terminated an employee over 10 yuan. Any kind of cheating was prohibited. Those who asked others to punch the clock for them, or who went out on personal errands on company time, were considered dishonest and were fired.

Kickbacks are a common phenomenon in many cultures and a well-known problem in China, but Liu never tolerated them. A serious case of corruption once took place in the major appliances department. After the guilty employee was fired, Liu was determined to solve the problem regardless of the cost. He would rather suffer a temporary performance loss and transfer people from other departments to fix the problem.

JD signed anti-corruption agreements with all its partners. It also distributed anti-corruption guidelines and provided clear mechanisms for reporting problems. At JD, employees could have meals with suppliers, but they had to inform the administration department and their direct supervisor. A major home appliance supplier reported that a JD warehouse manager went out for a meal with another supplier. An investigation showed that they had indeed shared a cheap porridge in a food stall. Still, the manager was fired. The department was fined 50,000 yuan, which was given to the informant as a reward.

In 2007, JD recruited a dedicated surveillance staff to fight corruption. Once a case of bad behaviour causing significant damage to the company was found, it would be reported directly to the police and handled by the relevant departments. Some guilty parties were found after they'd left the company; they were arrested. Liu was relentless and spared no one in this regard. If the case was not serious enough to register with the police, then the person would simply be dismissed. The company had an internal control compliance website that kept a record of offences, so the consequences were very serious. For a time, employees would turn pale at mention of the surveillance team.

Li Yayun, vice president of the internal control compliance division of JD Group, reported directly to Liu. With only 10 people, this was not a big group. Two of the employees were dedicated to training and education. Twice a year, training on criminal law provisions was carried out for high-risk departments – administrative procurement, product buying, delivery, spare parts storage and others. The team also went out to each region to provide training for suppliers. Many suppliers engaged in bribery because it was a standard business practice, not because they wanted to. They worried that their businesses would suffer if they didn't offer bribes or send gifts. Someone once paid a JD employee's 100 yuan telephone bill. The employee was so scared that he immediately reported it to his superior, who suggested he pay it back. On festive occasions, suppliers always brought gifts, all of which were to be turned over to the administrative department. A supplier once hinted to a director that he would receive 300,000 yuan if they could close a deal. "Buddy, the deal will advance in the normal way," the director replied. "If you say one more word about this, we'll have to stop talking." During training, the surveillance division told suppliers they were chosen based on price evaluation and quality of service. It was not only useless to send gifts, they would be blacklisted if they did.

The biggest corruption deterrent was the sight of police coming to JD to take away the employees involved. There were about three to five such cases per year. The most sensational one occurred in 2013, and involved more than 3 million yuan. After an anonymous tip, the surveillance team investigated IT department manager Zhou and discovered he had colluded with a supplier and was getting kickbacks. He was arrested and ultimately sentenced to five years and five months in prison. Two of the supplier's employees also were arrested.

The company set strict standards against corruption. Any employee who violated the rules would be dismissed, and both his superior and his boss's boss would receive demerits in their files. Anyone receiving two such strikes against them would be automatically dismissed. If one suspected his supervisor of wrongdoing and reported the matter, he or she would be exempt from punishment. Once, in a promotion activity offering free iPhones, an employee changed the winners' names to those of his wife and friends. His superior found it a bit strange and asked the surveillance division to investigate. The iPhones were taken back and the man was fired.

In recent years, JD invested great effort in fighting corruption, and as a result reported cases declined sharply.

PART III

2011-2015

By the end of 2010, JD had grown into a company of nearly 8,000 employees. Some 457 million Chinese people were now online, and more than 300 million of them were predominantly mobile users.

The Yinfeng Building in Beijing was home to the company as it quickly grew from JD Multimedia into JD Mall. When he originally surveyed the office space he'd secured there, Liu had said proudly to Sun Jiaming and the others, "Look, the tap water is drinkable. How nice!"

Employees who spent as many as eight years at JD's headquarters, however, would later remember the conditions at the facility less fondly. The elevator often stopped working and people could be heard calling for help opening its door. The single bathroom had long queues and its floors were often flooded. Cockroach traps were everywhere, even on the backs of computers. And employees soon learned never to drink from a water glass before thoroughly washing out the dust that had accumulated in it overnight.

To keep pace with its rapid growth, in 2010 JD relocated to North Star Century Centre, located on Beijing's 4th Ring Road. The upgrade to dramatically better office space reinforced everyone's sense that JD had become a large, successful company.

At first, North Star Century Centre's property management wondered whether JD could afford the rent. But by 2014 JD had leased six floors, each with 6,742m^2 of workspace. Every day, in the new building's Starbucks cafe and Subway sandwich shop, people with JD badges could be seen engaged in intense business conversations and working on their computers. It was not unusual to see employees in their 20s confidently interacting with suppliers and partners 10 or 20 years their senior, a notable exception to the hierarchical segregation that was the norm within many Chinese organizations.

On 30 March 2013, JD introduced a new logo and a corporate mascot: Joy, a glowing, silver dog with a big smile. The company changed its domain name from www.360buy.com to www.jd.com. At the same time, the word "Mall" was dropped and JD Mall became JD.

The strategic name change signalled that JD was no longer just a retail company. It was positioning itself to pursue lucrative business opportunities in financial services, logistics and cloud computing.

JD used the new logo announcement event to publicize its depth and breadth: 1 million square metres of warehouse space, annual turnover of 60 billion yuan, 30,000 employees, an inventory of tens of millions of commodities for sale and a customer base of literally tens of millions of active users.

The speed with which JD grew pushed its competitors to upgrade their offerings as well. Along the way, the company inevitably attracted its share of sceptics and critics. Rumours of debt and cash flow problems were relatively common, especially after a brutal home appliances price war in the summer of 2012. When Li Xi, later vice president of public relations, joined JD in January 2013, she conducted an internet search for "JD capital chain rupture" and found more than 6 million results. Anxious suppliers came knocking, asking for payments, and there was no shortage of negative commentary in the marketplace.

In the long run, JD's investors came to see that period in the company's history as its most vulnerable.

Despite the challenges, JD had no trouble attracting outside investment. From 2011 until just before its listing in May 2014, its total financing topped $2.026 billion. Shareholders included Today Capital, Bull Capital Partners, Tiger Fund, Hillhouse Capital, DST, Sequoia Capital, KPCB, Ontario Teachers' Pension Plan of Canada, Tencent and others. JD's public listing, and a round of positive news coverage that accompanied it, helped reassure investors and employees alike.

In March 2012, Hu Chun joined JD as financial manager for the Central China Region. Early on, Hu was asked to sign a stock option agreement, which she frankly saw as a worthless piece of paper. That changed after the IPO, when she and others were duly rewarded for their roles in the company's success. She had previously worked for a home appliance retail chain with locations across China. After six long years there, she felt her personal finances had not really improved. "JD represents fairness," Hu said. "If you work hard and make a meaningful contribution, you'll be rewarded."

In Hu's former company, the headquarters secretly dispatched supervisors dressed in street clothes to inspect stores and monitor employee sentiment. This caused discomfort and stress among employees. Even if you talked about management in hushed tones in the restroom, she said, your comments could be heard by the eavesdropping undercover inspectors and there could be repercussions.

At JD, on the other hand, she found that employees could discuss workplace concerns openly with colleagues without getting called out. An old saying in Wuhan goes like this: "Domestic chickens still circle around you when you beat them, but pheasants will fly away." The notion is that a chicken will relentlessly hold on to the yard as its home, despite the danger. A pheasant is different; if harassed it will flee and never come back.

Chief financial officer Sidney Huang was largely responsible for the investment community road show that preceded JD's public offering. Along the way Shen Haoyu, CEO of JD's consumer business unit, also took on an active role in the IPO briefings. The roadshow was completed in seven days and was well received in the capital market. Investor demand was several times greater than the amount raised through the IPO. The stock price was ultimately fixed at $19 per share, higher than the pre-roadshow estimate range of $16 to $18.

Huang joined JD as CFO in September 2013, with extensive experience working in IPO management and listed companies. He came to regard Liu as refreshingly outspoken and straightforward, with an aversion to secrecy and the uncertainty and doubt it sows in the workplace. Huang saw the tremendous value Liu placed on the free flow of business information, and how it benefitted the entire team.

A public listing would of course require the release of formal financial reports, and the preparation of performance data and business projections picked up steam. (Huang also saw value in continuing private placements.) When the financial report for the third quarter of 2013 was published, it reflected strong performance, with respectable revenue growth and a net profit. With those positive metrics, JD was qualified for listing.

Around that time, Alibaba experienced setbacks and delays in its effort to get listed in Hong Kong. JD had no desire to overlap with Alibaba and arranged to delay the planned JD IPO until after Alibaba was listed. But Alibaba was continually reworking its listing schedule. JD could not wait forever.

In October 2013 Huang discussed IPO timing with Bao Fan of China Renaissance Capital and with senior management from the Merrill Lynch VC Fund. In November, he made a detailed analysis of the pros and cons of launching an IPO. He submitted it to Liu, who decided to accelerate the process. On the eve of the Chinese Lunar New Year in 2014, JD submitted its first IPO application to the United States Securities and Exchange Commission.

The timing and announcement logistics were such that it caught the industry largely off guard, preempting strategic pushback and counter-measures by competitors and bringing more attention to the event.

China Renaissance Capital was one of the underwriters of JD's IPO; it had also served as JD's financial adviser when Tencent invested in JD. Initially, though, China Renaissance believed JD was a risky proposition and it declined the opportunity to participate more fully. Bao Fan, chairman and CEO of China Renaissance, first got to know Liu in 2008 when JD was raising funds. He has said he originally viewed Liu as domineering and ambitious, with a strong sense of loyalty to insiders and friends. In 2010, China Renaissance missed another chance to invest in JD. It wasn't until 2011, when China Renaissance helped the Russian investment company DST with an investment in JD, that the company finally came around. It had taken Bao Fan and China Renaissance Capital four years of watching Liu run his business before they were ready.

"It turns out to be the right formula: if you find a reliable man, you can find a great business opportunity," said Bao Fan. "If you pick the right guy, you have to keep an eye on him over time, even if it takes four or five years. Liu is resourceful and loyal to friends. We first became friends and then we did business together. Others might be capable, but they put their own interests above all else. They approach everyone with an interest only in doing business. If they think only about making money, they won't go far."

Over the years, Liu was more or less digging a hole. He jumped in, full of high hopes and boundless energy, but uncertain whether he could make it. Through hard work and determination, he slowly began to pull JD from the pit. Many who are ambitious and hungry to compete would jump into the hole, struggle, and throw money at the task, only to end up digging the pit deeper.

JD did research over time to see how much its competitors had spent to challenge Liu's upstart company. If Newegg had raised $50 million at that time, the result would have been hard to predict. In 2011, JD raised more than $1 billion. Who dared to burn through $1 billion to compete with JD? In the end, it doesn't take much to dig a deep pit. But to pull oneself out of the hole and move ever upward? By any measure, that really is something special.

The external challenges were formidable, but the greatest obstacles Liu faced were from JD's internal management. Over the course of four years, JD's workforce had ballooned from 10,000 to 70,000. Its suite of businesses came to span e-commerce, logistics and finance, among numerous other fields. With turnover of 260.2 billion yuan in just a few years, JD had become a retailing giant. But behind the seemingly miraculous success story, there were countless operational problems. Growth was king, and the company's annual growth rate of 100% to 200% overshadowed the considerable challenges. These problems would surface sooner or later, and they'd have to be dealt with.

By 2012, e-commerce had been growing for a decade and accounted for 5% of total retail sales nationally. In time its growth would slow and become more predictable. Over the preceding 10 years, as the e-commerce ecosystem had matured, the primary objective changed from desperately seeking scale at any cost, to achieving scalable, bullet-proof operational efficiency.

The age of extensive development had given way to a new era of intensive cultivation. The winners would be the master cultivators.

JD had three knives. The first knife cut prices. The benefit to consumers was self-evident.

The second knife cut costs. In contrast to traditional retail enterprises, JD worked to reduce costs by eliminating long, inefficient supply chains and strictly controlling its own costs. JD's calculation of costs was precise, down to the cent and the li (one thousandth of a yuan). Warehouse staff used to wield both RF guns, for data collecting, and paper order sheets they had to fill out. They eventually downsized order sheets from A4 to about half that size, for cost savings of nearly 45%. Annual savings jumped to nearly 100 million yuan when order sheets were replaced entirely by electronic forms.

The third knife concerned thought. Any idea that does not start from the consumer's point of view had to be pared away. Liu insisted that management improve internal processes using the customer experience as the starting point, not the company's costs and the profit. The needs of the consumer had to be the overriding focus. Managers' cost and expense issues were theirs to own and manage, secondary to thinking about the customer.

In 2012 it became apparent that JD employees responsible for delivery in the North China Region and the Northeast China Region were passing problems back and forth to one another without ever resolving them. For example, a load of goods was shipped from the North China Region to the Northeast China Region without proper tagging. The latter returned the goods to North China. In his morning meeting, Liu asked, "When you passed the buck, did you ever think of the consumers' interests?" When it became clear that the answer was no, the head of delivery for Northeast China was removed on the spot. At this critical moment, Yuan Wei, director of vehicle management in JD's delivery division, was entrusted with the mission. He was transferred to Shenyang to serve as delivery director for the Northeast China Region, a responsibility he carried through to May 2013.

To optimize the customer experience, JD purchased Mercedes-Benz truck engines at more than 1 million yuan each. That's roughly four times more expensive than ordinary truck engines, but the

Mercedes motors were considerably more reliable. On the highway from Beijing to Inner Mongolia, most trucks on the road were drab, lumbering and loaded with coal. It was particularly eye-catching when the red carriages painted with white letters "JD" sped by, their Mercedes engines purring. Compared to the normal traffic on that road, the JD trucks were so impressive that people took photos and uploaded them to social media sites.

The R&D department's top-to-bottom transformation of its user experience research paralleled the larger company's transformation. Prior to 2010, R&D got much of its intelligence by observing and interviewing customers at JD's pick-up stations. The largest pick-up station was on the ground floor of Yinfeng Building. When walk-in customers used on-site terminals there to place orders, the product manager would stand quietly nearby to see how they interacted with JD.com. The manager made note of where a customer paused, where errors occurred, and how users responded to prompts.

In early 2011, R&D rolled out the JD User Experience Room (UE Room) project. Three rooms were set up for interviews, tests and observation, respectively. The interview room was for focus group interviews, in which six to eight users sat together for a discussion moderated by the host. The test room was built to simulate a home environment so users could complete a series of online shopping steps in a relaxed, comfortable atmosphere. The user's mouse click and eye movement data were recorded via computer, using advanced tracking technology. The room was equipped with a one-way mirror, allowing product managers to observe user behaviour in real time.

The findings from this project prompted a rework that year of JD's front page aimed at attracting more female shoppers, and also laid the groundwork for an extensive redesign of JD's online shopping experience that commenced in 2012.

The Confrontation

J D's growth rate is best seen by looking at the market for major household appliances. Appliance sales experienced a surge beginning in 2011. Transportation of these products had belonged to the delivery department, but the warehousing department took it over and began logistics and construction work to integrate warehousing and delivery. After that an average of 10 warehouses for major appliances were built every year, soon expanding from seven cities to 40.

The growth of JD's home appliance business represented a bold incursion into the territories of Chinese retail giants Suning and Gome. The preceding 10 years had been the golden age of China's retail chain industry. In 2005 Suning Appliances had 224 chain stores with sales approaching 16 billion yuan and net profits of 351 million yuan. In 2012 it had 1,705 stores with turnover exceeding 98 billion yuan, with 2.682 billion yuan of net profit.

This booming decade for chain retailing was also prime time for Chinese real estate development. The Chinese commercial real estate market quickly overtook the chain retailing industry. In 2005, Suning's gross profit margin was 9.68%. It grew to 16.93 % in 2012, but with little change in net profit because of steep brick and mortar storefront costs. Chain retailers tried to maximize profits by squeezing the margins of manufacturers. As a growing share of the cost of chain retailing was passed upward and outward, not only were consumers feeling the pain, but so were manufacturers and even the chain retailing industry itself. This helped set the stage for e-commerce to emerge.

In the US, e-commerce began to develop only after traditional, offline retailing had fully matured. Conversely, in China, e-commerce development was synchronized with the offline retail business.

The Logic of War

On 15 August 2012, JD launched the first salvo in a major appliance price war against Gome and Suning. The campaign eventually grew into an all-out brawl involving both online and offline retailers. In that unsettled environment, with the wolves lurking at the door, JD experienced a particularly challenging period in its development. Viewed in retrospect, the so-called "15 August price war" marked a turning point in the history of Chinese e-commerce. Following the upheaval in the fast-growing market for major household appliances, e-commerce companies began attracting unfavourable attention across Chinese society. JD's confrontation with the chainstore giants was a sobering blast of cold air for the stakeholders of China's retail industry.

As these events began to unfold, Liu said on his microblog that "JD's major appliances are more than 10% cheaper than those in the chainstores of Suning and Gome", and this 'announcement' triggered all-out war between the three companies.

On the morning of 14 August 2012, more than 20 senior executives sat at either side of Liu in a JD headquarters conference room. The meeting lasted just 20 minutes. The strategy was articulated. Marching orders were issued. The troops were mobilized.

JD's major appliance warehouses in 18 cities across the country began gearing up for replenishment. Liu directed all executives who were away on vacation to return to their posts immediately. With the exception of chief operating officer Shen Haoyu, who was in the US, they all arrived that night. Liu did not leave the office until after 10 pm, following a teleconference with shareholders and group photos with colleagues from the major appliance department.

Early the next morning, Shen Haoyu landed at Beijing Capital International Airport. By 9 am, the price war between JD, Suning and Gome was well under way. And it wasn't pretty.

"For eight years we've been fighting with others every day," said Liu. "The team would wither without the fight." Indeed, this no-nonsense entrepreneur, taller than many of his peers, had the erect posture and bearing of a military man and was a fit commander..

"I knew there would be a war with Suning, I just wasn't sure when," Liu said somberly. On 15 August, after the 20-minute morning meeting, Liu had some time to himself. He published 30 messages on his microblog. "At the beginning of the war," he remembered, "I found everything was in order."

JD's provocation worked. Suning.com management was in a rage. The JD team, with an average age of 23, could not wait to mix it up. The conflict immediately spread. Suning.com, Gome, Coo8.com and Dangdang all joined the melee. The timing of the price war was subtle. On 8 August, Suning.com had held a press conference, announcing that 10 days later it would launch promotions to mark its third anniversary.

Divergent market forces had combined to fan the flames of the price war.

China's e-commerce companies listed on the US market, such as Dangdang and China Mecox Lane Inc, performed poorly from the second half of 2010 through to the second half of 2011. The American capital market was hesitant to embrace Chinese e-commerce companies that exchanged scale for losses, and had given them relatively low valuations. In June 2011 the growth of new users in e-commerce fell sharply and in the second half of that year venture capitalists curtailed their investments in e-commerce enterprises. The market's 100% growth rate over the previous decade had been driven by overall Chinese economic growth and the internet demographic dividend. In a context of economic depression, when demographic dividends disappeared, the rapid growth of e-commerce slowed, effectively returning to normal. That meant competition would intensify, as the major players frantically sought more market share.

3C products can be divided into major appliances, digital communications and IT products. The major appliances category accounts for the biggest volume, with annual turnover totalling between 700 billion and 800 billion yuan. JD needed to drive business growth before its listing. Investors valued sales, market share and gross margins, but at the end of the day they valued growth more than anything. JD had to maintain high growth for a successful IPO. Major appliances, inevitably, became its new growth imperative.

However, in its haste to go into battle, JD found it was not entirely prepared for the fight. It had anticipated a local skirmish, with limits. It did not expect an industry-wide free-for-all. But that's precisely what it got.

The hostilities were provoked by Suning. Rumours circulated online that JD no longer had the price advantage for mobile phones and digital products. Suning and Gome, the rumour mill suggested, had much lower online prices. The chatter continued for six months, becoming increasingly widespread. In fact, JD hadn't changed its normal low prices. But the other two companies were covering their losses on online phone and digital product sales with the profits earned from the major appliances offline.

In 2011, major appliances only amounted to a small percentage of JD's sales, lagging behind IT and the digital communication category. However, they represented a large proportion of Suning's sales. Suning chose to challenge JD head-on. How would JD react? A strong offence, they say, is often the best defence, and JD retaliated in the hope of undermining Suning's and Gome's main source of profits. That, the thinking went, would pull them down to where they'd compete with JD on the same level. It was the same tactic JD had employed when it had gone up against Dangdang in 2011.

In this price war, JD planned to limit the fight to offline major appliances. But Suning and Gome opened two new fronts, declaring war against JD in the online IT and digital communication spaces. Both sides knew they should avoid mortal combat in their main businesses.

Nevertheless, this unprecedented price war came to an abrupt end. Theoretically, Suning.com had wider population coverage and longer selling time, but its one-day sales were no more than about 300 million yuan. "It reached the all-time peak, but it was not a big victory," Suning vice chairman Sun Weimin would later say. "It was a price war unworthy of its name. Price competition is eternal, but I do not appreciate it played out in a lousy way."

Suning's main business was not online. A listed company, what its investors wanted were short-term profits and compelling financial reports. JD was not yet listed, but the online business was its principle focus and it could not afford a protracted, scorched-earth campaign. Neither side wanted to wage a long-duration war.

Jockeying for position with Suppliers

Sun Zhitao, general manager of the brown goods department in JD's home appliance business division, joined the company in 2011. He used to work at Amazon's Chinese unit, Amazon.cn. When Amazon.cn had requested funding for advertising, its US headquarters couldn't see why it was necessary. Some observers felt that American companies simply couldn't grasp how important it was for e-commerce companies in China to raise their profiles in the market. For its part, Amazon believed e-commerce was methodical work, best executed slowly and steadily. Between 2008 and 2010, Amazon chief Jeff Bezos traveled to China repeatedly to learn about the market, and he finally agreed to invest in advertising there in 2011. He could not understand why in other countries Amazon could rely on word of mouth without significant spending on advertising, but not in China. The truth was that if you didn't rush to claim a position in such a gigantic emerging market, and do it correctly, it would belong to others. When Bezos decided to spend on ads, it was already too late.

If Amazon.cn wanted to modify its systems, it had to vet changes through Bezos for approval. Only then would R&D teams in the UK and India begin working on the modifications. Sometimes that would mean at least a year between the request and actual implementation of important changes. Sun found the situation was quite different at JD. When he first joined the company it had 39 home appliance warehouses and it was difficult to say whether inventory data were scientifically accurate or just guesswork based on the judgment of the staff. He hoped to answer such questions by building an IT system that analysed historical data and existing inventory. The R&D team immediately began working on solutions, in sharp contrast with the bureaucratically sluggish reaction time he had seen at Amazon.

Back then, JD's major appliances sector was not as professional as it would become. Young buying staff lacked experience. When goods were out of stock, they would place orders with the manufacturers. If the wholesale purchase price for a product was 3,000 yuan, they might randomly add a mark-up of 100 yuan to the price without knowing that it went for 4,000 yuan on the open market. They did not think strategically and would react passively to the policies of the manufacturers. As a result, the sales volume of major appliances didn't meet expectations and gross margins were quite low. From 2009 to 2010, the manufacturers engaging in e-commerce on home appliances were outside of the mainstream. Beginning in 2011, manufacturers began paying much closer attention to e-commerce channels.

At that time, major appliances made up only a small part of JD's business. Sun Zhitao decided to take 10% off the price of the products, undercutting Suning. Sun asked employees to zero in on Suning's prices and to call the manufacturers to adjust them in response to any price fluctuations on Suning's side. JD's attitude was that it was fighting this price war to defend itself. The battle between JD and Suning.com made consumers aware of price differences between online and offline, and the effect was far-reaching.

On 15 August 2012, from 9 am to 1 pm customer traffic through JD.com increased 80% from levels on its 18 June anniversary sale day, and it logged more than 200 million page views. JD rushed into the price war even though its physical inventory was worth only 400 million yuan. The goods sold out before noon. With long lead-time production plans already determined, it was too late for manufacturers to increase output after sales skyrocketed. From September to October, the manufacturer Hisense adjusted its production plans five times to meet JD's needs.

JD paid a high price for instigating this price war. In some categories, the relationships between JD and selected manufacturers deteriorated. Some regarded JD as a spoiler and reduced shipments to the company. With no inventory and insufficient replenishment from the manufacturers, negative effects began to appear.

In retrospect, JD suffered setbacks in the price war, but it won strategically in the long run. Its intent was to impact Suning's and Gome's profits on major appliances so everyone could stand together on the same starting line. Following the price war, Suning and Gome owned about 30% of the market together.

Improving the Relationship with Manufacturers

JD's home appliances department had some very tough days. Wang Xiaosong was in charge of the department through a trying transitional period. When he took over, it was hitting just 80% of its sales target, so there was no bonus during a time when bonuses accounted for half of an employee's income. As a result, individual earnings for the people in his group were extremely low. Wang was reluctant to ask Liu to reduce his group's targets. It just wasn't his style, and he was embarrassed by the team's performance. Wang had previously been in charge of the mobile and communication department, which had achieved 120% of its target. After making a special arrangement with the staff in his former unit, he took 40% of that team's bonus and allocated it to the home appliances department. That addressed employees' immediate concerns about being able to afford food and clothing. The special bonus arrangement lasted approximately six months.

In 2011, JD's appliance sales JD reached 5 billion yuan. In early 2012, Yan Xiaobing joined JD as vice president of JD Group and general manager of the home appliances business division. Liu told Yan he did not need to ask for his approval for any order payment. Yan initially thought that would cause problems; he felt the need for higher level professional direction. But Liu had always prided himself on not unduly shackling those who worked for him. Yan could feel Liu's eagerness to develop home appliances in short order. It was easy to realize short-term sales growth, but quite hard to change the overall pattern of the industry. He found that JD had a lot of 'buy-and-sell' transactions, meaning people bought products directly from competitors and sold them on JD. This was particularly true with major appliances, and it entailed virtually no brand strategy. Meanwhile, they had to take discontinued models from dealers, and these were often out of stock too.

The newly established major appliance department lacked a pricing system and any significant relationships with manufacturers. Business controls were also lacking. The only rule was to sell at the price a JD employee would set. They sold products soon after receiving them.

What they focused on was rapid turnaround without considering the price system.

It took Yan a year to get the team to recognize what for him was a guiding principle – that the starting point for any business is the manufacturer relationship and that sales promotions should only happen when the supply is guaranteed. JD's practice at this time was just the opposite: everything started with the price, and this fostered poor relationships with manufacturers, unreliable sourcing, and little or no support from the manufacturers regarding promotions.

JD's major appliance department likely would still be a mess today had a new system not been established. The pricing system had to return to the groove that accounts for market norms and allows sustainable development for everyone. Home appliance manufacturers are in the front ranks of China's top 500 enterprises. They have strong price awareness and do not want wanton price-cutting to disrupt the market. Yan and his team had to talk with managers one by one to describe JD's business philosophy and unique cost advantages, and explain that price wars were not meant to disrupt the manufacturers' pricing system.

Sales staff needed product portfolios. Some products were cash cows and could be priced higher to make profits; others were fighters and needed to be priced lower to build scale. Not all products were fighters. Yan put a stop to the disorderly old practice of haphazardly lowering prices across the board. Employees questioned this, wondering why JD shouldn't automatically follow when rivals set very low prices. "As an industry leader, we have to be broad-minded," Yan told them. "Let's first stop the chaotic price wars and let the price return to value. Low price is necessary, but it should also be reasonable."

Liu rarely interfered with the process, remaining more concerned with results. While at a former employer, Yan once told management that the company was faring poorly because the power was centralized. No one shouldered responsibility. Everyone tried to shuffle things from layer to layer. But in JD, if the major appliances business was not successful, there was no one else to blame. Leadership had delegated the power downward and all eyes were on Yan alone. Had

Liu ever signed a payment order for Yan? No. Ever set a policy? No. The high level of trust allowed Yan to implement his business philosophy without obstacles.

Meanwhile, Liu also offered a lot of support to Yan. If he needed to create advertising for major appliances, Liu would ask the marketing team to allocate special funds. He understood the difficulties of the major appliances space and accepted the necessary cost of securing inventory. Seeking breakthroughs, Liu, who usually did not meet manufacturers face to face, made exceptions for Midea, Samsung and others.

Liu viewed JD from a customer's perspective rather than from that of a company employee or manager. He emailed Yan to ask why a certain beauty appliance was so scarce. Yan quickly checked and found there were only three models and two of them were out of stock. Liu was attentive even to such a small category.

There was a significant price range difference in home appliances due to the lack of transparent information. An electric rice cooker that sold for 99 yuan in first-tier cities would be priced at 119 yuan in the lower-tier cities and even 139 yuan in the more remote village stores. In the home appliances price system, the capital turnover for major agents might be two or three months, and a year or so for smaller dealers. So the profit margin for stocking a batch of goods had to be high enough to sustain their existence. JD stocked in from Beijing and sold nationwide. This had a strong impact on the price system. Dealers called manufacturers to complain about JD. One sourcing agent who secretly supplied JD informed the purchasing staff that he would be doomed if he ventured to supply more. In 2012, the manufacturers began enforcing a strict supply control programme. Agents would turn pale at the mere mention of JD.

In 2011, manufacturers of major appliances would seldom even mention JD in their meetings. By 2012, the manufacturers held a negative view of JD. They constrained JD with unreasonable terms and auditors assigned it the highest risk level. Yan had signed purchasing agreements in JD unlike any he'd agreed to before. In his words, they were "humiliating treaties".

After the price war in 2012, under pressure from Gome and Suning, some manufacturers stopped supplying JD entirely. Thus another round of communication between JD and the manufacturers took place. The relationship between the two sides evidently improved at the end of 2012. Manufacturers found they could make money by collaborating with JD and did not have to bear excessive costs. The key to improving the relationship with manufacturers, Yan believed, was to prove your values through your cooperation. "If you can satisfy their needs, which are making money and giving them breakthroughs in sales, then you are valuable to manufacturers," he said. "Otherwise, why should they do business with you?"

JD began to repair the disorder in its operations by prioritizing activity in this hierarchy of importance: manufacturer relationship, sourcing, sales and prices. Manufacturers could now touch the pulse of JD and began to trust the company and its employees. With the rise of e-commerce, the third-tier brands of home appliance began to impact the second-tier brands, and the second-tier brands the first-tier. Suddenly, competition among manufacturers grew fierce and they began more willingly to increase their supplies to JD.

Even if you're doing all the right things, you may not see the results immediately. Patience is necessary. When talking to Haier about cooperation, the home appliance department was told JD was not ready and that it should first try selling a Haier sub-brand called Leader. In a year, Leader achieved sales of more than 500 million yuan through JD, which was a pleasant surprise to Haier. By the end of 2013, Haier's full product line was put on JD.com.

Many manufacturers found it relatively easy to collect payments when they worked with JD; the turnaround was a quick 30 days and there were profits to be made. They began to embrace JD with open arms. But there were conflicts between online and offline sales. In addition to Gome and Suning, there were also the reseller channels in the third-tier and fourth-tier cities. With increasing conflict, the hard-won relationships between manufacturers and JD once again became unstable. On one hand, manufacturers felt JD had strong momentum when there was cooperation. On the other hand, they had to pull back at times when the price difference between the online and offline channels became too great. Later, they adopted a strategy of artificially segmenting models for online and offline sales to make it more difficult for consumers to make direct comparisons.

The strategy of model segmentation was first adopted in notebook devices. Tsinghua Tongfang supplied the devices at 2,800 yuan apiece to Dangdang, but charged JD 2,850 yuan. JD blamed the Tongfang sales manager for the gap. With notebook sales taking the lead, mobile phones and home appliances followed suit. For instance, JD was given a notebook model with a card reader that other retailers didn't stock. Not only were consumers unable to compare prices, JD and Suning couldn't do so either.

If the product was hot, model segmentation could not be done. Some suggested making it a head-to-head showdown. One would sell at lower prices, but only two units a day. Who could tell? There was no way to see an objective, fair and comprehensive comparison report.

Major appliances have large market scale. Once the barrier is broken, category growth can be enormous. With JD's surge in the major appliances space, talks between the company and manufacturers began to take place at higher, more strategic levels. It was not unusual for a manufacturer's vice president or even its president to come personally to negotiate with JD. In 2013 the company signed orders of more than 1 billion yuan each with Konka, Hisense, Midea, LG and others. JD expanded its scale with the power of capital and its position in the industry chain reversed from the downstream to the upstream.

A Formidable Trend

By August 2013 JD covered 22 Chinese provinces in home appliance sales, but its delivery coverage wasn't perfect. In Guangdong, Jiangsu and Zhejiang, the coverage reached prefecture-level cities and was countywide. In other provinces it had spread only to the capital cities. In the view of the sales network, there was still a lot of room to improve.

That year, besides bargaining with manufacturers, JD's home appliance department chose to invest its profits in services that would bring consumers visible, tangible benefits. It would have been pointless, after all, to wage the price war in a vacuum.

As a result, in 2014 first-tier brands like Midea, Haier, Siemens and Samsung began to increase their support to JD. They supplied high-end models and the companies' presidents took the time to visit. The online home appliances market had turned into a two-horse race between JD and Tmall.

JD comprised 30% of major appliance market share in Beijing, Shanghai and Guangzhou. For every 10 major appliances sold, JD booked three or more of them. "We've taken all at once the market they took more than 10 years to build," said Yan. "The concept of e-commerce remains vague in rural areas. Once it's understood, the impact will be greater." He suggested that the logistics network for major appliances cover the whole country. He estimated that by 2020, e-commerce sales would make up 40% of the entire home appliance market.

I asked Yan if JD would become the next Gome or Suning. "The one who is in charge must be clear that, as a channel, you have to know what you should have and what your share is," he said. "If you want to keep the characteristics of the advanced channel, you have to reduce the costs and get the gross margins to provide for sustainable development. You should not maximize your profits and compress your costs to the bottom. If you drive unlimited expansion and enlarge your cost with no limit – and pass it on to the manufacturers by turning yourself into a channel with higher costs – you'll be overthrown sooner or later."

Liu shared that philosophy on e-commerce. He believed every channel should earn its fair profit. Profit-maximizing would lower the threshold and attract 100 competitors to challenge a company. In particular, if distributors tried to seek profits by applying harsh policies to squeeze suppliers, then new business models and new competitors were likely to appear. If, over the long haul, a company hoped to become a century-old enterprise, it had to maintain unique competitive advantages. Instead of seeking profits from its upstream partners, it had to provide value by reducing costs and improving efficiencies. It had to provide the upstream manufacturers with a fast, efficient and low-cost sales platform, while providing consumers with the most efficient, affordable and convenient way to shop.

Many manufacturers viewed the rural market as an El Dorado. The first-tier cities were places to build reputation while losing money, they maintained, whereas the rural market could be a source of immense profits. The rural areas were destined to move online, eventually. But the cost of achieving concentrated buying across that dispersed population might be too high to sustain. Gome and Suning both opened chainstores at the county level, and both efforts ended in failure. In terms of cost and efficiency, the dealers' teams of manufacturers faced extinction in the face of JD's faster inventory turnover and deep pockets. Thus, manufacturers' reliance on the support of dealers for production became an obsolete operating model.

It is not that manufacturers didn't accept the internet. They rejected the overnight upending of traditional marketplace rules, out of fear it would cause confusion offline and damage the channel network they'd painstakingly built over decades.

JD needed a lot of support to work around entrenched interest groups. Flipping the online-offline pattern would take years of concerted effort. Gome and Suning accounted for 30% of the home appliance market. E-commerce had to own at least 30% market share to subvert the channel dynamic. Ownership of "last mile" delivery would break the channel lock-down.

In 2014 JD achieved seamless logistics network coverage for major appliances across Henan Province. An order could be placed from anywhere in the province, and the consumer could get delivery from JD. "The cost for seamless coverage is very high," said Yi Wenjie, the first GM of JD's South China Region. "We were stressed, because this was all new to JD and to the entire industry. Six months later, JD had a 50% increase in orders of home appliances in Henan."

He said Henan was chosen at that time because it was situated on a wide expanse of plain, while other provinces in Central China were mountainous. The Henan model was eventually replicated across the country.

When Yan Xiaobing joined JD there were just 13 major home appliance warehouses in operation. Some had been shuttered due to low order volume. Yan proposed setting up new warehouses to better meet consumer demand. It would be a costly but necessary move. In 2012 JD set up 15 warehouses for major appliances. In just one year, orders grew from dozens a day to hundreds and even thousands in areas where home appliance warehouses were in place.

Zhu Jun, manager of major appliance logistics for JD's Central China Region, joined the company in May 2010. At the time there were no independent appliance warehouses in the region. He established a 200m^2 facility with 14 employees in Wuhan. Daily orders totalled fewer than 100 and the goods were delivered to Nanchang, Changsha, Wuhan and Zhengzhou, four capital cities. By 2014 daily orders for major appliances in the Central China Region had reached more than 3,000. Out of 484 counties and districts, 367 were covered and 60 prefecture-level cities were in delivery range. There was full coverage throughout Henan Province, with customers in most prefecture-level cities receiving their orders the following day. The storage area was expanded to 60,000m^2. Soon there were five operations centres (Zhengzhou, Wuhan, Nanchang, Changsha and Xiangyang), each with more than 100 employees.

The storage of major appliances required big initial investments. JD's approach was first to consider how best to serve existing and potential customers and then expand services to win them over. The growth rate of JD's major appliances in third- or fourth-tier cities was higher than in key urban centres. Consumers in capital cities had more choice when buying home appliances. Some of the first-tier brands had not extended their delivery systems to third- and fourth-tier cities. Most of the local dealers only sold second- or third-tier brands.

With economic development under way in rural areas, newly prosperous villagers wanted to buy first-tier brands, but simply didn't have sufficient choices. Also, small dealers priced their inventory much higher than on the web. Even with some items routinely selling for 1,000 or 2,000 yuan above e-commerce prices, villagers wouldn't stop buying because the price was too high. They cared more about satisfaction. A lot of people found the smaller appliances they were able to buy from JD were inexpensive and not high quality. But when they learned that the major appliances could not be delivered to their villages, they called to complain.

As far as JD could extend its delivery zone, orders would grow accordingly. Once the service was available, it seemed, the sky was the limit.

From a supply chain perspective, JD had to stretch its channels to county towns since major appliances were missing in these places. The company worked with competent local dealers and set up authorized "JD Service Stores" that provided delivery and installation of home appliances, furniture and other products. Once properly certified, these stores could offer maintenance services as well. In addition, the "JD Co-Op" developed local marketing programmes, placed orders for customers and mounted special promotions. Local authorized stores made money through services. Major home appliance manufacturers had always cobbled together service systems on their own, wasting significant resources. By binding together the upstream ecosystem, JD solved the problem of local service for many suppliers by relying on a single store.

People drew a connection between JD's new silvery dog mascot character and the black cat logo launched by a rival a year earlier. Taobao Mall, a part of Alibaba Group, introduced its cat and was renamed "Tmall". In fact, the time had come for JD to face its most formidable opponent: Alibaba. The face-off was jokingly called "The Cat and Dog War".

E-commerce would not be a short-term trend, and fierce competition for the space was not about to end anytime soon. The jousting would likely last for a decade or longer as the market matured. Competitors covered all aspects of e-commerce: IT, order management, storage management, and customer management skills.

In 2013, Alibaba announced the creation of Cainiao Logistics through an alliance with numerous logistics companies. Cainiao built its top-down network around a powerful information system. Conversely, JD pursued a dramatically different approach: it would build its logistics network from the bottom up.

Quick Learning
vs. Experience

In April 2010, Hillhouse Capital invested $265 million in JD, marking the biggest internet investment to date in China. On a business maturity scale of 0 to 100, Hillhouse CEO Zhang Lei said he thought JD as a business was in the 0 to 1 range in 2010 but had hit the 50 mark by 2014.

Liu achieved a real breakthrough after 2010. At the time he had many basic, rudimentary ideas but no strategic roadmap for realizing them. After his investment, Zhang Lei took Liu to visit Wal-Mart headquarters and talk with the retail giant's controlling family. On his return from the US, Liu had a long talk with Zhang, excitedly telling him he wanted to transform JD and reshape it into an aggressive, dominant player.

Liu had always been open to learning from people with diverse backgrounds and perspectives. Zhang once said of Liu, "He has the magical ability to absorb knowledge, ideas and talents."

In 2010, Li Ruiyu, part of the third group of management trainees to join JD (and now director of investor relations), accompanied Liu to the US for a conference sponsored by JD investor Tiger Fund. Liu's English was far from perfect and he needed Li Ruiyu to translate. Liu carried a phrase book and English dictionary with him. When Li Ruiyu used a word that was new to him, Liu would ask its meaning. He spoke to her in his broken English: "Don't speak Chinese. I want to practise English."

This was the first time Li had taken a business trip with her boss. She was nervous and uneasy. To make matters worse, she misplaced Liu's bag, which contained important credentials and credit cards. The bag was eventually recovered, but Liu was angry.

Before arranging a second business trip with Liu, Li Ruiyu's supervisor, Miao Xiaohong, who later served as Liu's assistant, asked her how she was holding up under the pressures of her job. After all, her previous trip with him had been difficult and she had been scolded by the boss for losing his bag. Miao offered this advice: "If you don't know that you've made a mistake, he will tell you. You need to correct it and improve and he will be happy to see you do that. But if you repeat the same mistake without improving yourself, then you are not someone he will value. This is how he is."

Kate Kui, president of Paipai.com, at the time a JD company, previously worked in investment banking at Merrill Lynch. She joined JD in June 2012. A year later her focus shifted from finance to operations and she was put in charge of the entire Paipai business. This was a huge challenge for her. No one except the bold Liu would dare put her into such a senior position. It was the same with Shen Haoyu. Although he had no previous experience in logistics management, he was asked to take care of packaging logistics. He was named COO first and later the CEO of JD Mall. These examples illustrate how, in a fast-growing company, the ability to learn quickly far outweighed the value of past experience.

The boundaries of e-commerce continued to shift. The development of the internet had already subverted most traditional industries. The old business model was to make money by selling things. This would not necessarily be the way to make money in the future. Money could be made through other services. For example, a refrigerator could be sold at cost on the internet. With the consent of the consumer, an e-commerce company installed a detector on refrigerators to track eggs, poultry, meat, beverages, fruits and vegetables inside the unit, as well as other consumer data. That data could be used to remind customers when to replenish certain items, or even to place automatic re-orders. Certain data could also be sold to manufacturers for a handsome fee.

Strong execution had helped ensure the rapid growth of JD over the preceding 10 years, but it has also hindered innovation and stifled the nurturing of an open corporate culture. Liu wove "tolerance for failure" into the fabric of JD's culture. He saw the company as an infant. Going forward, failure to innovate would have been devastating. Now, as a dramatically larger company, Liu acknowledged that JD could be more innovative and more tolerant of failure.

At this stage Liu was most concerned about JD's future direction. Over the past decade the company had focused exclusively on e-commerce. Now, it had an enormous customer base, mass data, logistics and IT. Knowing this, Liu thought the company could pursue an even more innovative business model.

Senior executives, led by the CEO, had to dedicate the necessary strategic planning, funding and resources to the task of business innovation. When the overall pace of e-commerce growth slowed in China, Liu looked at the global landscape. The pressure to grow once again forced JD to change. A company with tens of thousands of people and revenue totalling of billions of yuan needed visionary, inclusive leadership.

Liu had a desire to study further in the United States. His last deep immersion training had been in 2009 when he studied at China Europe International Business School (CEIBS). There, Liu said, he learned how to know himself better through other people's feedback. In 2012, starting during the Spring Festival, Liu studied at Harvard Business School for more than 40 days and in 2013 he attended a programme at Colombia University.

JD's executives could sense Liu's transformation when he returned from the US. In August 2013, at the mid-year management meeting held in Jiuzhaigou, Long Yu, JD's chief human resources officer and general counsel, noticed that Liu waited to express his ideas only after everyone else had. Previously, the CEO couldn't wait to speak his mind.

Senior VP Xu Lei observed that Liu now spoke more gently. He used to carry himself like a soldier and could speak harshly to his executives, although he would try to make up for it by later by sharing drinks with them. Now he expressed sharp ideas with clear, direct language. Li Daxue, JD's vice president in charge of technology, also saw the transformation. "He had been impulsive, but now he was more tolerant." Once when Liu shared his thinking on globalization strategy and the intricacies of management, he told his executive team that the interests of investors and the media's influence on them deserved more focus. And the company needed an open, fair leader with a broader vision.

Steeped in Chinese education, Liu had been trained to seek a single answer: either black or white, good or bad, right or wrong. One of the things that most impressed him about American education was that 90% of the professors' questions were open-ended, aimed at inspiring students to view things from different perspectives. He realized that he had to adopt the mentality of open thinking and should not always try to change others.

I once met a US headmaster in Raleigh, North Carolina, whose school had training programmes for future global leaders. "The most essential thing for global leadership is to learn to listen and be inclusive of different cultures," he told me.

From Executive to Coach

Liu used to attend personally to virtually every matter, despite having 18 vice presidents reporting to him. He could go on and on, without a break, for months. If Liu believed something could be done, then it should be done. He felt others could not make it happen for him. But the company was infinitely larger and more complex now. It was impossible for the CEO himself to be personally involved in every decision. When Xu Xin of Today Capital was herself wrestling with this issue, Liu told her he planned to go study at Colombia University. "Wow," she thought. "This is the only way for Liu to delegate his powers. 'I'm leaving; it's your show now.' That proved to be the best way."

At subsequent management meetings she attended, she found that Liu had indeed delegated powers to lower levels, and executives had begun to take on additional responsibilities. Other investors were worried and asked Xu Xin whether the company would function properly with Liu absent for so long. Xu Xin told them, "If it doesn't work, Liu will surely come back. Because the company is running smoothly, he allows himself to stay over there. No one cares about JD more than him. It is his life."

Song Jianhui, head of the administration department of JD East China, was responsible for the renovation and relocation of that group's office building. In order to avoid paying a design fee of 500,000 yuan, he simply did the design himself. Yu Rui, GM of East China, had said, "Song, I trust you. Just go ahead and do it." Song had previously built the workshop of a large-scale woodworking factory and had been responsible for office decoration at other companies. But, he said: "This office in JD is like my real child. No one was there to supervise me. It was done entirely by me, working alone."

He had previously worked for Foxconn, where every move was prescribed. He did everything by following set procedures. At Foxconn, everyone copies CEO Terry Gou. Everything comes from Gou's mind and employees simply carry out his thinking. JD, on the other hand, provides direction. The company may say it needs a painting, but it is you, the employee, who decides how it will look.

Liu had dared to empower JD's workforce. The team responsible for constructing the new automated "Asia No.1" warehouse in Shanghai was young compared with the rest of the industry and was relatively inexperienced. At the time, there was debate among the management team over whether to hire an external design consultant or assign someone from inside the company to handle the task. Obviously, an experienced consultant seemed the better choice. But Liu insisted on developing the team from within the company. Purchasing and decision-making, he felt, should rely mostly on the existing team. Outside consultants and supervisors were to assist them. A young man born in 1984 was assigned to take care of the purchase of "Asia No.1" two weeks after joining JD. Under tremendous stress, he shed private tears. But he was ultimately successful on the job, matured quickly and is now a director.

The traditional corporate organization structure is a pyramid, with the CEO at the top. Those in the middle manage. The bottom tier implemented. Conventional thinking held that the CEO was most familiar with the industry, highly experienced and unlikely to make wrong decisions. But in the past, businesses were almost static compared with those of the internet era. Previously, a much lower premium was placed on the rapid flow of business information. In the internet age, the cost of information transmission was very low, and quick decision-making was of utmost importance. Opportunities could be missed if you waited for key business data to bubble up, level by level. Today's contemporary enterprise architecture is more oriented toward trust, with frontline employees empowered to make informed decisions. In this environment, the CEO should become a supportive coach and provider of resources.

By December 2014, after 10 years of rapid growth, JD had become a gigantic enterprise. It had nearly 70,000 employees, with a logistical network spanning 1,862 districts and counties across China (there are 2,860 districts and counties in the country). With this tremendous breadth it would be impossible for the company to reach new levels of success relying on Liu's leadership abilities alone. He learned to manage JD through the strength of the organization and the vigour of the systems he and the team had put in place.

Liu completed the distribution of C-suite talent and learned to delegate, rather than micro-manage. Decentralization became one of his key objectives. As a business owner well versed in every aspect of e-commerce, Liu created a workforce skilled at carrying out his vision and strategies. Now, after 15 years, he would dramatically change the way the business was run.

On 29 July 2013, at JD's open-platform partners' conference, Liu appeared on stage in his light blue shirt and beige slacks. He looked tanned and trim, and was in exuberant spirits. He told the audience of sellers to take control of their destiny. From April to August that year Liu had spent just five weeks in China. In August he left for the US again and stayed until the end of the year. Upon his return he jokingly told his executives, "I will be staying here this time for longer than a month, so you should make good use of my time."

He knew that decentralization meant he needed to mind his mouth. If he was the first to speak out, he knew the matter would essentially be finalized. He had to wait until after everyone else had had their say. Going to study in the US was the best way he could think of to achieve decentralization: to be away from the company's day-to-day operations meant he and the executive team could become accustomed to not looking for each other.

In the years that JD was headquartered in the Yinfeng Building, Liu would circulate through the office daily, observing employees at work and constantly checking sales data. After JD moved to North

Star Century Center, opportunities for the management team to meet and communicate with him become increasingly rare. Once competent executive management was in place, Liu seemed to distance himself from the nuts and bolts of JD's operation.

At a company of 30 people, the boss knows every detail at a glance. In a company of 300 people, it is impractical for one person to try and manage every detail. In a company with 3,000 employees, the CEO cannot realistically expect to manage more than a fraction of the daily decision-making. By 2013, JD had in fact become a company with more than 30,000 employees. Liu needed to consciously step back and push responsibility out through the organization. In the past, if he wanted to get something done, he would find the right person to do it, or do it himself. Now, he realized, he had to populate the business with the right people, let them decide what needed to be done, and let them do it.

Liu's early management style was to deeply immerse himself in detail. He was quick-tempered and domineering. His management team often received pointed, critical e-mails: "Change the product price immediately. Just do it. Don't ask why." "The page design is not good enough and it is unattractive to users." Executives would hear their phones ring at midnight and worry it was Liu.

Liu realized the time had come to loosen his grasp. He spread the word that he would not be involved in detailed matters and his employees should begin making key decisions by themselves. But old habits die hard. Sometimes he would intervene in a specific line of business. He was still learning how to delegate authority. JD executives would remind him when he became too deeply involved. It was not easy for someone like Liu to let go. At meetings, he would repeatedly remind employees not to ask his permission for things within their control. If executives asked for decisions they could make on their own, he would criticize them instead of praising them.

JD pushed a management system that emphasizes the fundamental "ABCs" of HR, finance, authority and accountability. This system had been at work to varying degrees in parts of JD but it was now systematized and uniformly applied across the entire company.

Liu's chief concern was whether the sense of empowerment was pervasive enough. If it wasn't, JD's response time in a fast moving market could become fatally sluggish. For instance, should company leadership ask permission before donating to the Sichuan earthquake relief? Who could comfortably make such decisions, and to what extent? Liu had spent an inordinate amount of time studying the value, limits and potential pitfalls of far-reaching authorization.

In April 2014, JD Group split into two subgroups, one subsidiary and one business division: JD Mall Group, JD Financial Group, Paipai.com and the Overseas Business Division. From then on, Liu only attended C-suite meetings of the topline JD Group.

Managing the Company by Relying on the System

Even when he was halfway around the world in the US, Liu remained close to JD. Relying on its information systems, Liu could see all of the company's data from wherever he sat. He could do so through a smart phone or tablet. Warehouse backlog numbers were at his fingertips. He could also see public comments about JD from microblogs and bulletin boards through the company's market intelligence system.

At the end of 2013, after he had returned to China, Liu called the buying and merchandising teams together. He asked them to develop a new service philosophy. He wanted them to become true service providers rather than bossy order-givers. Around that time, he felt the company had begun showing signs of arrogance. JD had won too many battles. Purchasing managers just a few years out of school had begun to rebuke suppliers who were decades older than them, upsetting hard-won relationships and bruising egos. Liu's remarks were heard loud and clear, and employees began modifying their behaviour.

"You had to solve a problem before he learned of it," said vice president of technology Li Daxue. "It'll be too late when he calls or sends you an email; the matter would be like a knife placed on the table by then."

As always, Liu remained focused on the user experience. Even while he was in the US, from time to time he would place orders with JD.com and send gifts to his friends across China. Liu would also try many products prior to release. Once, he summoned Xiong Yuhong, then head of the mobile R&D department, to his office and pointed out problems with making purchases with the JD music app. He asked Xiong to redesign the product and report back on the results.

Liu also learned not to dwell on visible details of the user experience, but to dig deeper and try to understand root causes deep within the system. A consumer from Chengdu emailed Liu directly, complaining of his terrible shopping experience. Liu forwarded the complaint to the appropriate executives, asking them to handle it immediately. A day later, the Chengdu customer advised Liu that JD had given him a refund and product exchange. Instead of getting the praise he expected, the manager who had handled the situation was chastised. "Deal with the problem from a systemic, generalized point of view," Liu told him. "No additional customers should encounter the problem. It has to be fixed once and for all. By only appeasing this one customer you're just fooling me instead of improving the user experience." His executives were dumbfounded. If the same thing had happened in the past, Liu would have praised them for their efficiency. Now, he clearly told them: "Don't tell me about the solution to an individual incident. What I want is the broad, systemic solution."

Amazon takes the same approach: never view a problem as a single, one-off incident. Coordinate with various departments, implement the necessary fixes, follow up and then report back. Be prepared to illustrate the crux of the problem, how you improved the process, and how you did it in just a matter of days. Inform the CEO in another week that the matter has been resolved. And, more importantly, affirm that similar problems will not occur again.

Wu Haiying, director of management support for the JD warehouse logistics department, joined the company in May 2011 as head of JD East China's warehouse department. He was in charge of multiple delivery centres for small to medium parcels in the region. At the time, the regional warehouse system had more than 500 employees who handled tens of thousands of orders a day. Two years later, the average daily order processing during peak times increased more than seven-fold. Yet, the staff had barely doubled, thanks to strategic re-organization, optimization of warehouse processes, introduction of new productivity equipment and adoption of more reasonable performance management metrics.

When he first got to East China, Wu had directly managed all of the warehouses, among many other duties. He held two mobile phones in his hands while his fixed-line phone rang constantly. At times there were multiple people standing beside him waiting for him to sign a document or render a decision.

At the branch level, JD began to build warehousing operation departments that would offer assistance by business function. The distribution and coordination of responsibilities were laid out in a detailed organizational structure. The head of warehousing, who once did everything, began to focus on planning, team-building and employee development. For three months, Wu worked seven days a week, sleeping just three or four hours a night. It took him six months to get the organizational structure right.

Liu had been resolute in the past. He sought quick solutions. When problems reached him through his subordinates, he would issue immediate instructions. Later, Liu found that many complex issues involved different sectors. Some departments could respond appropriately to a simple instruction while others could not. Horizontal coordination was needed. He began to ask different questions: who will take the lead? Which sectors should coordinate? How can we solve this systematically, pervasively, truly effectively?

Unfortunately, as the company's growth continued, cross-functional communication and inter-organizational efficiency declined for a time.

In 2009, JD signed the real estate agreement for the "Asia No.1" advanced logistics facility with authorities in Shanghai. By September 2012 the deal was concluded. JD took possession of the land, work began on a logistics design scheme and architectural planning commenced. The first batch of equipment was moved into the facility in

April 2013. In May 2014 the warehouse went live. Within six months the facility's order volume exceeded 100,000.

This was JD's first automated warehouse, and it required even closer alignment between various departments. A concerted effort was launched to foster cooperation between logistics, construction and other parts of the company.

During its expansion, JD made mistakes common to many large and growing enterprises. Should a certain department's requirements take precedent over another? If so, how should they be prioritized? Problems and disputes cropped up one after another. Responsibilities were not clearly delineated. Whose opinion should prevail?

For example, extensive storage equipment was needed on site. Because this equipment was produced and shipped from abroad, the Chinese Department of Government Affairs had to be involved and they proposed and listed the entry requirements. Moreover, the facility's entire production and delivery schedule had to be synched with the equipment import and installation plan. For the logistics team, this was a nearly impossible task. Departments reverted to passing the buck. Could these schedules be synchronized? If the equipment could not be there on time, there would be additional storage costs overseas. Who was to bear the costs? Needless to say, there was much internal wrangling.

The sales and marketing department needed to stock and replenish merchandise, but warehousing had to simultaneously carry out an assessment of area utilization. If too much inventory replenishment lowered the speed of turnover, warehouse operations would be affected.

By almost any measure the company was growing too fast. Everyone seemed to be overworked. Fewer were willing to assume more responsibilities. Previously, the company was small enough that departments could meet to hash out problems. Is it your part of the business? If not, is it his? Let's enlist the right people and get this thing done. But in the huge new JD, that dynamic was a thing of the past. Now the conversation became: is it your business? No? It's not mine either, so let's just forget it.

At times, effective cross-functional coordination in a large organization hinges upon personal relationships. For example, Xiao Jun, the executive from JD's operation and maintenance division, needed project help from Ma Song, head of marketing for the R&D division. "Sorry," Ma told him, "but my boss has me working on something else so you'll have to wait three months before I finish." Xiao Jun needed his project in a month. What could he do? If this dispute were brought to Liu, both sides would be scolded. Xiao Jun pleaded with Ma and his team: "Please, guys. Can you just do it for me?" He asked them to consider working overtime on weekends to get it done and offered to take them out for a treat and send some of his own employees to help if they were short-handed. He got the help he needed and both projects were completed on time.

JD added cross-functional collaboration to performance evaluations. Employees had to show how they'd collaborated with others across the business. Financial results typically accounted for up 50% in C-Suite evaluations. It was generally 30% for vice presidents and 20% for directors. Collaboration drove and helped optimize bottom line results. Nonetheless, real collaboration was a personal commitment and if employees remained too compartmentalized, collaboration was impossible. It was the company's responsibility to promote managers who had a big-picture perspective and were willing to help others.

Each employee needed to consider the challenges facing colleagues and think from the broader company's point of view. Henceforth, a marketing person would not be responsible only for his or her own performance.

As noted, between 2008 and 2013 JD grew from roughly 300 people to more than 30,000. With this growth, Liu realized he needed a strict management system to run the company. In the second quarter of 2013, JD applied key performance indicators (KPI) for the first time. From 2009 to 2010 the company had run fast and hard. The target was set at the beginning of each year and everybody hustled like crazy, doing the best they could, without regard for specific indicators. They were overworked but had a strong desire to succeed. At the time, the KPI for marketing department leaders was 65% sales plus 35% cultural assessment. Multiple indicators were eventually added for the evaluation of organizational performance.

In 2010, JD mainly focused on gross margin and sales. In 2012, the company began placing more emphasis on indicators like supplier management and inventory turnover. This mapped to JD's bigger strategic transformation: from 3C products to a full category range, from reselling to a platform model, from self-support to large customers, and to offering services to third parties and meeting social needs. This stressed JD's operating efficiencies. In 2012 the company significantly increased its investment in R&D to rapidly improve the operating system. As a result, order processing and order delivery per head and the call answering efficiency of customer service centres improved dramatically. "It was a big company now," said Xu Lei. "We had to check out our data quarterly, monthly and daily, and focus on our own target KPIs. We were under great pressure to make it work."

Along the way JD's processes became more and more rigorous. And that presented a paradox. If there was no standard process, people were likely to take advantages of loopholes. On the other hand, adherence to strict processes could reduce innovation, communication, and collaboration. In the past, with a "so be it" attitude, employees teamed up and laid into even the most challenging assignments. Now, with tighter business processes, they had to apply for permission once requirements grew beyond certain pre-authorized limits.

From management's perspective, it was hard to tell if KPI was an entirely good thing or not. Without KPI, management lacked control and visibility; with it, employee initiative was constrained. JD had arrived at a point where relying on the institution supplanted total reliance on the individual. There was, it seemed, no perfect management culture, only the one born and instituted at the right moment.

JD had a robust bonus culture in its early years. At the dinner table, it was not unusual for Liu to say: "Get your job done and meet the target. I will give you a car." There were many stories out of marketing and purchasing, pre-2012, of fabulous rewards bestowed at the CEO's dinners. During after-dinner drinks, those who exceeded targets could be promised year-end bonuses of 30,000 or 40,000 yuan.

Needless to say, everybody loved to dine with Liu. At most, human resources could only offer tens of thousands of yuan as bonuses. But dining with Liu, it was possible to get virtually anything. A reasonably fair and equitable system had been established by HR, but Liu barreled over it at will. The pay system was on an even keel, yet nothing compared with the excitement of dinner with the boss. However, it was impossible for every employee to dine with Liu. And the money spent certainly didn't please everyone. Even those who were direct beneficiaries of his largesse might not have a sense of greater security.

Through 2011 and 2012, HR raised repeated concerns with Liu, who felt overwhelmed and restricted by a tangle of rules and regulations. "Why am I in the wrong," he asked. "Why can't I spend my own money?" He later admitted it was reasonable and necessary for HR to insist on an equitable compensation and award structure. But at the same time it meant his freedom of action was being constrained. He stopped distributing money on his own and HR began to manage incentives relating to all projects.

Take the innovation award, for example. JD offers a prize of 8 million yuan, but there is a detailed, carefully monitored process for evaluating and granting these periodic cash awards.

Improving the Talent Pipeline

Liu had read many of Peter F. Drucker's business philosophy books, but in the past he did not buy into many of the ideas. After re-reading them more carefully, he found inspiration. Drucker wrote that a big company could no longer rely on a single person to manage; there had to be a formalized top management team.

In 2007, JD had only one vice president: Yan Xiaoqing. In 2008, a second VP, Li Daxue, was appointed. And in 2009, Xu Lei became the company's third VP. For a long time, Liu himself shouldered most of the burden of running JD. For 15 years he arrived at the office at 7 am and an hour later would preside over the morning meeting. But starting in 2013 he no longer showed up at the morning meetings. Shen Haoyu, chief operating officer, presided over sessions in his place. If Shen was not around, Lan Ye, chief marketing officer, would chair the meeting. The morning meeting usually took 15 minutes. General managers of the six regions and the customer service centre would report on warehousing, delivery, customer service and other daily operational elements. One day, for example, they would discuss an increased redelivery rate due to heavy rain in the Southwest China Region. On another they would focus on an earthquake in the Northwest China Region and its impact on employees and delivery stations.

Shen, who joined JD in 2011 as chief operating officer, was the first new C-Suite level executive. His arrival meant Liu could begin managing the company more like a modern CEO. There was now a true emphasis on process and empowerment, allowing Liu to spend more time pondering strategy. "Liu had scarcely worked for others," said Shen. "He started his own businesses early on. He was more concerned with thinking about what the CEO should do in a sophisticated company."

JD successively established the COO, CMO, CTO, and the joint chief HR officer and general counsel positions. In March 2014, after merging the e-commerce businesses of JD and Tencent, the company was restructured. JD Mall became a subgroup of JD Group and Shen Haoyu became CEO of JD Mall.

Zhang Lei said that Liu was unafraid of high-power talent. Many private entrepreneurs were wary of recruiting talent out of fear of losing control, but Liu was never known to lack confidence. Zhang introduced Liu to Shen and Yao Naisheng, now VP of the JD financial group's strategy department, one after the other. At the time, it was difficult for JD to recruit executives, because the company was still too small and the work was seen as intense, unrewarding and tiring.

Shen remembers Liu telling him: "This is not my business. You can make your own decisions. Don't ask me." Sometimes it was clear that Liu wanted to take control but he reconsidered, realizing that would not be the right approach. And he took a step back.

JD's management system had VPs sending daily reports to the C-suite. Liu gave VP Shi Tao responsibility for books and audio-visual products and international brand development. Shi Tao developed a planning report. After reviewing it, Liu told him: "I want you to manage the business directly, but from now on you will report to CMO Lan Ye. You can copy me, but do not bypass Lan Ye in your communication with me."

"He doesn't want those in marketing to drift too far away from the management system, which would be disrespectful to the CMO," said Tao. "He doesn't want confusion about lines of authority to create a wrong impression across the team."

JD set up delivery stations in 1,862 districts and counties across China, each overseen by a station agent. As JD expanded its delivery range, could the company provide enough station agents in the coming years? When staffing and operations grew quickly, a company needed sufficient management personnel to support the organization. After HR chief Long Yu joined JD, she began an extensive recruitment effort. She sought talent for the C-Suite as well as for VP, director and manager positions. She carefully examined, level by level, whether the talent pool could sustain JD's long-term development and whether there were enough qualified successors in line for managers at each level. She found that there was a sufficient talent pipeline at the VP and director levels, but significant gaps below that. She faced a tremendous challenge in trying to address this shortfall in a timely manner.

In 2010, Liu Meng (later VP of HR) joined JD. When she asked what human resource systems the company was using, she was told there were none. The HR management process consisted of Excel spreadsheets filled in manually. She couldn't believe it. She recommended buying a turnkey HR management system, but was told that JD could develop the capability on its own. Again, Liu Meng couldn't believe her ears. There were so many mature management software systems on the market, but the company was refusing to consider them. She thought the company was just too narrow minded, with a misplaced sense of self-sufficiency. Later, she was given a budget of

100,000 yuan to piece together a companywide HR management system, even though it was not unusual for other companies to spend 20 million yuan on their HR systems.

Working with what she had, Liu Meng began to build complementary systems, covering job grading, performance, pay, and so on. But with JD's rapid growth, initial plans for her system were insufficient even before they were rolled out. JD's headcount grew from 5,000 to 20,000 between the project's inception and its completion. More and more people joined the organization. Experienced outside managers joined JD and brought their own concepts of management and HR thinking. The project plan had to be adjusted accordingly.

There were monumental conflicts and heated debates over the definition of leadership. Operational departments emphasized efficiency, standardization and cost, while the R&D team prized creativity and technological innovation. Purchasing and marketing departments argued that strategy trumped R&D and was more critical because it charted future business opportunities and the direction of category expansion.

Nor could any consensus be reached on employee pay structure. The founding executives thought JD should pay B-class basic salaries for A-class employees, giving them preferred treatment only after they had shown top-notch performance. But newer executives felt JD should trust and reward the talent it was recruiting. Otherwise, the thinking went, new recruits wouldn't fully buy into JD's vision. The old guard believed employees first had to put in the effort before getting their due, since every penny was earned at JD with great effort. The new school couldn't see how ten of thousands of talented newcomers would unconditionally believe in JD without appropriate incentives up front. The debate grew intense and it was not uncommon for people to lose their temper and angrily storm out of a conference room.

Liu Meng thought JD needed to develop a system that reflected the current state of the business but was capable of scaling to its future needs. The salary system would better compensate newcomers while ensuring current employees would see their wages increase if they performed well.

In 2013, after the leadership model was established, JD began a sweeping talent inventory. Previously, employee appraisals were based exclusively on the boss's judgment. Newer thinking held that employee performance was better assessed through a mix of different perspectives, including input from one's superior, self and peers. A common, codified language was needed for these assessments, including basic components like a numerical performance scale.

The talent inventory began with a C-suite meeting in which the VPs were appraised. Liu Meng called in each executive to explain the meeting's intent. HR management consultants from Hewitt Associates emphasized the importance of JD's first-ever formal talent inventory. To keep things moving smoothly and effectively, the team and the consultants wondered, would it be possible to keep Liu away and ask him to watch the proceedings later, on video? Long Yu wrote a message to Liu, conveying the spirit and importance of the meetings. Liu replied: so be it.

On 8 June 2013, Liu silently observed while JD's CFO, CMO, COO, chief HR officer and others evaluated the skills and potential of more than 30 VPs. Liu had trained most of them himself and probably knew them better than anyone. Several times, he felt the urge to speak. But he swallowed hard and let the process proceed at its own pace. When it had concluded six hours later, Liu had used his power of veto in only one case.

The talent assessment shocked Liu; he hadn't expected such a frank and comprehensive discussion. A senior adviser at Hewitt told Long Yu that the consultants had not really expected JD executives to embrace and successfully implement the new, highly transparent model, but they did.

While attending seminars abroad, Long Yu often found that those who sat quietly in the corner were the real leaders. In 2012, when she first attended JD meetings, she had observed that Liu was often the only one to express his views. The others were silent. And that, she thought, was a recipe for disaster. JD's evolution over the coming decade would depend on collective wisdom and the team's diverse skills and talents, not Liu's opinions alone. In August 2013, at the semi-annual management meeting held in Jiuzhaigou, Liu listened with uncharacteristic patience. He shared his thoughts only after everyone else had done so.

Human-Oriented Management

On 17 August 2012, Liu hosted an evening banquet at the Yugong Yupo Seafood Restaurant in the Asian Games Village. It was to honour employees who had worked at JD for five years. Each table was set with treats and ornate bottles of a popular brand of baiju, the potent Chinese liquor. Liu invited me to attend this party, where I spoke casually with various employees. A man in his 40s named Xu Wenyi had joined JD's delivery team in August 2007 and initially worked at the Maliandao Delivery Station in Xicheng District. At that time, JD operated just three delivery stations, each with four or five employees. In 2012 he worked at the delivery station in Xinfa District, and had a monthly income of more than 5,000 yuan. Four of his co-workers in that initial group are still with JD.

Liu arrived at the restaurant casually dressed in a white cotton shirt, blue trousers and black rubber-soled shoes. He greeted each and every one of the more than 80 employees present by name and correctly referred to each one's business unit.

"It's been five years," Liu told them. "When you first came, we would gather a few times a year for a drink together. Now, it's hard to see each other that often, let alone share a drink. Five years ago we were on Suzhou Street and JD was a small company. Today we have become a well-known domestic business. I believe in the next five years JD is bound to become a remarkable and widely-respected enterprise."

His remarks became more personal. "I hope the single colleagues among us can find their other half in the next five years. And I hope the married ones can raise a child of their own."

Liu took turns making toasts with each of the employees around the table. He said to an older employee, "We haven't seen each other for two years, right?" The man said, "Three years." Later, while chatting, Liu said, "We are all in our late 30s now. We have to pay attention to our health. I run three to five kilometers every day. I run even if I get home at midnight."

Before the end of the party, there was a drawing for prizes that included 10 iPads, 10 iPhones and an envelope containing 50,000 yuan in cash. Deliveryman Liu Xiaoming, who joined JD in June 2007, said, "I've been here for five years, but I've never won a prize in the lotteries." At that moment Liu called his name as the winner of an iPhone. He was so excited that he ran up and hugged Liu.

In JD, it was well known that the capable rose and the incompetent fell. In the talent inventory meeting, some VPs were downgraded. They had turned in middling performances and didn't show much potential. But in discussing these people, Liu said: "JD is big enough for them to find their own places. We shall never say, 'Sorry, you don't fit in my organization. Please leave.'" A certain VP had been in the company for a long time, but his thinking failed to keep pace with the company's development. Liu spent time talking to him personally. He was given responsibility for a less prominent department, where he performed well and was praised in meetings. Such moves ensured the normal operation of the business and at the same time helped older employees save face.

Chen Yanlei, warehouse director of JD South China, had been with the company for eight years. A young man with little formal education, he nevertheless started as logistics manager overseeing a warehouse of approximately 3,000m². Today he manages warehouses of 20,000 to 30,000m² and has a team of more than 2,000 people.

In 2007, JD set up the South China Branch. Two months after Chen joined JD, the company built the first warehouse there, with an area of more than 2,000m². Liu rented a temporary apartment suite in Tianhe, Guangzhou. He regularly dined and had drinks with employees there. For the time he was there, he effectively made Guangzhou JD's temporary headquarters. In those days, Liu was quick-tempered and liked to make decisions quickly. In choosing the site of the warehouse, he called Chen and made the decision on the spot. This was quite unlike Chen's former boss, who would have to sort through many options before finally choosing one.

In fast-growing companies like JD, individual growth either kept pace with or outran the company's development. This could sometimes be cruel, but it was also realistic. Management was rational and there would inevitably be those who stayed and those who left. While one's previous contributions had to be acknowledged, employees could not coast along on what they'd done in the past. Management needed to be flexible, but if too many emotions were involved, the health of the entire team suffered.

When Chen Yanlei and other older employees gathered together, an underlying concern seemed to be: "Will we be washed away by the tide? How can we do better?" At a strategic seminar, while speaking about regional organizational structure issues, Liu told the regional managing directors: "If you find someone is hindering our development or is incompetent, don't hesitate. Replace them." But at the same time Liu always tried to give older employees special consideration on salaries, help identify suitable positions for them and even help them resolve family difficulties. It was clear he cared a great deal for these older workers.

Chen Yanlei's performance was seen as mixed at best. His managers were strictly results-oriented and didn't appreciate his abilities. Fortunately, thanks to Liu's concern for older workers, Chen Yanlei got one more chance. In 2012 he was full of anxiety and worry, but his performance was ultimately ranked first nationwide. This, of course, boosted his self-esteem and changed how colleagues felt about him, which further motivated him. His case bolstered Liu's belief that older workers really can change, adapt and succeed.

More Freedom for the Post-90s Era

It was hazy at 6 am at the JD Jinjiang Express Centre. Situated at the Wangjiang Oak Grove Community gate in Chengdu, this was JD's largest delivery station in China, with more than 1,000 delivery staff. Its vans were painted in red with the silver, smiling dog mascot. Deliverymen in red uniforms lined up and relayed parcels on their electric scooters.

In early 2013 the southeast delivery department chose to build a large-scale delivery station in the eastern district of Chengdu. By chance, Long Hui, manager of the southwest delivery department for the eastern district of Chengdu, saw a storefront that was for lease. The monthly rent was listed at 230 yuan per square meter, but it was reduced to 180 after a bit of bargaining. In May of that year, the Jinjiang Express Centre was established there. On the 18 June anniversary sale day in 2014, 12,000 orders were distributed from the facility, smoothly and without incident.

In this 700m² space, there were separate lounges where deliverymen could have their meals, unlike at the much smaller, original location, where they could only eat while crouching in a doorway.

The cramped former site had had a heavy order load. A dozen people would have to work in a narrow space where they hardly had room to turn around. The movement of outgoing orders was slow and inefficient in the morning. The new Jinjiang Express Centre was open in front and offered easy parking. Unloading efficiency had improved and the electric scooters no longer blocked the doorway. It also had a more presentable image. Customers who visited felt it was a proper retail store.

By combining five stations together in the eastern district of Chengdu, the Jinjiang Express Centre saved management and manpower costs of more than 20,000 yuan a month. There was only one station agent instead of five, and four assistants instead of five.

Wang Wu, born in 1990 in Mianyang, Sichuan, was station agent for the Jinjiang Express Centre. He used to work in DTW Logistics. Back then, when he made a delivery to JD, he was impressed by how nice the warehouse was, so one day he went to JD's southwest branch office and said: "I want to join JD. Any job is just fine with me." He was hired as a deliveryman for the East Gate Delivery Station and began work there in May 2011, feeling very lucky.

Three days later, Wang was transferred to the new Wenjiang Station. That facility handled just 30 to 40 orders a day when he first arrived. There were four deliverymen and each was assigned a mere seven or eight orders a day. But the distances were great – up to

20 kilometres for each order. Wang would chat with customers after the deliveries were done. At the end of 2011, Chengdu Station was expanded and he was transferred to Yanshikou to work as the station agent. In March 2013 he returned to the East Gate Station of Chengdu, where he had begun his JD career. All told, he had been station agent at all but one of the stations within the Third Ring Road of Chengdu. JD was developing rapidly and every day brought something new. Some older station agents could not keep up with the changes and left the company. By 2013, the transfer of station agents was quite common.

Wang had personally met Liu twice. The first time was when he joined JD in 2011. They briefly shared the lift in the southwestern branch building. Wang didn't know who Liu was, but as they exited the lift he heard everyone say: "Hello, President Liu!" He would have shaken hands with him had he known. At the 2012 annual meeting, Wang formally met Liu when the boss was taking photos with the southwestern region staff.

Not unusual for an employee hired in the post-1990s period, Wang Wu is assertive and resolute at work. There are more than 100 employees in the Jinjiang Express Centre and the deliverymen come from different age groups, regions and backgrounds. Some began their work lives in the 1960s and 1970s. They come from both rural areas and big cities. Some joined the company to make money, others with an eye toward social security, and some simply because they liked the company. With such a varied workforce, managing effectively could be especially challenging. But Wang had many tricks up his sleeve.

He believed information was the best antidote to mistakes. He would take time to speak with deliverymen who'd made a mistake. But the deliverymen were often quite anxious during those discussions because they preferred to use that precious time to make more deliveries and earn more money. If an order sheet was not signed, Wang would ask the deliveryman to copy his name 100 times. If there were customer complaints, he would ask the responsible deliverymen to write summary reports of at least 500 words. Most deliverymen would rather be fined than have to sit at a desk, wracking their brains over a report.

After becoming successful at this job, Wang bought a house and a car. He felt he had done quite well compared to his peers. "All thanks go to JD," he said. "Everything I have now has been given to me by JD." His father also came to visit him at the station and told him how impressed he was by his achievements.

Wang came to Beijing headquarters for training and learned that there were more than 100 regions across the country, so he had a lot of opportunity to get promoted. This made him excited about the future. "There are so many opportunities in JD," he said. "I have to aim higher. My goal is to join the C-suite."

Li Junxiang, born in 1991, joined JD in November 2011 and later became supervisor of the Central China Region's small appliances warehouse. Following his first night shift, he was cold and hungry. As he was walking out of the warehouse he checked his phone and saw many messages. Most of them were from his new colleagues, saying things like, "Thank you for your hard work. We've prepared hot water, milk, bread and fruit for you." He was really moved.

In 2014, Li was awarded a trip to Taiwan as a top-performing employee. Only three people from the Central China Region, 0.15% of the region's employees, had won the trips. Each had a unique story to tell. Li felt terrific. He traveled around Taiwan, seeing the sights and having fun for eight days and seven nights.

When he joined JD, Li had started out as a merchandise picker in the warehouse. He wanted to be a group leader and thought he could get there if he picked faster than anyone else. He spent most of his time in the warehouse. After he became team leader, he found it was not enough to know how to work alone. He had to learn how to coordinate the actions of the team.

When the small appliances unit in JD Central China was established, Li stayed in the warehouse from 9 pm to midnight every night, without a break, for two months. He was responsible for general department operations and had to take care of everything, from leaky roofs to computer failures and invoice problems. Li was always more of a listener than an eloquent speaker. His team enjoyed interacting with him and often told him when they were having difficulties. He would help them solve their problems if he could, and if not he'd help out by running errands for them. His supervisor once said: "Li Junxiang spoke the least among all the managers, but he won the recognition of all through his actions."

He organized informal events every Friday in the small-appliance warehouse. On festive occasions, he'd buy moon cakes, watermelons and a variety of small prizes for games among employees. For those who couldn't go home for holidays, there would be a party in the warehouse. Li organized badminton competitions, inviting people from other departments to join in. Some deliverymen even stopped by after work. "The small-appliance warehouse was in a separate office park that's far from the other departments," said Li. "Cross-function coordination could be slow. These workplace social activities helped everyone get to know one another other and pave the way for cooperation."

During the massive 2014 "Singles Day" or "double 11" promotion on 11/11, some 1.2 million orders were processed by JD North China. Employee morale and engagement were high. There was a sense of excitement as everyone vied for new orders to fill, sometimes literally grabbing them from the hands of managers. But leadership carefully managed order production because it had to keep the whole production chain in balance. Some picking centres had lost power and storage production had to be moderated. Some employees even begged tearfully for more orders, saying they felt sorry for customers who might not receive their orders on time. A number of workers asked for sick leave two days later because they were so stressed by the ordeal.

The post-90s hires were not overly money conscious. They didn't have family pressures. When they first joined the company they were told by HR that, unlike civil servants, no-one in JD knew what they would be doing when they reached their 50s. JD would offer them a rotation system. After two or three years, whether they want to stay with the company or seek employment elsewhere, they'd be fully rounded talents. Managers needed to be mindful and do a good job on staff training. There had to be room for promotion in addition to making money, which helped ensure that employees would be competitive when they pursued new opportunities years later. If employees came away with more than just a salary, they would be more satisfied with the company.

How to manage the post-90s hires became a hot new topic for management. They were free, unrestrained and assertive. And they did things in their own way. This was truly a generation of individuals. Management needed to consider their self-esteem while teaching them the organization's needs and the impact of their mistakes.

Yang Tao, manager of JD's East China "Asia No.1" Warehouse in Shanghai, asked his employees to make a formal presentation at the morning meeting if they'd made a mistake the day before. Many were quite shy, and feared going on stage more than the prospect of being fined. "The company wanted them to face their mistakes openly, not to suppress them," said Yang. "Fines were useless. The staff would think an error is a one-off phenomenon. Moreover, if the company chose to deduct money for each mistake, employees would become resentful." Yang firmly believed that a lively morning meeting set the tone for a passionate workday.

A board that hung on the wall of the warehouse charted the facility's error rate. Younger employees were proud and valued positive recognition but were loath to see their names appear on the error list. The post-90s hires had a strong sense of participation. They hoped to promote change and see results when they found a problem. They needed a platform to voice their opinions and assumed their suggestions would be taken seriously and adopted by their own and even other departments. JD realized management had to pay more attention to recognition and incentives, and shed the rigid management style of the past. Examples of success also needed to be publicized so employees would see they could do as well as their most successful peers.

Respect in business was seen as increasingly important, and it had to be a two-way street. Know-it-all preaching was outdated and supervisors were discouraged from pulling rank. The post-90s hires embraced a shared management style. They hoped their superiors could be more like coaches and friends, willing to share their own experiences and offer advice. They were more self-centred and more emotional. They weren't short of money, they were strong willed, and they were not afraid to quit their jobs.

One morning a warehouse employee came directly to Yin Hongyuan, JD Group VP and general manager of JD South China, and said: "I want to quit, because my supervisor won't let me have my meal." Yin took a look at the time. It was only 11 am, and the normal lunch time was noon. "It's still work time," Yin said. "Why are you in a such rush for lunch?" "I'm hungry," he replied. "I was in too much of a hurry to have my breakfast this morning." "Everyone else is working. If you go out to have a meal, what do you think others will say?" Yin asked him. "I work faster than them," the employee replied. "How is your performance this month?" Yin asked, "Are you in first or second place?" "It all depends," the young man answered. "If I want to be first I will be first. And if I want to be second, I will be the second. I don't like my position now. I want to be transferred to something else."

Yin then told him: "I'll give you 10 minutes right now to have your meal. But you have to get into the habit of having breakfast from now on, for the sake of your health. And, if you can be in the top three performers for three months in a row, you can choose to go to any post you like."

This young man chose to return immediately to his work instead of breaking for lunch. Later, whenever Yin met him, she asked how he was doing that month. "His supervisor might have neglected his needs," she said. "I can't just tell him to take a break whenever he likes. And it's pointless to reason with him about the rules and regulations of the company. You need to resolve his inner resentment with his own language."

Zhou Hang, who was born in 1991, can be very emotional. She joined JD in 2012, and is now operations manager of the JD National Customer Service Centre. In 2013, on the evening that JD launched its new logo, "Joy", the smiling dog mascot, and Zhou was browsing social media sites, searching for an image of the dog. When she saw Joy on her screen, she was moved to tears. This is our company, she thought. And today it is showing itself to the world.

Beyond performing their assigned tasks, few employees voluntarily offered up helpful business suggestions. But if they wanted to be seen as future stars, they needed to be more open and forthcoming. In meetings, management would ask: "What would you do under such circumstances if you were in charge?" They would brainstorm, find ways to work out an approach, and then assess its feasibility.

When Zhou Hang first came to JD, the call centre lacked tools to ensure uniform solutions when the same question was raised by multiple customers. Zhou's manager said: "Customer service is proposing different solutions to the same problem. What should be done when that happens?" The company eventually introduced a knowledge-based system managed by a single, skilled individual and as issues were raised and resolved, the findings were constantly documented and updated. This was the most meaningful change Zhou observed in her initial period with the company.

Zhou was promoted to supervisor. One of her employees, an 18-year-old woman, was frank and lively, with a positive, can-do attitude, but she was not particularly well spoken. Zhou thought the employee needed to change her "little girl" voice and conversational style, or her future as a customer service representative would be limited. Zhou asked her to arrange a party for the team and the employee did a great job; everyone had a wonderful time. She told Zhou: "You can assign things like this to me from now on." Zhou said her time at JD taught her that if employees were empowered they would grow and mature quickly, freeing up supervisors to consolidate the team and focus on new issues. It was a lesson she embraced.

After Zhou moved into management, she encountered a particularly rebellious employee. When his supervisor tried to teach him how to perform a new task, he for some reason took offence. One day, he was unexpectedly absent from work. He had not asked for leave and did not answer his phone. Zhou worried that something may have happened to him. She asked HR for his emergency contact and finally found him in the boys' dormitory. He appeared to be OK.

"What do you think about the task your supervisor taught you," Zhou asked. "Was it helpful or did it pose a problem for you?" The employee had no opinion. He said he felt his supervisor was watching him all day and it annoyed him. "Why are you absent from work," Zhou asked, "when you could have requested leave?" "I just don't want to come in," he replied. It hadn't occurred to him that the company had rules and regulations, like the need to actually show up for work. "If you give up this job, you'll have to go to other companies and interview. With your attitude toward work, do you think other employers will hire you?" "No," the employee admitted.

After this incident, Zhou asked supervisors to be clear in their communication with employees and to take the time to explain the company's expectations.

Lv Luyi is from Ganzhou, Jiangxi. She joined the JD call centre in 2009 as an intern. Her family disapproved of her move to Suqian and kept encouraging her to return home. She had difficult conversations with her parents in the beginning, but soon came to realize they were worried about her safety. She needed to prove to them that her independent work life had helped her become a responsible young woman.

The development channels in the call centre include three paths, designated "OPM". 'O' is the operation sequence, in which the ordinary costumer service representatives become experienced service experts. During this process, calls are escalated based on degree of complexity, from general consultation through complaints and, ultimately, critical incidents. 'P' refers to professional talent tapped for questions on quality control, data analysis, finance and other matters. 'M' is the management sequence through which a matter goes up level-by-level to supervisor, assistant manager, manager, senior manager and director.

When Lv Luyi first became a manager, she was quite inexperienced. In less than a month, nearly half her employees had doubts about her abilities and many left the company. A senior manager was sent to assist her. They held panel discussions and took measures to stabilize the staff. Lv Luyi also reflected on her style and realized she was too impatient. She had assigned newly trained workers to the front lines and was too strict with supervisors. The supervisors in turn put pressure on employees and disregarded their moods and feelings. After this, Lv Luyi realized she had to take greater care of her employees. Only when they felt stable could they trust her and do the work as directed.

Lv Luyi eventually came to speak with passion and assurance about her own management philosophy. "You need to know how the younger workers think," she said. "Some thrive on high performance; some are looking for a bigger stage; some want to be recognized for their expertise. You need to work out transparent performance incentives and help employees break down their targets and share status reports on a regular basis. For staff that prefer it, performing to a clear target tells them how much money they can make in a month, and they will become more motivated."

For those who wished to go into management, the first step was to assess whether their personality, skills and thought process were compatible with a supervisory role. The second step was to tell the candidate he or she had to perform at a consistently high level. Each candidate received an initial administrative assignment for practice. Certain employees possessed special talents and expertise, which they'd be asked to demonstrate. The post-90s hires were decidedly not money-conscious. They wanted to do the things they liked and they were happy if they got recognition from others.

"The biggest achievement as a manager was not to show how strong you were, but how well you could guide your team's development so more employees felt fulfilled," Lv Luyi said. She used to have 12 employees when she was the supervisor. Two-thirds of them later became supervisors themselves.

"In JD, I felt fulfilled," she said. "Before, my mother often asked what the point of being so far away from home was and asked me to come back home. After I became supervisor and manager, she stopped urging me to come home. I asked why, and my mom said, 'There is no need. You can decide for yourself now. You are more experienced.'" When she chatted with others, her mother had found that many children relied on their parents to find job connections. Her daughter found the job on her own and was happy with her work. "I supported myself and even had shares of stock," Lv said. "Besides, I could buy things for them. They were proud of me."

Liu once said: "When we talk about people of each generation, we are always filled with fear. A decade ago, we said post-80s hires were lazy. Now we say post-90s are the lazy generation. I believe after another seven or eight years, we'll say the same about the post-2000s. People from the post-50s and post-60s generations said that we, the post-70s, had not experienced the Cultural Revolution and the struggle. I think each generation has its own distinctive culture. Each generation will demonstrate their personality and have different pursuits. But there will always be 1% of each generation that's career-oriented. It is not just that someone wants to travel the world, or buy a big house and many cars. In any generation, there are people who hate wasting time and are willing to fight for careers and enjoy success. Therefore, my responsibility is to pick that 1% of people who will become the company's executives, regardless of which generation they are part of."

Liu's management style did not change in principle, but it varied subtly across different generations. "For instance, the post-90s hires value freedom, so I gave it to them," he said. "Post-90s liked to express themselves. So at each meeting, I left time for them to share their opinions. After they finished, the whole team would return to the same theme. The purpose of discussion was to reach a consensus."

Morale Built Through Triumphs

On JD's 18 June company anniversary in 2012, Guo Xinwei, senior manager of storage for the North China Region, felt like a puzzled onlooker when he should have felt in control. Products he was responsible for had been wrongly inventoried and he was disoriented. His supervisor had to transfer all of JD's North China leaders, assistant managers and above, to support his warehouse. Guo was embarrassed and felt terrible. His team was so demoralized they hadn't recovered by Spring Festival the following year.

After the Chinese New Year holiday, Guo steeled himself and invited his team to dinner to discuss the coming year. A manager said: "Guo, we can't have too many voices in the team. We must unify our thinking. For any decision, we'll listen to your idea first and we'll discuss it together if it does not work out. But we need a unified approach. No matter if it's right or wrong, we must carry on or none of us will do a good job." After two months of consolidation and alignment, the team had a sense that it was getting better and better.

On 18 June 2013, Guo Xinwei was in the warehouse by 5 am and with tears of relief reviewed the preparations his team had made. Inventory that a day earlier had been haphazardly stacked in mountainous piles had been neatly arranged. Equipment was wiped clean and polished. The vans were fueled up and parked in a neat row. Most importantly, employees were in high spirits. They were ready for action. "Don't worry," they told him. "We'll win the battle today."

That day, Guo's warehouse became the first in JD's history to complete 100,000 orders in a single shift. The proud team won a silk banner.

For Guo, who had been so discouraged, it seemed like a miracle. "I felt a sense of belonging; I was with my team. We all need friendship and want to be recognized. Both the general manager and the director of the region recognized the team. They gave me more self-assurance and more space and encouraged my team and me to move forward with confidence."

On "Double 11" in 2013, Guo stayed in a modest hotel for four days while working long hours at the warehouse. His team cleared

150,000 orders in a single day, a feat that normally took four days. By "Double 11" in 2014, more than 200,000 same-day orders were completed. At that point his team was actually smaller than it had been on the June anniversary in 2013, when it fulfilled half as many orders.

The most dreadful situation for a team is to have low morale in the face of a battle. Morale is built up when a team realizes one victory after another. It has to be inspired for the next hard fight. Discouragement has to be reversed with victory. Otherwise, the team will feel frustrated, lose heart, and won't rise to the occasion.

Two warehouses under Guo's purview were reorganized into three, and the managers of two of them remained on his team. This showed employees that they would have more space if they worked hard and got things done. Then the team entered an entirely new cycle.

In June 2011 DHL chose to withdraw from the domestic Chinese market and sold some of its assets. Shao Jiwei, who was then with DHL, felt lost. He considered JD. At the end of his contract with DHL, he completed a round of seven interviews with JD in a single day. On 16 December 2011, he accepted a position as JD North China's director for delivery. His new supervisor asked him to come to the office at once. Everything was ready for him. Shao finished his in-processing formalities in half an hour and rushed to the office by taxi. As soon as he walked through the door, his superior asked him to write the 2012 work plan. The annual meeting would be held in a week. He was totally overwhelmed. How would he handle it all?

At lunch with his assistants, he could not relax and said he had to go and look around the warehouse. There was a serious backlog in the Majuqiao warehouse and the arduous process of stock moving began. Warehouses that normally had 80,000 to 90,000 orders were suddenly swamped with 120,000. Originally, a third party was contracted to handle up to 50,000 orders, but this proved to be beyond its abilities. So, the goods were left unclaimed and piled up in the warehouse. There was no space for new merchandise and it had to be stocked in other places.

Every day, wearing his headphones, Shao moved goods while listening to conference calls from 6 am until 8 pm or 9 pm. He just put his head down and worked as hard as he could. He felt he couldn't really give anyone orders because no one knew him. If he asked others to do something he would be scolded. Dust was everywhere in the warehouse and his entire body was caked with it. After he had been moving stock for 10 straight days, his wife began to feel uneasy. She questioned what kind of place he was working in and worried that he might even be out of a job.

Shao was born in 1980. On 20 June 2014, he met Liu for the first time. Liu told him that nothing in the world was worth doing more than e-commerce. Liu asked: "How old are you? Where do you live? Do you have children? Who are your parents? Do you have a house of your own?" Shao replied, "I do not want to buy a house with a mortgage. I feel too pressured and can't afford to buy one now." Liu said: "Just work hard. In the future, you'll be able to buy a house anywhere in the world."

After chatting for half an hour, Liu ended by saying, "What if you take over JD North China?" In July, Shao took that job. Three months later, he faced yet another a tough challenge.

In November 2014 the APEC (Asia Pacific Economic Cooperation) Summit was being held in Beijing. Security was tight. Many streets had sentries posted every 10 steps. Traffic controls were enforced in the capital and in many cities in Hebei and Shandong as well. Many companies gave employees time off on 7-12 November. With the coming "Double 11" on 11 November, JD faced great challenges. In preparation, Shao began looking for resources and reserved 1,200 vehicles. Although there were eight days to go before "Double 11" and the inventory volumes had not reached their peak, it was preferable to lease the fleet early than fall short when the need was most pressing.

On 10 November, JD commenced its "Double 11" activity ahead of time. Jiwei pressed the full workforce into service in the early morning hours. Authorities were allowing vehicles with different number licence plates on the roads at different times. So cars with numbers outside the traffic controls were put in operation from midnight to 6 am and those with controlled plates started from midnight to 3 am.

To deter theft, each delivery site was guarded by employees and their families overnight. They would watch the loaded trucks at the gate and then deliver the cargo to the sites after 5 am.

At 8:08 pm that evening JD North China became the first major region to produce one million orders. In the four provinces and two cities in the North China Region – an area of 2.2 million km^2 ranging from Wuhai in Inner Mongolia in the west to Weihai in Shandong in the east, from Chengde in Hebei in the north to Zaozhuang in Shandong in the south – 90% of the orders were received by customers the next day despite the impact of the APEC Summit.

During those few days, employees were so worn down that they dozed off while having meals. Some fell asleep on the ground in narrow gaps between the towers of stocked goods.

A corporate culture's origins could often be traced back to the founder of the enterprise. The dedication of JD's management came from the spirit with which Liu had started from the very beginning. If Liu could personally unload goods and reply to messages at night, why couldn't they?

Liu's focus on the basics provided a solid foundation. Not every enterprise could manage 70,000 people. JD had strong executive power, rooted in concern for employee wellbeing. The company's values were embraced by everyone, from top to bottom. Everything was undertaken to meet the needs of the customer and the company, while never going against the fundamental interests of the employees. If employees weren't happy on the job, a company's vaunted values were, in the end, nothing but empty talk. There had to be incentives, such as money and recognition. The sense that you'd be rewarded for your contributions was the source of employee passion and commitment.

The rapid expansion of the workforce threatened to dilute JD's foundational culture. The old ways inevitably conflicted with thinking, attitudes and work habits brought in by new employees. In early 2009, JD had about 1,000 employees; by the end of the year there were more than 2,000. Even then, values could still be passed on from old employees to newer ones. In 2010 the number of employees jumped to more than 7,000. How did a big business carry forward what was valuable about the old while absorbing the new? In 2010 in particular, JD introduced many people who had experience in large companies and a set of values acquired from their professions. They were not blank pages. They were fully-formed individuals, with skills and track records in the marketplace. A collision with the values of the company's old guard was to be expected.

Should the existing corporate culture acquiesce to what new employees brought with them? Or should the new employees concede to the existing culture? Neither won over the other entirely and new, melded values were adopted and internalized. This was a painful process, as the realities of a fast growing business and dynamic marketplace drove change.

It would have been naïve for an enterprise to hope its employees kept the founding spirit through decades of growth and change. It would have been be foolish to expect new employees to gladly accept low wages, hard work and tough management.

In China, as elsewhere, entrepreneurs worked tirelessly. A talented leader with a couple of reliable helpers could make things happen. Remember how Liu worked out JD's back-end system with only one engineer? In the start-up phase, an entrepreneur could accomplish much with one or two colleagues, and then do even more with ten or 20 people earning high salaries. The cost-performance ratio was high, but real progress could only be achieved by experienced, and often highly-paid, employees. The company simply had to accept the cost. During the start-up phase, the founder was like a company commander who led his troops at the front. When the company grew bigger, he became the commander in chief who looked at the whole picture, not the outcome of a single battle.

The "38th Army" of JD

In August 2013 Sun Jiaming took over the general merchandise category, JD's largest business, but one that had performed poorly in the past. From 2010 to 2013 the person responsible was replaced each year.

JD's general merchandise line-up included six sub-categories: mother and baby products, cosmetics, food, wine, clocks and watches, and cars.

There were no clearly defined values and the group lacked team spirit. Employees from the early start-up period were demoralized after the loss of three consecutive supervisors during a time of operational strategy problems. Young white-collar professionals were the main target customers, but for some reason they bought neither snacks nor cosmetics from JD. Liu had to acknowledge JD's weakness in general merchandise. It worried him. He shared his concerns to Sun Jiaming, who said: "No problem, I'll go."

The difficulty for general merchandise was that the brands were less concentrated, with top suppliers numbering more than 100. In contrast, there were just 10-12 top suppliers in the computer category. Sun was back to square one again, as he was when he first began selling IT products. "We were shooting for first place only and we'd find ways to get there," he said. "We could not yield if we wanted to surpass the competition." Sun predicted that sales of general merchandise would reach 100 billion yuan sooner than the 3C category.

Sun transferred experienced staff from the IT category's purchasing and marketing section, JD's so-called 38th Army, so they could teach employees in general merchandise by personal example and help them understand the company's values.

The executive team was made up of professional business managers, while first-generation employees were the backbone of the company. The professional managers, with their accumulated work experience and expertise, brought perspective and insight. A closed system would not contribute to JD's success. Older workers, on the other hand, had a strong sense of responsibility and were endlessly diligent. They were devoted to work and ready for the fight, but their knowledge could be limited. Yet, these were the people who could rise to the challenge in difficult times.

Guo Xiaobo joined JD in March 2006 and first worked on webpage maintenance, concentrating on perfecting product images and text. Later he became the director of mother and baby products in the general merchandise department. "The development of JD," he said, "was really driven by the employees who compete with each other. If one of them rolled out a special offer or made a creative deal, others would do the same tomorrow, just for face-saving." Liu frequently asked what good deals they'd cut today. He pressed them on their sales volumes.

Guo was responsible for marketing a computer bag, which was sold at 49.9 yuan. He expected his inventory would last seven days, but rapid sales meant they were on track to sell out in just two. He raised the price to 59.9 yuan, thinking he could sell out and also bring in more profit for the company. Liu learned of this approach and criticized Guo during a meeting. "Short-sighted," Liu said. "You just think of earning money. Have you ever thought of the feelings of the customer? You suddenly boosted the price. Do you know how many customers that would hurt? You've made a few bucks in a short time, but you've lost heavily on the customer front."

At that time, Guo addressed Liu as "Manager Liu". At one point in 2007 he told Liu his performance would be good that month and that he'd surpass his colleagues. Liu promised to reward him with a digital camera if he made his numbers. A colleague beside him said that he could accomplish the same. Liu wanted them to compete and said the winner would get the camera. In the end, Guo received a Ricoh camera and his colleague got an LG phone.

At a team dinner, wine glass in hand, Liu queried buying and merchandising staffs on their performance targets and promised bonuses of 300,000 yuan if the targets were met. In Liu's eyes, only 100% counts. The target is the target and 99% achievement is not a win. There is a clear distinction between the completed and uncompleted, which to those present at the dinner meant the difference between 3,000 yuan and 300,000 yuan. Generous rewards can rouse people to heroic heights.

In 2011 and 2012 Guo won annual bonuses of 300,000 yuan. Once, his team set its target at 1.1 billion yuan. In December, 110 million yuan had to be booked. There were seven members on the team. Every day, tasks were assigned. Some took care of warehouse coordination, others handled payments, and some helped customer service process orders. No one was to be off duty before they finished their tasks. They ultimately closed on 160 million yuan that month. Guo got the 300,000 yuan bonus and his team members' bonuses varied from tens of thousands of yuan to 200,000 yuan. "Liu never breaks his promises," he said. "These bonuses were well beyond what was budgeted."

In August 2008 the market went into a downturn due to the global financial crisis. The price of computer displays dropped 150 yuan a month. In two months, the company lost 1 million yuan. Guo Xiao-bo was too worried to sleep. Liu told him: "This experience is worth more than MBA training. Here you can actually experience the cruelty of the business in person."

Zhang Li, general manager for food business in the general merchandise department of JD Mall, joined JD in 2010. When he first came to the company he was fascinated by the prospect of turning ideas into reality. If an idea struck him at night, he could put it into practice the next day, and by the afternoon he'd know if it was right or wrong. That year, Zhang overshot his target. He received 400,000 yuan as a year-end bonus even though he was then just a department manager.

At the end of 2010, Beijing began enacting automobile traffic controls. JD's domain name was still 360buy, and to demonstrate their pride in the company they'd helped build, many employees bought cars with a licence plate number ending in 360.

Wang Na, who later became manager of the food and oil group in the food department of general merchandise, joined JD on November 25, 2005. At the time the company had only a dozen people. In August 2013 she joined the food and oil group when its sales totalled several million yuan a month. Looking around in a supermarket one weekend, Wang noticed that rice and cooking oil were not discounted, but that shoppers still spent half a day going there to buy those items and carry them home, burning time and energy.

This made her think about what JD could do differently to succeed in this segment. Wang said: "In the short term, JD's rivals in the food category were Wal-Mart and Carrefour, but in long term, the rival was JD itself." She introduced promotions and other modifications that paid off. In October 2013 her group achieved sales of 10 million yuan; a year later sales had multiplied fourfold.

I was impressed by the employees who'd transferred from IT purchasing and marketing because they had a common understanding: create profit or create great sales; bring in new users or make existing customers more loyal.

Sun Jiaming said, "Why does JD make it? It has had hard workers for a long time. And the number is increasing. They have become the mainstream. They have to be matched up with corresponding work and incentives. Employees have to know there is a difference between working hard and not working hard. If someone works hard but others don't, and the result is the same, then why should anyone work hard? Liu has created a relatively fair playing field. Those who work hard are treated differently from those who do not."

When you achieved through effort, you got a raise. Everyone knew how others were performing. When Sun became a leader, he paid special attention to this. Why do you keep pressing onward over time? In his view, it's because you'll be recognized by your supervisor. The most important thing is not how much money you received, but whether he recognized you, whether you achieved a higher material standard of living, whether you learned more and broadened your horizons. This was the first step. The second step was that there must be a just and fair environment. Those who worked hard needed to be treated differently from those who didn't. Most enterprises did not do well at this.

JD performed an inventory twice a year. There was a salary raise in the middle of the year and at the end of the year for those who worked hard. Who would get a raise? How much would it be? Sun would gather all the directors and department managers together to discuss this, over and over again. Previously, when there were just a dozen people, he had a clear picture in mind for each. But for 100 people, he couldn't possibly know all the details and had to rely on democratic decision-making. In the end, those who worked hard got a raise and those who fell behind worked at catching up. Those who seemed not to care would be dismissed.

In many enterprises, if there were ten people, every individual would give 100%. But when there were 1,000 people, perhaps some would give less than 80%.

Systems could be copied. You could replicate organizational structures. Conversely, recreating a successful corporate culture was not a cookie-cutter proposition. For an enterprise to stay relevant and successful, it did not need something standardized. What it needed was something different. Something almost spiritual.

What threatens a company's ability to grow is not necessarily the competition, but the organization itself. Could the factors that contributed to past success be carried forward? Could tens of thousands of people continue to identify with the original organizing principles? If a company failed, it was most often because of internal factors rather than external ones.

Sharing Comes After Consensus

Could the spirit of the "38th Army" be carried forward? JD's corporate culture circa 2007 was created by Liu alone. In 2013, Liu was the culture's head cheerleader and most ardent practitioner. But it was no longer what he'd originally created. The founder's personal influence had diminished. New values were emphasized based on collective wisdom. There was now unprecedented focus on placing the customer first, along with collaboration, integrity, passion and innovation.

Throughout 2013 Liu continued searching for top-notch executive talent. When he was in the US, he'd invite people in for interviews. For each C-Suite post, he would interview at least 10 people, and often 40 or more, asking detailed questions of each. For example: "You've worked in your company for eight years. Would you want to invite your most capable subordinates to come along to JD? With them at your side, you could work more rapidly and efficiently. If not, you'd have to begin anew, with new subordinates, and the process could be very painful." If the executives said they would bring along their old subordinates, Liu would not consider hiring them.

The executives Liu expected to hire were those who had leadership skills, who had their own special charm and who could find ways to integrate with the new team. His key requirement for new executives was simple: successfully blend in with JD's culture, or leave.

In July 2013, when Liu returned to China, he was quite pleased with how things had progressed during his time away. But he was not entirely satisfied with the level of coordination across the business. He believed JD was showing signs of those creeping big-company maladies: poor cross-functional coordination, low-efficiency decision-making, and the appearance of factions. He saw dangerous signs of the dilution of JD's culture. The company's history of results orientation and rapid response was weakened. Instead, too many departments had reverted to passing the buck and the approval processes became more and more cumbersome. The result was that decisions could not be made in a timely manner. Liu wanted to smooth out the management process and improve efficiencies across the enterprise.

When the organization grew to a certain stage, Liu's personal charm wasn't enough to cement the team. Fewer and fewer people could directly make contact with the entrepreneur. For the vast majority of middle- and lower-level workers, Richard Liu was the enduring symbol of the company. Over time, the vision, mission and values of the company had become more prominent.

JD's modern management emphasized consensus and sharing. Sharing came after consensus. When trimming the corporate culture in 2012, JD invited more managerial staff and employees to take part in the project. It also carried out an externally managed survey via questionnaires and anonymous interviews. With a promise not to reveal names of positions, the company issued 4,000 questionnaires and conducted in-person interviews with more than 200 employees. They documented behaviours the people of JD appreciated and those they disliked. Finally, at a survey debriefing attended by senior executives, the old and new versions of JD's corporate culture collided. The debate was heated and aggressive. When the argument came to a stand-off, Liu said: "Enough. I'll have the final say." It is worth mentioning that Liu spoke little during the meeting except when it was about to conclude, which at the time was a departure from his usual style.

In the end, JD's corporate culture was defined as "one centre and four basic points". The core tenets were customer first, integrity, teamwork, innovation and passion. At the end of March 2013 Liu began to speak about corporate culture with those at director level and above. Afterward, each participant had to stand on the stage and reveal what they'd learned. Only through retelling could they truly internalize, Liu believed. By the end of August, Liu's remarks on corporate culture were publicized to all the employees. Each department got its customized lesson of the company's culture and values. In the call centre it was: "Let customers hear you smile." Everyone put a small mirror in front of them, to see whether they spoke with smiles or not. In Shi Tao's department, directors and senior managers were thoroughly familiar with the culture and values, but ordinary employees knew perhaps 50-60% of the message. "This was a big transformation," Shi said.

In 2013, Liu worried about whether the intermediate-level managerial staff, such as inspectors and senior managers, understood the new corporate culture. He personally conducted training with high-level executives. Deliverymen had senior employees teach them. Moreover, Liu liked to visit lower-level employees. In the coldest days of winter, he drove to Heilongjiang delivery station. He was not familiar with the 300 or so directors in the middle management ranks, and many of them didn't know him. It was necessary for Liu to personally spread his ideas to employees to achieve pervasive understanding and buy-in.

The company needed a mechanism to pass on values and culture. In the end, the culture had to be as homogenized as the sea, which had but one salty taste.

From Binary Opposition to Binary Fusion

When Liu decided to self-build logistics, Xu Xin suggested it would be near impossible for Liu to manage the development team. Some delivery drivers were thieves, she argued. It was harder to manage blue-collar workers than to manage engineers. After the logistics system was built, Xu often bought things from JD. When she chatted with the deliverymen, she found that they really cherished their work and were proud because they could make enough money to buy an apartment in their hometown. On the other hand, JD was known for its strict discipline. Deliverymen were fired if they got two complaints. Sometimes, they'd actually ask customers not to file a complaint after they'd made a late drop-off.

On each "18 June" and "Double 11" day, deliverymen from many courier companies were eager to work for JD. In Chengdu, the monthly income for JD deliverymen was about 4,000-6,000 yuan, in the middle-to-upper range for similar jobs. The salary in many courier companies at the time was only 2,000 to 3,000 yuan a month.

Wang Lianwei, a courier in the Chengdu Jinjiang Express Centre, previously worked for ZJS Express for eight years. He was the company's recognized pacesetter, but his only year-end bonuses were items like toothpaste, a toothbrush or soap. He was greatly disappointed. After he joined JD, he always rushed to the front at unloading time. And he was always among the first three in KPI appraisal. He'd never received a traffic violation and always provided the best customer service. If his customers had a problem, they'd come to him directly instead of turning to customer service. He was always ready to help other couriers in need, without hesitation. He also won the pacesetter award in JD and received a year-end bonus of 10,000 yuan.

JD's couriers held their heads high. Where did this pride come from? The company brand was strong and they wore the work uniform proudly. The company offered them a relatively fair market rate and social position. JD paid into social insurance and housing funds and salaries were disbursed on time. These things were all an advantage in the logistics industry, where they certainly weren't the norm.

Internet companies faced a dilemma similar to China's urban-rural binary opposition. Before 2011, Liu felt there were obvious gaps in the company. White-collar workers looked at the deliverymen the way urban dwellers might see rural people as country bumpkins. They were on different social levels and neither cared to interact much with the other. In 2011, things changed. The key driver was the disappearance of China's demographic dividend. The deliverymen began to make more money. Some made 6,000 to 7,000 yuan a month, more than some office workers earned.

Liu shares the blood of the peasants. At a meeting on sharing values, he bowed to the executives and said: "Thank you, all of you. You come from the elites. It is easy for you to find a similar position once you leave JD. Our blue-collar workers come from rural areas. They are not very well educated. They can make a good income and have a stable life working for JD. If JD encounters difficulties, these workers will be the first ones affected. It would not be not easy for them to find opportunities like they did here."

When Liu saw the news that a young person who'd been left alone because his family worked elsewhere had killed himself before the Spring Festival, he decided to subsidize those whose children were not with them when they worked during the holiday. Each child would be subsidized to the tune of 3,000 yuan. Xu Wenyi, the JD deliveryman I'd met during the banquet to celebrate five-year employees, had a brother-in-law who also was a JD deliveryman. He had three children and had to be on duty for seven days during the Spring Festival. He told Xu he didn't believe the subsidy really would materialize. "President Liu said so and it will be done," Xu told him. "I promise you, you will have the money." Sure enough, 9,000 yuan was soon transmitted to his account.

Xu was one of JD's first ten deliverymen. In March 2014, I met him again in JD headquarters. For this interview, he was meticulously dressed, with a grey baseball cap, a dark grey woollen coat that was unbuttoned at the front to reveal a light grey V-neck sweater, and a grey-blue shirt with check pattern buttoned at the collar. He was wearing a pair of khaki casual pants tucked into tightly strapped black boots. Only his rough, dark skin hinted that he was a weathered manual worker.

Xu was born in Fuyang, Anhui Province, in 1971. He joined JD in August 2007 as a courier. He was doubtful at first because he had never been exposed to online shopping. It was not until he rode his bike to see JD's rented Playwell Warehouse in Beijing that he felt assured.

On 25 August 2007, JD delivery officially launched. Beijing was divided into four regions with the following four stations: Tuanjiehu (east), Panjiayuan (south), Asian Games Village (north) and Maliandao (west). Xu was one of only two couriers in the West District. His basic salary was 1,500 yuan plus three yuan "push money" for each order. On his first day, there were only three orders to be delivered. He rode on his bike for an hour to deliver a computer mouse from Maliandao station to No. 1 Luhua Road, some 12 kilometres away. The next day, he had seven orders to deliver. A month later, as volumes continued to increase, Maliandao upped its delivery team to seven.

In 2008, Xu's daily orders increased to 50. Whenever the company launched a promotion, there would be warehouse overloading. JD's order volume increased dramatically with the rapid development of its delivery stations. Today there are 21 sites in the West Region of Beijing, each with 20 or 30 deliverymen. They can earn average incomes of up to 5,000 yuan.

Yang Fangying was Xu's first station agent. Xu brought his daughter to Beijing to stay for a while. Yang, later head of quality improvement in the delivery division of JD North China, invited Xu's daughter stay with her for a month. "How could a little girl live in the dorm with you?" Yang asked Xu. For a long time, Yang was the only female station agent in JD. She was a very thoughtful manager. In two years in that position, her deliverymen were essentially free from all worries. Most of the deliverymen who used to work under her are still with JD.

Areas like Xuanwu, Caoqiao and Jiaomen had many residential addresses. Xu was responsible for these areas. Other young men all rushed to deliver the goods so they could get home early. Xu was never in a hurry and would sort products according to the type of addresses. He arranged his schedule efficiently, knowing when to deliver to companies and when to deliver to homes. Sometimes, he would still be making home deliveries at 8 pm. He was patient and maintained good relations with his customers. The relationships were built on trust and reliability.

The first time Xu spoke with Liu face-to-face was at the anniversary dinner party for five-year JD employees, when Liu took turns drinking wine and chatting with each of the workers. Xu thought Liu was an upstanding man who valued his word. He never turned a blind eye to problems. "He took good care of the lower level workers," said Xu. "At every annual meeting, he would mention the deliverymen. He also personally made deliveries sometimes and carried parcels up and down stairs. He may not know me, but I always respected him."

In addition to his brother-in-law, Xu's brother and son also worked as JD deliverymen. His son was born in 1993 and began to do courier work at 17. He later became station agent for Badachu Station in Beijing. Xu knew little about computers and said he got dizzy looking at the screen, so he could not become a station agent. Colleagues who worked with him at the Maliandao delivery station became station agents, one in Tangshan, Hebei, and another in Shandong. Yang Fangying, Xu's former station agent, later became the senior manager of JD North China. She often urged him to go home to visit his family.

But Xu hadn't been home to Anhui Province for seven years. He was eligible for annual leave, but had never taken his days off. "I really felt sorry for my family," he said. "They live in poor conditions in the village and it isn't easy to find a good job." His wife and daughter stayed in his hometown in Anhui. His sister had a computer at home. He talked to his wife and daughter once a week via video call. His wife had never been to Beijing because of the cost. His 12-year-old daughter came to Beijing during her last two summer vacations.

Xu earned 6,000 yuan a month. He kept 2,000 for himself and sent the rest to his family. He lived in the delivery station, also serving as its gatekeeper. He had two meals a day, one in the morning, the other at 6 pm. At noon he had to unload goods and was too busy for lunch. "I felt fulfilled having something to do. If I was too relaxed, I'd suspect there was something wrong with my body."

It is about 900 kilometers from Beijing to Fuyang and it would take seven hours for Xu to go home by the fastest train.

His father once called to ask Xu when he would visit. He was unloading merchandise at the time and said: "I'm busy right now." His father quickly hung up. His cell phone was a Huawei, a gift Liu gave to all attendees at the dinner party for five-year employees. "I miss home and I miss my parents," he said. "It's been almost seven years. There must be big changes. They are over 70 years old now. I should go home to see them. I know I'll burst into tears when I see them." At this point in the conversation, Xu's eyes are already welling up. "My parents don't want to increase my burden. They told me that everything was fine at home and asked me not to worry. They said they were proud of me."

Jiang Anming, station agent at the Shanghai Zhangjiang station, joined JD in November 2007. In September 2008 he was promoted to his current position. He kept the Excellent Station Agent certificate of merit awarded by Liu. Many deliverymen who joined JD in 2007 received shares, and Jiang was given a bonus of more than 7,000 IPO shares.

When I interviewed Jiang, JD's share price had just risen. He said he'd sold a few shares just to see if he could really turn them into money. "Were you afraid of being fooled by Liu?" I said jokingly. He replied, "If Liu wanted to fool us, he would have done so before the listing." This rural, middle-aged man who started as a deliveryman was full of gratitude.

In 2007 JD had five stations and seven deliverymen in the four districts of Changning, Xuhui, Luwan, and Huangpu of Shanghai. Each worked about 50 orders a day. Jiang took care of half of Luwan District plus a small part of Huangpu District. At the time, each element of the process was done manually. At 7 am each day he began unloading goods with the station agent. The picking, registration and entry were all finished manually. The regional manager said to him: "You don't want to be just a deliveryman, do you? You have to make plans for your future. You need to learn how to use a computer."

Jiang was clever. He soon learned whether his customers were office workers, or had a spouse or parents at home. Of those who had a child, he knew what time the client would go out to pick them up. With this in mind, he would arrange the optimal delivery sequence just by quickly scanning the addresses.

For a time, he was transferred to the outskirts of Minhang to make deliveries for two schools. In his eyes, the students were educated and cultured, and deserved a higher level of service. Later, the students came to call him Old Jiang. In September 2008 he went to Zhangjiang to set up the station and serve as station agent there to this day. Daily orders in Zhangjiang station ranged from 2,300 to 2,400. About 700 to 800 of these were from third-party sellers and most were paid cash on delivery. Deliverymen could get a monthly income of 5,000 yuan or so after working for six months. This station publicized a delivery guarantee that mapped to three delivery times a day. The morning orders were delivered by 3 pm, and the other two periods were 3-7 pm and 7-10 pm. The Zhangjiang station now had 27 employees. A half dozen of them ultimately became station agents elsewhere.

Jiang did not play favourites at work. He did not dine out with certain colleagues in secret, so as to be fair to all. When they went out to eat together, he gave a treat to all the deliverymen and never let others pay the bill. He never took sides at work. He brought everything to the table and discussed the rules and regulations with everyone. And there were rules to follow when someone made a mistake.

If there were only a few outstanding players on a team and the others weren't so capable, it was not a good team. Everyone had to be good enough to help carry the load. If a deliveryman couldn't meet the expected target, Jiang would ask him to explain. If necessary, he would ask others to complete the task, show the original person the result and give him pointers on how to improve. He'd give him another week to try, and kept him on board if things worked out. If no improvements were made, the deliveryman would have to leave the team. Every year JD assessed its deliverymen. If they failed to achieve the target KPIs, they were dismissed. It was all consistently applied and based on objective data.

Labour disputes are common in labour-intensive enterprises. Money was usually the major issue. For lower-level workers, salaries were calculated according to piecework, with their base pay usually fixed. The more they worked, the more they got. The key was that the KPIs had to be transparent. There needed to be detailed records:

"You delivered five orders today and I delivered ten, so you'll be paid less than me. I made a mistake today but you didn't, so my points will be deducted." Everything was recorded and clearly accounted for. If "A" got 300 yuan more than "B", the reason could be verified and confirmed in the accounts and everyone knew where they stood.

Many JD employees had families to support. If they felt their income was unfair or opaque, they reacted negatively. These people with a monthly salary of 3,000 to 4,000 yuan had to send money back home while at the same time raising their children. A 100 yuan gap made a difference.

JD had a high-temperature allowance in summer, 300 yuan each month for three months, in addition to free beverages. There was also a low-temperature allowance in winter, which ran for three months. In 2014, JD introduced snacks for warehousing and delivery systems: a daily five-yuan snack allowance per person. The company provided specially prepared porridge, cookies, sausages and more. This kind of welfare was common among white-collar workers in Chinese office buildings. They were fewer in number and had relatively high incomes. The value they created per capita was relatively high. But in labour-intensive companies, such benefits were extremely rare.

The majority of the public regarded deliverymen as low-level workers who ran simple errands. Therefore, they were assumed to have low self-esteem. Zhanng Weifeng, director of the corporate culture division at JD Group, told me his team had made a film called *JD Speed* that focused on the value generated by front-line operations. For instance, although those responsible for packaging would never have contact with customers, the way they packed the products directly affected customer satisfaction. Packaging quality influenced the customer's mood when the goods arrived. The film showed why JD had such quick turnaround and how the goods were delivered to customers so rapidly. It not only satisfied customer curiosity about JD, but helped make tens of thousands of lower-level JD employees feel valued.

Liu was born in a rural area. His fate was changed through education. He was well aware of the huge gap between Chinese rural and urban populations. I once spent five months researching Wenzhou's factories and got to know how difficult it was for Chinese blue-collar workers, mostly peasants, to survive in big cities. JD offered more to the front-line staff than the vast majority of labour-intensive enterprises did. From the way JD treated these employees, we catch a glimpse of Liu's sensitive, caring side.

Be Schoolmates with Richard Liu

In the past, when they were still located in the Yinfeng building, Liu could easily gather everyone together to have dinner and share experiences over wine. By 2012, JD had become a company with tens of thousands of employees. The small workshop model, where the more experienced people could personally pass their knowledge on to the newer ones, was no longer practical. How could Liu share experience and knowledge through the company?

Eventually, the idea of JD University came to him. In February 2013, Ma Chenggong, now director of JD University, joined the company and set about establishing the education and training programme. Ma had previously worked for Wanda Group. According to published data, the advent of e-commerce triggered a 30% drop in foot traffic through the Wanda Plaza shopping complex. Realizing e-commerce was a powerful force, Ma was determined to get on board. Before Wanda Group, he had worked for the Li Ning Company, and enterprise that was struggling because it could not keep pace with the changing needs of consumers. Before plotting out a strategy, one first had to identify the big trends.

The first problem Ma found after joining JD was that 40% of training costs was for business trips. As JD's workforce is spread nationwide, trainers had to travel extensively. He realized it was not feasible to continue spending so much on travel.

He researched the sales-oriented Taobao University. Taobao innovated by putting its curriculum on a platform where six million sellers shared their own experiences. Participants could prepare a summary of their own business expertise and submit it to the university, where, after additional research, it would be refined into theory. Taobao mobilized social resources to help the sellers think, rather than amassing existing material and packaging it as course work.

Ma divided JD University into two parts. The first followed a traditional training methodology where classes provided training on leadership and professionalism, aligned with different management positions. The other part was a learning platform: a JD Talk modelled on TED (the private non-profit institution in the US). In the popular TED lecture series, a topic is discussed by a person with a unique perspective, on stage before a live audience, for 18 minutes. Many of those talks attract tens of millions of views via social media. The idea behind the JD Talk was to organize monthly speech opportunities in each region where JD employees could share their work experience.

Every year, HR organized surveys on employee engagement. Survey results showed that front-line employees had a low opinion of company training, and in fact thought there was hardly any training at all. Ma wondered why. Each region had launched the courses, so why did people say there was no training? After further inquiry, lower-level employees said they viewed the sessions more like business meetings because they were held in the conference rooms. And, they said, these could not be regarded as training because there were no tea breaks.

Ma realized that white-collar and blue-collar staff had different definitions of training. Office workers thought training was learning, and what mattered was whether the lecture taught a concept effectively. Lower-level workers, on the other hand, paid more attention to the format of the session, whether it actively demonstrated physical work processes and whether they were respected by the trainers. After reviewing this feedback, in 2014 JD University altered the format and also increased the budget for tea breaks.

Ma hoped his experience in white-collar training could serve as a basis for improving training for blue-collar employees. What he needed to do first was define the budget and methodology.

In 2013, trainers from all regions gathered in Beijing for a fact-finding session led by Ma. He asked how they conducted front-line staff training. They complained that there were no resources, no teachers, no funding and that leadership was not paying enough attention. Ma persisted, but the meeting devolved into a heated complaint session. He immediately changed direction and dedicated a 100,000 yuan budget to selecting the very best training programme.

There were only five months left in 2013. With a 20,000 yuan incentive package each month, all the regions were to submit training plans to headquarters for assessment. The best submission would get 10,000 yuan, the second best 6,000 yuan and the third runner-up 4,000 yuan. "I just want to know the highlights of your training, because I have no experience on the front-lines," he told the regions. "You want money, right? OK, you can have the money, but it's my game and my rules." Under the incentive programme, the regions developed many new tricks, working up formulas, drawing comics and carrying out joint training with local colleges. All the cases were publicized so trainers from each region could see how others did it. Properly inspired, creativity has few limits.

In JD, there was little direct interaction between blue-collar and white-collar workers. They enjoyed the same treatment and received the same insurance and housing subsidies. But managing them posed a challenge, since it was as if two languages were needed to address these two very different groups. With white-collar employees, topics needed to touch on ideals, dreams, life and travel, as well as product management and creative thinking. Blue-collar workers were more inclined to be concerned with their children's schooling, the health of their parents back in their home villages, and how much money they could send home each year. Cultural identity was tapped into through segmented socio-economic language.

Internally, corporate culture was perceived through a variety of hardware, systems, processes and a leader's style and actions. The company's stakeholders, including customers, media, investors, suppliers and others form opinions about a company's culture through the services it provided. Consistency with all these audiences was necessary if a culture was to take root. If perceptions were inconsistent, there would be confusion and wasted energy. If a company stressed "customers first", but failed to deliver good customer service and seemed focused only on cutting costs, nobody would be convinced. Both the consumer and the employees would feel the sloganeering was superficial. If you stressed that you were a responsible corporate citizen but customers saw that you or your supplier ran a sweatshop, your truthfulness would be questioned.

In the past, an employee skill competition launched by the corporate culture division was based on a memory test. In September 2014, JD launched the "Warehousing All-Around Master Hand", a live contest staged in various regions. The finals were held in Wuhan. About 30% of JD's warehouse employees competed in specialty areas including standardized operation demand, efficiency and safety. Players had to comply with the rules in their operations or points would be deducted. Speed required familiarity with the job and employees' personal skills. If scientific management specified all the details of a process, then the staff's initiative would be affected, so employees were given room to be creative while still complying with the rules.

Actions speak louder than words. Perhaps you were the best in your region but you thought there was always someone better somewhere else. For many people, scoring high in this competition would be the pinnacle of their career. Efficiency and morale were factors, and the objective was to advance without using force or hurting others. Soft methods were encouraged to inspire participants to win, because competing and winning were thought to enrich people's lives. No person is a purely economic being. We all live in society and have to have both material and spiritual needs met to lead a balanced and healthy life.

Some people enter this world with a silver spoon in their mouth, while others have just a straw. If inequality at birth were a constant until death, then life would be very constrained and disappointing. Society as a whole has to address the problem of social mobility and the capable need a chance to rise to the top, regardless of their family or where they grew up. It is the same in a company. Opportunities have to be provided so people from any background can rise to become technical experts or members of the management team. JD gave young employees opportunities to win honours they could be proud of. But the company needed to let them know that if they didn't get the glory, it was because they just didn't have what it took at that moment. It wasn't because they didn't have the same opportunity to succeed as their peers. If they wanted to excel, they had to work at making themselves stronger, smarter, more capable.

JD's talent promotion channels included a management sequence (M), professional sequence (P) and technology sequence (T). Each JD employee had clear development channels to pursue in this system. For white-collar staff, there were dual channels (M and P). Blue-collar workers were afforded a three-channel development track. When someone reached the top level of T sequence, if he or she still had potential, JD would provide a learning opportunity so the employee could get into the M or P sequence. Building the fast track for talent identification and training was the focus of HR chief Long Yu's work. In 2013, Liu proposed that 70% of company managers should be promoted from within, and talent had to be retained. At the end of 2014, 52% of management had been promoted from within.

The company had prepared a path upward. But without good education you'd be handicapped in your efforts to succeed. What options did these employees have? JD University introduced learning platforms and provided channels through which they could earn their bread today and better food tomorrow.

Many lower-level employees had little idea about higher education. JD University launched a short-term training project called "Be Schoolmates with Richard Liu". It was something like a summer camp. Sixty or so excellent employees were selected to study and hang out in Beijing for a week. JD rented a classroom at Renmin University and the lectures were given by the teachers there on self-brand management. That was the notion that the impression you make on others is your personal brand. The opportunities at your disposal depended not so much on how you saw yourself, but how others perceived you.

Since the biggest pain point for front-line employees is their lack of formal education, JD University introduced the "I'm Studying in University in JD" project to cooperate with universities in e-commerce-related subjects. JD employees could get tuition discounts and complete course work for college and university degrees, including a Master's Degree in Engineering from Beijing University of Aeronautics and Astronautics. JD University mobilized the staff. Many people borrowed money to get married, buy a house and raise children, employees knew. So why shouldn't you borrow money for an education? The tuition was 8,000 yuan, but employees paid just half. In order to encourage them to stay in JD once they get academic certificates, participating employees could also get job promotions. One-third of their tuition costs would be returned to them if they got one level of promotion, and half was reimbursed for two levels. Their entire tuition would be covered if they received three promotions within three years of completion.

If a company was willing to spend money on training, it created an internal pipeline of good prospects. JD was growing fast and needed to allow its people opportunities to recharge for future development. Otherwise, it was prone to crash if management capacity couldn't keep up with expansion.

JD also selected particularly promising employees for private training. JD staff had to understand the company's direction and its condition, and know the essence of their work. And because these topics were so important to the smooth functioning of the company, they also had to understand warehousing, picking and transportation logistics. One had to jump outside the box and get to know the bigger company story in order to foster cross-function collaboration. Teachers from outside JD were invited in to talk about management theory during the closed training sessions. For managers who rose from the first line, experience was not enough. They had to improve their grasp of theory and strategy or they wouldn't be able to manage well.

Wang Hui, head of JD's delivery business, joined the company from S.F. Express in September 2011. He noted similarities between the companies' cultures: both valued talent in labour-intensive industries and both had done well in recruiting, training, managing and evaluation. Further, both showed great concern for product quality. S.F. Express sought high customer satisfaction through exceptional service quality, which in turn supported higher prices and generous employee benefits.

In 2014, the most pressing matters for the JD delivery division were standardization, staff training and the promotion channel. "We now have 52 areas and more than 100 areas are under development," said Wang Hui. "JD employees have many opportunities for recognition and wealth. You have to paint a picture of the future so they know what's out there for them besides money. I don't want our employees to work for two or three months and then quit; the cost to the enterprise is too high."

JD's corporate culture seems to have had a great impact on professional managers from foreign companies. Non-Chinese companies did things step by step. They wouldn't usually give an instruction at 6 pm and expect a data report on it at 8 the next morning. Foreign companies had processes that laid out precise timing for raising a request and submitting a report. JD was different. If you were told tonight to turn it in tomorrow, it had to be done. If you were slow, you'd be left behind. A fast pace could inspire the fighting spirit.

JD as a company grew up with this temperament. When everyone was of one mind, almost anything could be achieved. When there was a big sales promotion, employees were easily mobilized to give their best. In some foreign companies, if the production target was 10,000 orders then the result would be 10,000 orders. They would not expect you to handle 15,000 orders. Again, JD was different. It always tried to make the impossible possible. When employees were exhausted, they would tear up cartons and lay them on the ground to sleep. But this sort of culture also had its negative side. Managers of front line employees could be too arbitrary, announcing at the last minute that staff would have to put in overtime that night. Employees often had to put aside family obligations because they were told to stay and work.

In an environment where everyone fought to be first, the KPI ranking also became a priority. If production in the labour efficiency competition among the regions was 10,000 units a day and there was a total of 100 people, the labour efficiency rate should be 100 orders per person. But in a performance evaluation, the goal would become

110. If a region produced more, it set a new benchmark and all others would be ranked based on this standard. This made competition especially brutal.

As JD grew, developed and matured, did it still need KPI competition? JD employees had ample opportunity to rise from group leaders to supervisors, and become managers. JD's fighting capacity could be improved through automation, management and innovation.

At peak times, front-line employees at times had to work 12 hours a day and 26.5 days a month. This was high labour intensity and their free time dwindled. These people were loyal and idealistic. But given the nature of the work some experienced physical pain. When they got foot cramps and stumbled, they would get up, walk it off and go on with the race. When asked if they were tired, the answer was often no. But ask again, are you really not tired? The answer would be yes, of course I am. This could be ignored in fast growth periods. But it was only right that JD employees shared in the fruits of success as they and the company grew together. And that would ultimately be reflected in the improvement of an employee's quality of life.

Take packaging and picking, for example. Since experienced employees could be more than twice as efficient as a newcomer, they should be rewarded appropriately and should help train the new hires. If the company didn't encourage this, the new employee was likely to quit and pursue a better paying job. The company had to think more about its employees and let them feel they were cared for by the enterprise. This encouraged employees to stay and serve the company over the long run.

The conditions in JD's rented warehouses were slowly improving. In the past, it was messy everywhere and staff had nowhere to eat their meals. Staff restaurants were added, as well as air conditioning and chairs. Facilities such as basketball courts and fitness centres were also provided. Since no open flames were allowed in warehouses, JD worked with local government officials to introduce snack bars where employees could have more food choices. Employees came from all corners of the country. Northerners preferred noodles, while southerners love rice. It was difficult to keep everyone happy.

The Shanghai warehouse wanted to add a cinema in the multi-function hall for training films. It also planned to set up a public-address system to praise high achievers, provide good news about family milestones, wish people a happy birthday and the like. Some thought this was no more than show. But ordinary employees had a completely different mentality. If they were remembered on their birthdays and a song was played just for them that everyone could hear, it could be better than a 1,000 yuan bonus. In such labour-intensive enterprises, concern for them as human beings imparted a sense of family when they were often far away from home, family and friends.

Liu said: "Balance is always important. You cannot choose between the two extremes, the Chinese model or the European model. If I were to make the choice, I'd choose neither of them. I'd choose the American model instead, because it can ensure well-being, time for relaxation and happiness for the employees. At the same time, it leaves no room in the company for lazy employees."

If employees chose to quit because they were too tired, Liu said, then the team's performance would be affected and the manager would be unable to survive. "He would be faced with two choices: either changing his rough management style, or leaving the company. If his subordinates are happy and can be late for work and reject overtime, then he can't achieve the target, and he will also choose to quit. If you ask employees to work overtime every day until 11 pm, will anyone keep working like this? It is impossible to work like that for three to five years. But it is possible for a short period of time if necessary. I cannot promise any employee he'll never have to work overtime. If you have this idea, please leave the company."

Expanding
Sales Channels

Vying for Third- and Fourth-Tier Cities

In Zaojiao Town, Shifang City, 70 kilometres north of Chengdu in Sichuan Province, a peasant was driving his agricultural tricycle along the road. Massive golden rapeseed flowers along the roadside were in full bloom. On the other side of the road there was a red brick wall. On the wall was painted in white: "Work Brings Wealth. JD Helps Saving" along with "JD.com". At the end of 2013, JD began displaying these ads in urban-rural transitional areas.

The first-tier city market was gradually becoming saturated. In 2014, JD launched a channel expansion strategy. The internet and mobile internet had begun to reach rural China, which opened the door for more pervasive e-commerce.

Rural economic strength was lower than in capital cities, but the online shopping expenditure, frequency and proportion could exceed that of big urban centres. As the business was not as developed, many goods were not available or not affordable, or else quality was low and prices higher. And consumers encountered many fake products. In third- and fourth-tier cities, due to limited resources, the competition between JD and Suning had become white-hot. JD Central China posted a huge billboard in the downtown area of Xiangyang, Hubei, just above a Suning store. Suning's employees splashed ink on it and removed the billboard. The property belonged to a private owner and had nothing to do with Suning. After negotiating with the owner, JD restored the billboard and again it was splashed with ink. After this happened several more times, JD Central China moved the ad to the Xiangyang railway station.

In 2013, JD set up a regional buying and merchandising team, and staff was allocated in each region to carry out low-cost marketing work. For instance, resources were exchanged with McDonald's restaurants. JD distributed McDonald's leaflets with customer deliveries, and JD advertisements were displayed in McDonald's restaurant windows.

The first step in channel expansion is to understand everything about the supply chain. JD hired third-party researchers to survey the brand share of companies in the third- to fifth-level administrative areas and found there was a high concentration of standard brands. But for food and beverages, personal care products and other non-standard goods, the regional preferences differed. So, JD had to design supply chain management flexible enough to account for brand preferences in different regions.

If merchandise inventory and logistics fell behind, the marketing team would find it hard to attract customers. Marketing was the last step in channel expansion. "Even when effective publicity is in place, if the goods and services are not there, then the traffic conversion rate won't be very high," said Xu Lei, senior vice president of sales and marketing. "Supply chain and logistics are the most pressing matters and have to be done at once." In 2014, JD extended its logistics network to nearly 600 districts and counties. The work was done in less than six months; in the past it would have taken two years.

On the morning of 9 March 2014, after I arrived at Chengdu from Beijing, I met Yang Tao, manager of the terminal management department in JD's southeast delivery department. The company had nine deliverymen in Lhasa's Chengguan Station, most of whom were from the Tibetan areas of Sichuan and Qinghai. JD's goods were shipped to Lhasa from Chengdu via the Qinghai-Tibet Railway. It took seven days for a customer to get delivery after placing an order. Yang hoped to reduce the time by using air shipments.

Yang had joined S.F. Express in 2003 as a driver. Later he moved to Chengdu as the station agent responsible for the Hehuachi area. He came to JD in September 2011 and began as station agent of Longwang with a team of seven. A week later his team expanded to 14 people. Headcount hit 30 by the end of the year. Yang witnessed the rapid development of JD in Sichuan. Mianyang originally had three delivery stations with daily orders of 700. By March 2014, each of the central stations in Mianyang had an average of 1,300 to 1,500 orders a day.

On 18 March 2010, JD Southwest China was established. There were a total of five delivery stations and the actual delivery range covered the southwest and northwest of China, including Xinjiang and Gansu. By the end of 2011, the stations had increased to nearly 40, expanding to 80 in 2012 and 115 in 2013. As of early April 2015, the southwest China business covered Sichuan, Yunnan, Guizhou, Tibet and Chongqing with 273 delivery stations in operation.

Unlike East China, where the terrain is flat, the cities in this region were dense and the highway network extended in all directions. The southwest featured complex geographic environments, with more desolate areas farther southwest. Northern and southern Sichuan were relatively developed and more stations were built there. In western Sichuan, the cities were far apart and there were fewer stations. Panzhihua station was the farthest from Chengdu, at a distance of 700 kilometres.

It sounded like a crazy fantasy: in a country of 9.6 million square kilometres, could any company provide a network for 1.3 billion people that would get goods to them within eight hours after placing an order?

It took a great deal of investment for a business to scale to this level, and it required courage. It was a great opportunity, but also a great challenge. It seemed that Liu and JD were the closest to realizing the dream. By 31 December 2014, JD had seven major logistics centres across the country and 123 large warehouses operating in 40 cities. There were 3,210 delivery and pick-up stations, covering 1,862 districts and counties. All were self-supported. In 134 districts and counties JD offered guaranteed same-day delivery, and in another 866 districts and counties it provided next day delivery service.

In 2007, despite opposition from investors and executives, Liu had been determined to have JD build its own logistics systems. This was one of the most important strategic decisions in the company's history. Now, when people talk about JD's core competitiveness, they say it is logistics.

"President Liu's logistics strategy is very clear," said a regional executive. "He doesn't need to say too much. If he says OK to the programmes we've planned, we will be able to rely on his support." In 2013, JD spent 100 million yuan on cars. It built a fleet of 1,500 Scania trucks 7.6m-9.6m long, and added Mercedes-Benz long-haul trucks.

Before 2014, JD adapted a parallel storage model. It took central warehouses in Beijing, Shanghai, Guangzhou, Shenyang, Wuhan, Chengdu as the core, and divided the country into six regions: North China, East China, South China, Northeast China, Central China, and Southwest China.

In January 2014, a central warehouse was established in Xi'an, marking the establishment of a seventh region: JD Northwest China. JD was now able to deliver products nationwide, as long as there was inventory in any of the warehouses.

Later in 2014, Liu wanted the logistics system's coverage range to expand from 1,300 districts and counties to 1,800. As of 31 December 2014, JD logistics covered 1,862 districts and counties nationwide. In order to expand its reach, JD launched the Pioneer Station Programme. All deliverymen, nearly 20,000 employees, could apply for the programme and return home to set up stations. These were often places with daily average orders of 20 to 40 products. Normally, JD would send people to set up stations only when daily volume topped 50 orders.

This was seen as a creative way to expand the network while offering new paths to employees. Deliverymen could return home to break new ground. They could act as station agent and deliveryman at the same time. If orders increased, they could call on family to help. If the order volume was normal these outposts could be turned into regular stations. If family members wished, they had a chance to become regular employees after training.

"The biggest difficulty for channel expansion lies in transportation security," said one logistics executive. "The pioneer station had to ask families to line up branch road transportation from the shipping centre, collect the goods and then return to the delivery station." About 300 people applied for the first stage of the pioneer station programme. In some places, two or three people vied for the position. Some managers even wanted to be considered so they could return to their home towns.

Rapid Expansion Based on Standardization

In the pre-dawn hours of 11 March 2014, it was cold in the urbanized area of Chengdu. The highway was bathed in the orange light of street lamps. The occasional large truck rumbled through. At 4:20 am I arrived in Baowan Logistics Park on Shunyun Road, Xindu District, Chengdu. There was a JD warehouse here, storing 3C and small appliances.

The Xindu facility comprised two individual warehouses, 12m high, facing each other. They covered an area of 10,000m². In front, there were five red Iveco vans. Drivers in red uniform were pulling trailers to load their goods. The roller-shutter door was fully open and the shipping area was visible. The light of white lamps illuminated the desolate warehouse. Sealed yellow boxes were stacked, filled with packed parcels. It took the drivers about 40 minutes to go back and forth between warehouses, loading the vans. At 5 am, more Iveco vans arrived. The loaded vehicles drove away and others immediately took their place. By 5:40 am some 40 vans were in place. They were bound for Deyang, Mianzhu, Shifang, Jianyang, Meishan, Qionglai and other areas in peripheral Chengdu. Customers usually received their deliveries a day or two after placing an order. The vans going to Yunnan, Guizhou and other southwestern regions staggered their departure times.

Drivers usually started working at 5 am and finished 12 hours later. Wu Chaoxi, 34, wore a plaid shirt with the red uniform on top. "Aren't you cold?" I asked. He patted his chest, saying: "From the boss. Very warm." Wu lived nearby. His salary was 3,000-4,000 yuan a month, on par with the wages of local civil servants.

The southwest area is home to four office parks with seven warehouses that cover more than 100,000m². In 2012, when Ji Jie, now warehouse director of JD Southwest, joined the company, there were only two parks, 50,000m² of storage area and some 400 employees.

Goods shipped from Beijing, Shanghai and Guangzhou all transited from Wuhan to Chengdu, over a period of roughly 108 hours. Two drivers took turns at the wheel, four hours a shift. Local JD staff called this stretch of road the Cheng-Wu Line.

After the goods reached the warehouse via the Cheng-Wu Line, the workers opened the cartons and spot-checked the products. Some items were checked one by one. Employees filed them in the tracking system after scanning, then moved them from the receiving platform to storage areas and shelved them. Cheng-Wu Line transport relied largely on third parties. If the loss rate exceeded 0.1%, the delivery vendor's payment was reduced. The loss rate of JD's own trucks on trunk transport lines was held to a maximum of 0.05%.

Customers placed orders on JD.com and the picking system assigned goods to customer addresses and distributed them to the appropriate warehouses. After orders arrived at the warehouse, they entered the picking process. If items were on high racks, employees used reach trucks or counter-balanced forklifts. If they were in general storage, workers would do the picking and scanning manually. Products were then moved to the review area for reconfirmation; invoices and delivery notes were printed; and then the goods moved to the packaging area where they were packed according to product specifications. According to Ji Jie, the warehousing process generally took an hour, or even a bit less in the Southwest Region. Orders that came in at 11 pm had to be completed before midnight and no work was left unfinished overnight.

Merchandise was loaded onto vehicles for shipment to the next-level distribution centre or transfer station, where it went through a second allocation process until it was given to the couriers for delivery to customers. Parcels could be tracked through eight distinct delivery phases: receiving, picking, dispatch, departure, receipt at the station, inspection, deliveryman receipt, and delivery confirmation. Liu named this detailed tracking process the Green Dragon System.

"With the decentralization of management, will the entire process be carried out with efficiency and stability? If there is no coordination it will be in a mess," said Hou Yi, former director of "Asia No.1" project. "This requires power information systems, including an accurate monitoring system so operations in different warehouses, involving many employees, can be monitored in real time. And this logistics system has been deployed across the country."

JD assigned 100 people to develop the Green Dragon System, and on 11 November 2012, it was rolled out across China. It could support millions of orders with no downtime or data management issues. The former 23-second response time when a product was scanned with a hand-held device was cut to just three-tenths of a second. And the accuracy of an automatic deployment function in the pre-picking system was improved from 70% to 98%.

The point of sale (POS) device used by deliverymen was tied into the Green Dragon System and featured a geo-positioning function. The trajectory of all parcels could be monitored. Details could be obtained immediately if something went wrong. The system could automatically generate a report and the appropriate delivery VP, director, regional manager and station agent had a clear view of their team's performance at every level. In regions with complex terrain and inconsistent transport, like the southwest, the cost for management to supervise stations in person was too high. But through the Green Dragon System's wealth of data, they could stay on top of each site's operations.

Station agents' biggest headache in the past was the need to fill out data manually and issue reports. They would have to work into the early hours of the morning to finish it all. Now they could export data from the system and finish their reports in ten minutes.

"Logistics is the lifeblood of retail," said Hou. "It is the core dependency for supermarkets, shops and large chain stores. At that time, none of the outside logistics providers could meet JD's standards. DHL practised an asset-light strategy and would never buy if it could rent. But it built its own network without inviting other courier companies to cooperate. The network was the lifeline. The warehouses could be rented but the workers had to be your own."

Trial production for the "Asia No.1" Shanghai facility started in March 2014. The first phase facility covered about 100,000m^2. Most product inventory was in the middle range – items such as laptops, small appliances and the like. Daily order processing capacity was 100,000 units, and the facility could store 4.3 million items. With no case studies for reference, JD joined with suppliers to research their joint needs and create the procedures. Liu might have underestimated the complexity of the construction project when JD announced the facility in 2011.

Hou Yi said that with an investment of 1 billion yuan, if the project goes wrong, "the loss could be catastrophic." Nonetheless, given the project's complexity, he said Liu was tolerant of errors. He faced losses of millions of yuan due to design flaws and construction delays. When JD first tackled logistics for the book category, storage racks that should have been moveable were bolted down. This resulted in the loss of 10,000-20,000 racks and hundreds of thousands of yuan. The design of a two-story warehouse in Nanxiang, Shanghai, proved to be terribly inefficient. The building was torn down and rebuilt, at a cost of more than 1 million yuan.

"If we don't tolerate failures, no one will want to innovate," said Hou Yi. "Everyone would rely on existing models. But JD is changing so fast. I've estimated that when orders reach 2 million, internal coordination will be much more complicated and organizational and management modes will have to change accordingly. It will be a matter of more than warehouse construction. JD is changing minute by minute. If you don't encourage innovation and change, the enterprise will have no future."

When Huang Xing, warehouse director of JD East China, joined the company, there was no long-term plan for logistics networks. What should the warehousing logistics structure in East China look like? No one knew. Not long ago the Shanghai depot was scattered across seven or eight different office parks without coordination. Resources were difficult to align and efficiency was low. Middle management (managers, deputy managers and supervisors) was in short supply. If middle management could not raise its field of vision, bottlenecks became inevitable.

Logistics network planning had to be based on the very big picture. With a decentralized management model, a logistics park had to be extraordinarily efficient. JD once set up eight warehouses in Shanghai because future needs were unclear. If the company knew it would need 100,000m^2 next year, 200,000 the year after and 400,000 in the third year, it would have chosen parks with expansion potential. But since there was no long-term plan, those responsible just added 10,000-20,000m² of warehouses whenever they were short of space. The result was a multitude of independent warehouses.

Besides, JD was inexperienced in logistics and it was hard for it to find large-scale facilities. Leasing discussions generally began when the construction of a large-scale park was 60% complete. It wasn't easy to enter the queue without getting involved during the early phases of construction. You had to find a park and begin to look for the next one while the first was under construction. When the first was put into use, the second was under construction and the third was in planning. This sequential process had to be diligently pursued.

By May 2014, JD had completed the construction of seven logistics centres. The project had taken seven years and a great deal of manpower and material. When a company has just tens of thousands of orders a day, it might make sense to engage a third-party logistics provider. When JD launched its full-category development strategy and customer demand skyrocketed, there was simply no existing company that could handle the responsibility. JD would have had to spread the work across many logistics companies, and would have been unable to maintain the level and quality of service.

One of the most important warehouse logistics developments was the establishment of standard operational procedures. Through better organizational structure and the ordered division of labour, the complex production process was divided into modules. The warehouse and terminal chains were broken into numerous segments, each consisting of many steps. And each step was then standardized. The monitoring and reporting systems had to ensure that the business could be controlled by the group. If it relied on individuals of varying skill levels, it would be unstable at best.

JD was able to quickly grow the logistics system because the operations process was scientifically designed and its information management capabilities were highly reliable. These two elements were essential. Without a standardized system, each of the newly opened warehouses would be a mess. Some e-commerce companies failed due to the poor management of far-flung teams following large-area expansion. But not JD.

In 2013, the company began to recuperate. More attention was paid to operational costs, whereas before all eyes were on absolute logistical measures like quantities and speed. In 2013, JIT (Just-In-Time) and ALMS (Automated Logistics Management System) capabilities were developed. Additional focus was placed on labour efficiency and area efficiency (turnover generated on each *ping*, with one *ping* measuring about 3.3m^2). Also scrutinized more closely were maximum capacity per person per day and maximum capacity per unit area. Headquarters had full control of information flow and standardization. Thus, the operational processes were kept in shape through end-to-end monitoring.

However, business growth can be unpredictable, and planning can lag the actual pace of development. And so, warehouse overloading became common in JD. In the South China Region, in just 18 months there were 38 instances where inventory had to be shifted from one warehouse to another. Liu Tiebiao, warehouse manager of JD South China, oversaw a 38-hour period of uninterrupted warehouse moving and production. At that time, there was no well-organized moving process, although today it can be done in hours. Liu Tiebiao said every JD warehouse manager had experienced the move ordeal.

Yang Lei, who became manager of JD East China's major appliance warehouse, joined the company in 2010 as a management trainee. He was later assigned to what was then the Shanghai warehouse for major appliances. In May 2011 the stock in JD East China's warehouses ran short. It happened to be a hot season. Air conditioners were in demand and the warehouse was overloaded as a result. Yang Lei and others were told to move the warehouse in three days, so he cleared out 60,000 TV sets. A team of about 30 people worked for three days and three nights. On the third day, Yang almost fell asleep while standing upright. Orders flew in. One more day of backlog would crush the whole operating system. Employees would work until 2 or 3 am and then take a short rest in the warehouses or book a hotel room. At 6 am they'd be back at work. And management would have to stay behind to deal with shelf clearing, in addition to moving the stock, to keep everything orderly.

In the second half of 2012 a two-phase project to establish a 200,000m² warehouse in Wuhan's Haihang Park, in the Central China Region, was set to begin. But the other party could not deliver the building as scheduled. As a result, an existing JD warehouse of just 40,000m² elsewhere in the region ran short of space. There was simply no room for incoming products. JD was constrained by its real estate contract for Haihang Park and could not find a sufficiently large new warehouse. By the end of the year, the warehouse overload problem reached its peak. Some 90,000 electric oil heaters were moved to a 20,000m² food warehouse in Huangpi. That facility's normal production capacity was 10,000 orders a day although volumes could spike to 120,000 at times. However, promotions for food and electrical oil heaters were happening simultaneously and affecting the Huangpi food warehouse.

The electric oil heaters were very heavy, and this was the first time a food warehouse had handled such goods. Production was backlogged for more than a week, and employees became dejected. Yue Xuan, warehouse director for JD Central China, had no option but to allocate additional resources to overcome the problem.

On 18 June 2014, JD Central China produced 170,000 orders with a workforce of 1,500. After five months of work to improve labour efficiency, output during the annual "Double 11" promotion hit 300,000 orders with 1,200 employees. Regular shifts for storage staff during non-promotion periods were 8 am to 4 pm for the first shift, and 4 pm to midnight for the second shift. The workload per hour was not saturation capacity and there was no need to combine shifts. On "Double 11", in order to cope with 300,000 orders, the shifts were readjusted. The warehouse was put on a 24-hour production schedule. The morning shift worked until 6 pm and the evening shift was brought forward to noon, with the 6 hours in between slated for combined shifts.

In 2014, based on the company's experience in 2013, JD Central China Region increased the pace of new warehouse building and the segregation of different categories. It built eight new warehouses in a year, double the preceding year's number.

Encroaching

At 6 am I joined Zhang Donqin, a driver in the JD Southwest Region, as he left Baowan Logistics Park in Xindu in his red Iveco van. It was loaded with 85 parcels that included cooking oil, computer mouses, cell phones, shampoo and other items. He proceeded down the 108 National Highway. There were no streetlights, and Zhang's headlights pierced the darkness ahead. Even though I could not see it, I knew the farmland we traveled through was filled with large fields of golden rapeseed flowers.

At 7:10 am, as the sun rose, we arrived at Deyang delivery terminal. The handover was completed at 8 am. Zhang bought a bowl of noodles with shredded pork and mustard for seven yuan and hurried back to Chengdu. After taking a break for two hours at home, at noon he arrived at Xindu warehouse and from there he set out to Deyang again at 1 pm. After unloading his goods at Deyang that afternoon, he would go to stores in Deyang to collect merchandise and return to Chengdu at 4:30 pm. At 5:30 pm, he called it a day. His monthly income was 3,000-4,000 yuan. Getting up at 4:30 am every morning, he was miserable in the first months of work. Now he was used to it. He went to bed at 8 pm every evening.

Zhang Donqin, who was 38 when I met him, used to be a car mechanic. He did not think his work in JD was difficult and he was treated well, with insurance and a housing fund. He took a day off every three working days. He didn't know of JD before, but today he has a 55-inch Skyworth TV, microwave and electric stove, all purchased through the company and on his company wages. His friends envy him.

The JD logistics system was divided into three parts: warehousing, transportation and the terminal. The terminal was the delivery station and transportation via the trunk and branch road systems. JD referred to the cross-regional highways as trunk lines and roads within the region collectively as branch lines. Xu Shuai was responsible for transport management in JD Southwest. There were 118 vehicles and 172 drivers in Chengdu, and 26 vehicles and 33 drivers in Chongqing. Except for the periphery of Chengdu and Chongqing, the other branch lines were largely covered by third parties.

JD Southwest was a major client of the Chengdu Branch of Sichuan EMS Logistics Company. There were 330,000 orders in 2010 when Xinjiang, Gansu and other northwest areas were covered. In 2013, Xinjiang and Gansu were put under the umbrella of JD Northwest. That year, JD Southwest delivered 1 million packages, 70-80% of which went to cities below third-tier. Orders to Aba, Ganzi and Liangshan prefectures were all delivered by EMS Logistics, which had a special team of 18 people dedicated to JD.

JD rapidly expanded the reach of its self-support logistics system. It basically covered logistics in the Yangtze River Delta, the Pearl River Delta and around Bohai Bay without relying on third-party providers. In the Southwest, third party involvement was also very limited. Li Hailong, station agent of the Emei delivery station of Sichuan, used to send mail by YTO Express, but didn't find the people there to be very friendly. Before the Emei station was established, parcels to Emei were delivered by YTO Express. Now, JD's Emei delivery station had the surrounding area covered, from Shengli Town, Huangwan Town and Eshan Town to Fuxi Town. In the urbanized area the farthest deliveries were about 10 kilometres from the delivery station. The Emei station now had three deliverymen with daily orders ranging from 180 to 230. Li Hailong predicted excitedly: "Orders will still increase. Along the road from Jiajiang to Emei, there are already JD ads that say 'Work Brings Wealth. JD Helps Saving.'"

Dai Qing, former delivery director of JD Southwest, had worked at DHL for more than ten years before joining JD in 2012. "The big whale will squeeze out the little fish and eventually swallow the market," he said. "In the future there will only be the big whales, the shrimp, and nothing in between."

The entry threshold in China's logistics industry was very low. A couple could enter the business having little more than a Jinbei van.

There were estimated to be many hundreds of thousands of large and small logistics companies operating across China. Because of price wars, the industry's profits remained extremely low. A logistics boss said jokingly that when he golfed in Shunyi, Beijing, his friends would receive phone calls concerning hundreds of millions of yuan in business. But the logistics field being what it was, his customer discussions more often involved trimming pennies off the bill.

Zuo Renhui, born in 1991 in Deyang, Sichuan, is a deliveryman. He finished his education and went to work in 2009, opening a small supermarket. He also signed up with an express company as a partner. The express company settled accounts daily, but its big clients often took up to six months to pay their bills. Zuo had to pay the express company in advance and he could not sustain his business over the long run.

Zuo joined JD in February 2014. He liked that it was a big company that offered five kinds of insurance and a housing fund. He felt good wearing the red uniform, and he earned more than his peers. He could get 1.5 yuan push money for each order, and more for bigger cartons. He delivered merchandise in his Dongfeng van, a second-hand vehicle he bought for 20,000 yuan. The farthest point in his service area was Bajiaojing Town, 20 kilometres from Deyang station.

On 11 March 2014, I joined Zuo on his delivery rounds. He greeted customers in a friendly, respectful manner. By 2:30 pm he had finished the morning's 50 orders. He had a plate of rice fried with pickled beans and minced meat before driving back to Deyang station to begin afternoon deliveries at 3 pm.

Fighting for the Last Mile

On 12 March 2014, I went to the delivery station in Mianzhu, a county-level city under the jurisdiction of Deyang. Due to its small size, it was also called Linglong (tiny) Station. The 66m² facility was equipped with a separate bathroom and a bedroom with a bunk bed. The station agent and three deliverymen took turns on the night shift every week.

At 7:25 am a 5m-long red Iveco van arrived at the door. The unloading process took eight minutes. By 7:45 am the inspection was completed. There were a total of 111 orders in 118 packages. The driver signed the sheet and began his deliveries. The delivery areas were plotted out on both sides of the Mawei River, which ran from north to south.

Wen Tao, with a round, boyish face, was responsible for the northwest area. He had 40 orders. Lin Zhongcai, a thin, long-faced young man with narrow smiling eyes, was responsible for the southwest area. He had 35 orders. Liu Guanjun, a square-faced, honest-looking man, was responsible for the area east of the Mawei River and the outer suburbs. He had a total of 36 orders.

The rent for the station was 1,500 yuan. In February, Linglong Station used 7.2 yuan of electricity more than the company standard. The difference was covered by the site's employees. Delivery stations were the logistics competence centres and the final link in the logistics chain, culminating in direct, face-to-face interaction with customers. As such, JD expected the stations to play a marketing role as well. In this case, the site needed a better location. Some customers coming in to pick up orders complained to Peng Jiajun, the station agent, that the place was too hard to find.

The rental contract was due to expire the next month. JD had specified that the new workspace should be no more than 90m^2 and the monthly rent less than 3,000 yuan. As invoices were necessary for reimbursement, a 28% tax would be added to the payment. If the rent was 2,000 yuan per month, the actual payment would be 2,560 yuan. Peng worried about finding a proper space so quickly. He viewed several options but they were either too small or poorly located.

Peng Jiajun was born in 1987. He is well-groomed and looks rather refined when he wears his glasses. He joined JD as a deliveryman in May 2012. After the "18 June" anniversary promotion in 2013, Linglong Station's average daily orders stabilized at just over 100. At the time, the station had two deliverymen. Each took care of half the city and had only one meal a day, usually after 8 pm. Jiajun's personal record was delivering 120 orders in a day. Typically, to help ensure a better user experience, daily orders should total fewer than 80. In January 2014 he was promoted to assistant agent of Linglong Station, and he'd soon be named station agent.

The station agent needed to submit a production report every day along with handling taxes, social security and the mandatory housing fund. Before noon each day he had to deposit into the bank payment for products he received. He was allowed accounting errors of less than 20 yuan. When he first became assistant, Peng felt there were too many things to be done in a day and he was overwhelmed. He now feels much more comfortable with the requirements.

Responsibility for JD's delivery system cascades from COO to VP, director, regional manager, station agent and deliveryman. The station agent is the front-line manager. As has been the case in everything we've discussed, JD's rapid expansion also caused problems in the delivery process. The organization had to be supported by adequate front-line workers. All newly opened stations needed station agents. But how should the company foster and develop them?

Yang Tao used to manage 30 station agents. "The company needed speed and a growing volume of orders," said Yang. "That's the bottom line. As a station agent, you can play within the framework to make it all happen, but there's a line you cannot cross. Anything questionable involving money, such as withholding reimbursement, will get you fired."

Yang communicated with his 30 station agents via live video stream every week but at times he wondered whether they were even listening. "It's no way to manage the details," he said. "It's not like in Chengdu, where I can drive right over when something goes wrong."

With the increase in the order threshold for free shipping from 39 to 59 yuan and the normal slowdown following the Spring Festival, orders in Mianzhu declined. The three deliverymen saw average daily orders dwindle to just 40 each, although the station's target was 65. Peng Jiajun was most troubled by this. "What if we can't meet the labour efficiency target? We have to find a way," he said. "Yang Tao said he would let me know if he had a solution. In the meantime he asked me to do the best I could and let our actions speak for themselves."

Zhao Zi, who was Deyang station agent and later became Guizhou area terminal manager in the southeast delivery department, said: "We can keep the customers as long as they don't receive any damaged commodities. We have to spread that important message."

Zhao joined JD in August 2011, having previously worked for Deppon Express. He began with JD as reserve station agent and established the Guanghan and Wenchuan stations. Later he worked in the stations in Leshan, Dazhou and Pujiang. He later became Deyang station agent and group leader for the Deyang area, in charge of Mianzhu, Shifang and Guang'an stations. In his eyes, JD's station agents were capable of fighting the tough fight.

He had a strong desire to see Liu in Beijing. In January 2014 JD held its annual meeting at the Jiuhua Resort & Convention Centre. There were 300 tables. Zhao Zi sat at table number 89. He could see Liu on stage about 40m away, and remembers him saying: "The first decade of JD can be described as amazing, and the second decade will be even more amazing."

On 12 March at 8:30 am, I set out with Liu Guanjun in his Chang'an Star van. He was of course wearing the red JD uniform jacket and blue jeans. At his waist there was a "JD Mall" branded satchel for cash.

Liu Guanjun was born in 1980. He had been a barber for 11 years. His working hours back then were 8:30 am to 9 pm every day. Haircuts were 7.5 yuan for men and 25 for women. His monthly income was about 2,000 yuan. But he was locked in a room all day and could not enjoy the sunlight. He'd had enough. On the first day Liu Guanjun became a courier for YTO Express, he felt "like a bird flying out of the cage and into the sun".

He spent 14,000 yuan buying his used Chan'an Star van. YTO Express's Mianzhu station processed more than 600 orders a day. On average, each of the four deliverymen handled 150 orders a day, and as many as 200 during seasonal peaks. At times he could deliver an order in less than a minute. He just threw the package at the door and left without seeing the customer. For each YTO Express delivery drivers got a 0.5 yuan commission, regardless of the size of the parcels.

Their base salary was 600 yuan, plus 300 for fuel and 150 for their phone bill. All told, they could earn more than 3,000 yuan a month.

In December 2013, after three months with YTO Express, Guanjun made the jump to JD. His fuel subsidy was now 1,000 yuan a month, since his territory included some outer suburbs, and there was a 1.5 yuan commission for each order, more for large cartons. He took home 2,400 yuan in his first three weeks on the job. In January 2014 his income was more than 4,000 yuan.

At midday I waited for Liu Guanjun at the door of the Mianzhu's Municipal Bureau of Finance, where he was making a delivery. There, I met a ZTOExpress courier in a grey suit who wore glasses and rode a delivery tricycle. He'd worked in ZTOExpress for more than a year and said he was planning to quit. He pointed to the tricycle loaded with packages. "Between 150 and 200 orders a day," he said. "Sometimes several orders in a minute. I just drop the parcels and go. Orders pay 0.7 yuan apiece, for more than 100 yuan a day. I heard JD pays 1.5 yuan an order, and more for large and heavy parcels. A friend who was with YTO Express once said to me: 'I hear JD's pay is high and there are five kinds of insurance and a housing fund. I wonder if they need more people.' And he made his move; he just joined JD."

At 2 pm Liu Guanjun returned to the delivery station to service customers who were picking up their own parcels. He bought a pack of Master Kong instant noodles for lunch. I came to visit him at 4:30 pm and he was still working. He had to wait for customers to pay and then personally settle up for the day with the station agent. At 6 pm he drove his van home, where a hot meal was waiting for him.

JD's total order turnover in Mianzhu was a little over 1 million yuan a month. In February it was 980,000 yuan, 30% of which came from sales of phones, computers and 3C accessories. Two product categories – daily necessities and mother and baby products – were on an upward trajectory. There were 50 to 60 digital mobile computer merchants in Mianzhu. Many of them hated JD because it siphoned off a considerable amount of their business. Some would place orders at JD during sales promotions and then resell their purchases to village customers. So JD limited sales during promotion periods to two units per IP address.

Mr Zeng runs a 20m² computer store along the Mawei River. When I entered the store he appeared to be extremely bored. There was a time when a computer sale could bring 200 yuan in net profit. Now it was just 100 yuan. His business peaked in 2011. After the Wenchuan earthquake, victims needed to buy computers after moving into new houses. "It's been four years now," said Mr Zeng. "It should be time to replace the old computers with new ones. Why is the business still stagnant?"

E-commerce has put a mind-boggling selection of merchandise into the hands of people across China. It was a symbol of fairness and efficiency that spanned all levels of society. Search engines had done the same with information access. A brand that could be easily bought in a Beijing store was usually unavailable in a small county town in Sichuan. But through e-commerce, people living virtually anywhere could buy just about anything and have it delivered quickly to their door. Products had always been more expensive in remote areas. But JD's value proposition was amplified in those far-flung areas because the company demolished the old delivery model that layered on extra cost at every step in the process.

Supply Chain

L ogistics and the supply chain were matters of life and death for retail companies. The competition among retailers came down to how strategic they were about their supply chains.

Where did Wal-Mart's competitiveness lie? Superficially, in its well-publicized everyday fair prices. To keep prices low Wal-Mart invested significant resources in information technology to keep optimizing the supply chain. In 1969, Wal-Mart was the first large retailer to use computers to track inventory. In 1980, it was the first to use barcodes, and in 1985 the first to engage in electronic data exchange with suppliers. In 1988 it was the first to introduce wireless scan guns.

In the 1980s, Wal-Mart not only connected its own stores with distribution centres, it linked itself electronically to suppliers. Its distribution centres adopted station-crossing management, screening and repackaging suppliers' products before distributing them to retail stores. As warehousing and storage time of goods shrank, the flow of products and capital turnover accelerated accordingly. Wal-Mart's distribution cost was about 2% lower than its competitors, which could amount to hundreds of millions of dollars in lower distribution expenses. That's what made "everyday fair prices" possible. Those prices attracted more customers, driving greater sales per unit across product categories. The use of electronic data exchange and distribution centres also greatly improved Wal-Mart's supply chain efficiency. Suppliers could obtain data from Wal-Mart computers daily, including sales, unity quantity, store inventory, sales forecasts and remittances. They could replenish Wal-Mart stores through distribution centres based on real-time order volume. The order-to-delivery time, which in the past had been a month, was now 24-28 hours. This rapid-response system fundamentally eliminated out-of-stock problems.

What was JD's core competitiveness? Its supply chain. Sales forecasting, the integrated warehousing and logistics system, post-sales service and other elements came together in a supply chain matrix that consistently met and exceeded customer expectations. A huge IT infrastructure supported it all.

Supply Chains Driven by Technology

In May 2008, Li Daxue joined JD as vice president of technology, the young company's second VP. JD had 400 employees, more than 20 of them from the technology sector. By the end of 2014, the technology department employed more than 4,000, divided between group R&D and business R&D. The former was responsible for group development and management, cloud computing, big data and development and research on the architectural level. The business-oriented R&D team dug down into purchasing and marketing, operations, and functional development in closed business units.

Those in e-commerce circles said Li Daxue's major contribution to JD was SEO (search engine optimization), which saved the company significant advertising costs. "SEO is central to the overall structure of the site," said Li. "The first thing I did at JD was complete a revision of the JD.com site. After that there was a lot of research on the significance of this revision. It found JD was quite unique in SEO. Later, at SEO conferences orchestrated by Baidu and Google, JD was used as a case study."

Prior to the revision, JD's IT system had reached its limit. Li rented a villa where over three months, sleeping just three or four hours a night, he led a team of 12 in rebuilding the system. The system was designed to handle 100,000 orders. At the time, JD's daily orders numbered less than 5,000. Everyone thought 100,000 orders a day was a huge number. On 1 November 2008, when the new system went online, JD's order volume immediately surpassed 100,000. This was the first orderly, integrated modification of JD's architecture.

In 2010, JD's core trading function was still using the .net system. In 2008, after Li Daxue and his team had carried out their development work in the villa, more than 30 subsystems were still used in JD's trading system. It was difficult to upgrade and had to be supported by adding hardware. Operation and maintenance costs were rising. In 2011, the network system architecture was upgraded and Java replaced the .net system for two reasons. First, as many domestic and international websites used Java technology, a lot of experience could be borrowed, as could mature open-source frameworks, saving engineers from having to create new systems from scratch. The second factor was cost. The .net language itself was free, but the Windows operating system wasn't and Visual Studio development tools were not cheap.

In 2011, Li proposed upgrading the architecture to handle 10 million orders a day. At the time, the daily trading volume was 500,000 orders at its peak. The company's rapid development presented a huge challenge to the R&D department. The system had to run smoothly, and that would require a new infrastructure. More and more requirements were added to the system as the business expanded. It was an enormous, risky undertaking and Li was deeply troubled.

Before the upgrade in 2011, there was a book sales promotion and the old system crashed. The promotion was concentrated in a three-hour period. Users had added books to their shopping carts ahead of time and waited to submit orders when the promotion started. So many people submitted at the same time that the system froze. No one could make payments, which led to massive numbers of complaints. Liu posted a photo on his Weibo social media account of two cups of tea and silverware, inviting Li, who was responsible for the front-end, and Jiang Haidong, in charge of the back-end, to have tea with him. Li Daxue was on a business trip, so he regretted being unable to accept the invitation. When he returned to Beijing he went to Liu and apologised.

For an e-commerce system providing services to users around the clock, trading system upgrades were all but impossible. The R&D group compared it to trying to change the wheels on a speeding bullet train or changing the wings on a plane at 20,000m. The R&D team designed a complex switching mechanism for the front-end, where customers added products to their shopping carts.

At first, they configured closed user accounts to conduct internal tests with a small number of JD employees. Then they switched by types of business, with online payment first, followed by COD and self-collection. Later they switched to customer pickup orders, then to the third-party orders, and to the orders that didn't use any credits. Next in scope were orders that used coupons, gift cards and credits to pay. They switched by regions and imported the northeast's traffic into the new system. They switched by quantity, first turning to the new system to place 100 orders and observe what happened. The orders went to the warehouses and the merchandise was successfully delivered. They then switched to the new system to enter another 1,000 orders. Finally they tested by percentage of traffic: 1%, 5%, 10%, up through 100% . The testing took more than a month.

At the end of April 2012, the new system went online. The design capacity was 10 million orders. Li Daxue estimated it would be sufficient for three years. On "Double 11" day in 2014, orders to JD Mall were 2.3 times higher than the same period in 2013. Orders via mobile devices (using the JD App, JD WeChat shopping, JD mobile QQ shopping, etc.) accounted for 40% of total orders.

In 2008, after rapid development, JD's logistics systems gradually built up barriers to competition. Liu hoped shipping information would be clearly visible to customers so they could comfortably await delivery. In 2010, at Liu's suggestion, product managers responsible for order display started designing an order tracking function that showed key nodes across the delivery system. Whenever customers accessed the site, they could see the status of their orders, who was responsible for delivery and how to track it.

It looked like a simple information display. But behind the scenes the tremendous power of JD's information systems was churning away. The flow of products was accurately displayed by connecting the order system, storage system, allocating system, delivery system, site management system and deliverymen. Order tracking is today a standard component of e-commerce, but JD was a pioneer in this area.

JD built it and made it work. After the order tracking system went live the rate of incoming calls for customer service dropped significantly. The sense that everything was under control and the ability to track their packages eased customers' anxiety as they awaited their deliveries. By 2012, with the enhancement of warehousing and delivery systems, improvement to the processing system and the accumulation of big data, JD launched the order-time based Promise System. According to inventory status, warehouse location, location of the delivery, when the order was placed, delivery capability and other factors, the system could accurately predict arrival time well in advance.

Central to JD's business model were considerations such as how to acquire the right quantity of quality products at a low price, within a precise timeframe, from reliable suppliers, to satisfy and delight the customer. All this relied on data analysis. Big data drove JD's entire supply chain system.

Sales forecasting directly affected automatic inventory replenishment as well as other links in the chain, such as internal allocation and delivery. And sales forecasting relied on big data. How to extract the necessary data? How to predict future sales volumes more accurately based on these data? In June 2011, R&D set out to answer those questions. An open source distributed framework was selected whose key advantage was that with two application servers added, more servers could be applied to improve performance when necessary. After the migration, daily computing time was compressed to an hour or less.

In the second half of 2013, the sales forecasting team rebuilt the historical data and prediction module. Four months later, a complete historical data system was established. A more accurate price model, seasonal model and decision-tree model were put online. The accuracy of sales forecasts improved by 20% and JD gained control of this key indicator.

An automatic replenishment and sales forecasting system was constructed in the same period. Better sales forecasting made for better purchasing and replenishment. JD's book department had the strongest demand for automatic replenishment. By 2011, book SKUs had exceeded 1 million, a volume that made manual replenishment impossible. Amazon and Wal-Mart both had sophisticated automatic replenishment applications. Amazon's had an especially high degree of intelligent automation. Most of its purchasing behaviour was driven by the system. Automatic replenishment emerged as one of the core systems in Amazon's supply chain.

After the automatic replenishment system's introduction, the number of specialized purchasing staff in the book department decreased. In the first half of 2012, the system began rolling out to other categories, first auto accessories and mobile phone accessories, and then to IT categories. In 2013, CMO Lan Ye suggested promoting the automatic replenishment system in the trading of all self-support business. When promoting the automatic system, R&D also created the automated-purchase-order-placing system.

100 Million Yuan in Returned Inventory

In 2008, JD had a spare parts store larger than 200m^2 in Fengtai District, Beijing. Goods were piled haphazardly, and the facility was dirty and messy. The IT buying and merchandising team would go to the store on weekends to clean up damaged parts. Two 6m trucks brought cartons of products that had been sent back for repair to the door of the warehouse. There were motherboards, heat sinks, power supplies and just about every other imaginable part. The process was disorganized. The damaged parts piled up unattended. When they first arrived, marketing employees were shocked by what they saw. They sorted carton after carton of parts, by category and model, well into the night. Many products were in brand new packaging, but the team discovered they were badly damaged when they opened the boxes.

For a long time, JD had no post-sales information system. It relied completely on spreadsheets. The maintenance process involved reviewing the list and receiving merchandise in the morning and then taking items to Zhongguancun for repairs in the afternoon. In the evening, products would be delivered piece by piece.

The process could take 30 to 50 days. In 2009, Liu demanded that the post-sales service loop be compressed to just five days. The post-sales executive Wang Danghui thought that was crazy, and prohibitively expensive. Getting damaged products from customers required a day or two. Returning them to manufacturers for repair took another day. It was unrealistic to expect manufacturers to do repairs in such a short time. The alternative would be to give up on repairs and just send out replacements. Repaired goods would be sold to offline buyers at a discount. Any other way was simply burning money.

Wang expressed his view to Liu but got this reply: "What are you thinking? You can't keep up with customer demand."

Not until 2010 did he completely understand that the company relied on services to attract customers. Before then, JD's inventory tracking system was clearly outdated. There was no way to trace previous steps, and many elements were still entered manually. In 2010, the post-sales department got its new system, the last department to upgrade. It was divided into several modules to distinguish the before and after steps of the process.

At the end of 2010, Li Chen joined JD as national operations director for spare parts. (He later became general manager of JD Southwest China.) Liu joked that he was the company's highest-paid director. At the time, JD's sales exceeded ten billion yuan and returned inventory had a value of more than 100 million yuan. This became Li's issue to resolve. He had previously worked for Dell, where he'd been responsible for post-sales network planning. He found JD's returned-inventory management to be shamefully disorganized. The turnover of the returned inventory took more than 60 days because there was no standardized disposal channel. Normal turnover rates ranged from 10 to 20 days.

Li thought the warehouse looked like a dump on his first visit. Profit would suffer if this situation couldn't be fixed.

Li's approach was to increase sales through discounts and liquidate as much inventory as possible. In accordance with industry standards, manufacturers were obliged to bear the losses associated with returned goods unless they bought out post-sales inventory at favourable prices. This meant the marketing staff had to ask suppliers to liquidate 80% to 100% of the returned items or replace them with new products. Li's biggest headache was internal coordination because the return process was so cumbersome. The marketing team had responsibility for the effort, and it was under tremendous pressure to get it right.

It took Li a full year to standardize the process. The stop-loss target was achieved in the first year and 400-500 million yuan in returned inventory was effectively disposed of, saving more than 100 million yuan. By the end of 2012, returned inventory approached 120 million yuan. Later, even when the company's business had grown by a factor of five or six, returned inventory remained stable.

Internal Process Optimization by Customer Service

On 10 September 2012, I traveled to Suqian for the first time. JD Suqian Information Science and Technology Park is located in East Hongze Lake Road in the Suyu District. The first phase of construction at the site, covering 60,000m², had started seven months earlier. The facility became operational in 2013, with 5,000 employees. The second phase provided an additional 100,000m² of workspace, to accommodate some 12,000 people.

At the time, JD's National Customer Service Center Headquarters was located in an office building in Suyu's economic development zone. Due to limited space, the call centre could hold no more than 400 employees. More than 1,500 people had to work in a toy factory on Yandandshan Road. Call centre workers said they were very busy and in urgent need of additional staff. But it was not easy to find qualified recruits. Most of the workers were local Suqian people. They got 1,200 yuan a month in their first year and then monthly salaries of 2,000 yuan a year later.

In December 2014, when I returned for the second time to Suqian, some 3,000 JD employees had moved into the Phase I section of the call centre. The 19-story Phase II was under construction. The first four floors were office space, and floors 5-19 were staff dormitories. The dorms were built to standard, with six people to a room. With an area of 60m², each dorm was equipped with a separate bathroom with hot water. Staff accommodations posed a big problem for the company. The centre generally hired people from surrounding schools. Many workers lived in the countryside, beyond daily shuttle bus range. In accordance with company policy, workers who lived more than ten kilometres away could apply for space in staff quarters.

Huang Jinhong, vice president of JD's customer service department, had joined the company in July 2011. Under her watch the customer service staff grew from 600 to more than 7,000 in three years.

At the time, JD customer service was not a high-quality operation. There were only six managers, and only one or two of them had a grasp of call centre professionalism. JD's business developed rapidly, but workforce recruitment in Suqian was a major bottleneck. Management mounted an aggressive recruitment effort, going to provincial secondary schools and colleges on Sundays in search of talent. At the same time, they recruited directors who would be responsible for training and operations.

Huang had a hard time finding qualified supervisors. Cao Ke, director of JD's national customer service centre headquarters, told Huang her standards were too high. He told her she had no choice but to take those who were available. Huang insisted that management trainees receive instruction in Suqian and began recruiting reserve cadres. Some 30 people hired in 2011 went on to manager-level positions.

Back then, the look and feel of the workplace was downright depressing. Huang spent tens of thousands of yuan on renovations to create a warmer, cozier environment. One small but important change was that employees found toilet paper in the washroom.

On National Day in 2011, in Suqian, Huang met Liu for the first time. Liu asked what difficulties she was grappling with. "First, employee pay is too low," she said. "The average salary is only 1,300 yuan. Some of our competitors have put up recruitment banners in our neighborhood." Second, she asked for an employee shuttle bus to address problems with traffic congestion. "I had to make exorbitant demands," she said later. "The boss rarely visits, so when he does I have to overcome my fear and speak out." Liu told Huang that all of her requests would be granted.

Cao Ke joined the Suqian call centre in 2010, and a year later was promoted to senior manager. In 2012 he became deputy director, and in 2013 chief inspector. JD pushed him to develop quickly. Exceeding his own expectations, in less than five years he went from an entry-level position to being in charge of a call centre with more than 3,000 employees.

Good service makes it unnecessary for customers to call customer service in the first place. To this end, customer service is central to driving the company's business process improvement efforts. Initially, order inquiry calls took up more than 30% of customer service's time. That suggested that the details of promotions were not clear, forcing customers to call in for information. The call centre joined with marketing to standardize the entire promotion process. In 2014 the inquiry rate dropped to between 9-0 %. While JD's overall business volume doubled, customer service calls remained stable. Except during big promotions such as "Double 11," the number of inquiries remained level.

The call centre summarized and analysed inquiries to optimize the process and reduce the recurrence of the same questions. For example, customer complaints revealed that the third-party courier company in charge of Inner Mongolia was inexcusably slow. Customer service communicated with JD North China regarding the problem, cut the volume of business done through the courier and eventually replaced it entirely. Problem solved.

In June 2014, complaints emerged from the Southeast Region about limited transport capacity. During this time, employees had been asked to deliver goods using their own cars. But they weren't familiar with the routes or the shipping process, which impacted efficiency. JD Southwest China did a much better job when faced with transport issues. Management there turned to moving companies that were good at handling larger goods and charged reasonably. The customer service department recommended that method to JD South China and this allowed them to resolve their delivery issues before "Double 11".

The most troublesome case Cao encountered involved milk powder. A father found that his child had loose bowels after consuming a product he'd bought online. The father called to file a complaint and the case was passed to Cao. It became apparent that the milk powder had become damp and gone bad because the consumer had left the can open for too long. The child became ill after his grandfather fed him the formula. But the old man did not accept this explanation and insisted that JD, as the seller, was responsible. The child was hospital-ized and his grandfather looked after him there during the day. He had no cell phone and could only be reached after 8 pm. Cao tried to comfort the old man every day and gave him step by step sug-gestions about what to do. Once the child was in a stable condition, Cao offered the grandfather a refund. The father had originally paid on delivery and had no bank card or online payment account. Cao had to transmit the money through the post office. It took a week to resolve the issue and the child recovered fully.

The customer care department was set up in the call centre to handle health and safety complaints relating to general merchandise and mother and child products. Customers became increasingly de-manding. In the beginning, the answered-call rate was low. When that improved, customers said they wanted to be greeted with a better atti-tude when they called. They then complained that, although attitude had improved, their problems remained unresolved. The call cen-tre asked customer service to develop at least two solutions for every problem. In 2014, attitudes and solutions were better and so was the advice to customers on how to avoid such problems in the future. In 2014, with the channel expanding, a large number of new customers flooded into JD. The elderly in third- and fourth-tier cities, whose children worked outside town, also called to ask how to shop online. The call centre had to teach them fundamental computer skills.

If something went wrong with a Taobao customer's purchase, he would be advised to call the manufacturer. But people call JD even if they've bought things from one of its third-party sellers. Alibaba's philosophy was to make business easier, while JD's was to make life easier. Customer service staffers were under mounting pressure. Front-line people were blamed for everything. JD did not have psychological counsellors to help customer service staff cope with the pressure, but supervisors tried to help these employees understand that it was JD that the callers are cursing, not them, and that they shouldn't take it personally. The first three months on the job were the most difficult for customer-service personnel. If they could survive this period, things got easier. Managers and supervisors monitored the workplace to see who stayed on the line for a long time and whose tone of voice was changing. They would pat their shoulders and offer reassurance to help calm them down. If there were problems beyond the capacity of customer service, they could pass them to a higher level.

In January 2012, JD's online customer service capability went online. The new real-time communication channel linked website visitors with JD's help desk. Taking Chengdu's online customer service centre as an example, the normal workload was 160 customers during eight working hours a day. On 18 June that year, the staff worked from 9 am through 11 pm. The customer flow reached 400 to 500 at once during peak hours. Each employee opened three accounts, as there was insufficient headcount. They stayed online even at meal times. Managers and supervisors served them water and boxed lunches. There was a strong sense of competition within the team. If one employee handled 240 customers, others would vie for 300. Unfortunately, the office environment was relatively inhospitable. The outside temperature was 36 degrees (98 Fahrenheit), but there was no air conditioner. Water bottles were placed on each employee's desk.

After 18 June, Liu came to Chengdu and rewarded the team of more than 100 with 500,000 yuan, saying he was amazed by their remarkable performance. In 2008, Yan Xiaoqing, then VP of customer service, had urged Liu to develop online customer service. Liu thought that would not be necessary; he felt the call centre was enough. In 2010, after Wang Zhijun took over customer service, he also encouraged Liu to move it online. Wang told him online customer service would be the trend, driven by efficiency and cost factors.

In October 2011, JD began assembling its online customer service development team. A planning process that would normally take three months was completed in a single night. Chengdu was chosen as the location because it had everything. First, the phone company was located there, which meant better resources and the support of the Chengdu government. Second, it was a source of student talent. While Chengdu online customer service was under construction, newly hired employees were sent to Suqian for training.

It took only three days from the decision to do online customer service to the appointment of the first manager. Team-building took less than 15 days. In January 2012 online customer service started as a trial operation in Chengdu, and in March the operation began in earnest.

The ideal setup was self-service first, and routine inquiries accounted for 30-40% in services. JD R&D developed automated customer service for some departments and the solution rate reached 26%. Further, many customers wanted to solve problems on their own and didn't want to request help unless they were stuck. A number of customers were willing to share knowledge and help each other online. So if a problem could be solved online, then just guide the client to do so. The means of contact was there, but a telephone conversation should be the last resort.

In November 2014, after the JD National Customer Service Centre Suqian Branch had been running for eight months, it passed the industry's COPC (customer operations performance centre) international standards assessment, making it the only e-commerce company to be so certified in China.

Employees elsewhere in the company asked Huang Jinhong how they could accomplish what she'd done. She told them to focus on doing simple things well, again and again, until they become experts. Do things with your mind repeatedly and you'll be a winner.

At the end of 2012, an employee in Chengdu online services received an inquiry from a customer in Beijing. The caller said she lived in a basement, was in a dark mood and had a quantity of sleeping pills. It could have been a prank, but customer service checked her receipt address and found that she indeed lived in a basement. They immediately advised a supervisor, who called the police. When the police and the woman's friends rushed to the basement, they found there really was a troubled individual and a cache of sleeping pills there. The Chengdu employee may well have helped avert a tragedy.

A friend of the woman later sent JD a message thanking everyone involved for their concern and extra efforts.

---

* The content of this section draws upon the book *Secrets of JD Technology* written by JD's research and development team.

Open

I n 2010, some e-commerce professionals began to have doubts about what they were doing. B2C e-commerce companies all seemed so similar and they weren't performing particularly well financially. Was there no better way forward for e-commerce? At the time, the common understanding was that the trading of merchandise was really the only way to make money in e-commerce. The third-party seller platforms and big data had not yet made an appearance.

In 2013, JD removed the word "Mall" from the formal company name. In 2014, the company was divided into several subsidiaries, including finance and Paipai.com. It crossed beyond the borders of retail, creating new business by using the open platform model to leverage supply chains.

JD's value still resided in its network. First, by constantly improving the user experience, e-commerce solved the problems of information asymmetry and information immediacy. Offline retailers could make money from goods they bought from Wuhan and sold in Chengdu, because asymmetric information produced price difference. But through e-commerce, price information, delivery paths and production information all became transparent. Second, logistics management brought powerful efficiencies. Third, it all facilitated capital flow. And everything needed to be supported by powerful information systems.

On "Double 11" day in 2012, JD's database blew up. Customer orders were unaffected, but the back-end of the sellers took a hit and recovery was slow. The Beijing North Star Century Centre was in disarray. The R&D team's phones just kept ringing. Everyone was running up and down the hallways. Learning from this lesson, R&D worked up a comprehensive troubleshooting plan. On "Double 11" in 2014, they could finally say with confidence, "let the orders come." On that day orders from the platforms under JD Group exceeded 14 million and the system withstood the test.

People asked whether JD's system could be replicated and sold commercially. Actually, many JD platforms included external services. Someone wanted to buy inventory management, or someone needed a delivery system to use on cloud platforms. JD handled large trading volumes well, and it had a long value chain. The JD team was skilled and experienced. So if a company bought a JD system, they were actually buying the team's experience as well.

JD was best at supply-chain technology, encompassing the whole system from front-end marketing to back-end services. The business characteristics in the past were obvious and technology was basically led by business. JD had been optimizing its systems with business as the focus. Over time, the technology was able to walk in parallel with the business. Later, technology began to lead the business. Marketing, purchasing, pricing, and IT were automated and driven by big data. The human workload was reduced to a minimum. Departments that collaborated well with technology tended to have better performance.

In March 2013, the company reorganized and the R&D department became the business division. In 2014, the R&D effort was divided into two parts covering operations and marketing.

JD's business originated online. The IT system was its lifeline. The bottom – the cloud platform, together with the operation and maintenance system – supported the applications on top. "We thought we were an e-commerce company, but now we think we're a technology-driven company," said Li. "Technical services will become one of our sources of income."

CMO Lan Ye oversaw the marketing work that had a direct influence on sales, gross margin, cash flow and the company's other key financial indicators. Separately, he focused on buying and merchandising management. JD was trying to make its product offerings richer, and the prices more competitive, so more and more people would visit JD.com to browse and buy.

In 2013, JD upgraded its relationships with suppliers. Now it would not only sell their products but also act as a route to market and help them manage their own customer relations. If you were hired to sweep the floor, you were paid as a cleaner. If you were hired to do babysitting, you were paid as a nanny. If you were hired to educate the child, you'd be paid more. JD not only helped you sweep the floor and look after the children, it even helped with money management. The more value it contributed, the more profit it made. In 2015, JD classified performance marketing into two categories: the release of promotion information through the network; and digital marketing, also known as programme marketing. This approach placed higher demands on technology, relying on big data to carry out one-to-one marketing across mass populations of users.

This required a more targeted system for advertising. The traditional marketing method was to split 10,000 customers into affiliated groups like fashion enthusiasts, newcomers and so on. The goal was to then reach different customer groups in different ways. The more accurate marketing methods held that there was no need to try and classify the 10,000 customers, because everyone was different. It was impossible to carry out one-on-one communication with 10,000 people, but targeted communication could be done through the system.

The home appliance department of Samsung, which had been paying attention to offline channels, had shown little interest in JD over the years. In early 2014, Samsung asked JD to prove its capabilities. Samsung offered a special washing machine for baby clothes, an expensive model that cost more than 5,000 yuan. JD identified a subset of customers who were high-end milk powder consumers and went after them with precision marketing. In Suning and Gome, sales might have been less than 1,000 units, but JD sold more than 2,000 in two months. An organization's value is reflected in the things it can do that others can't.

POP and Paipai.com

On "Double 11" in 2013, Men Jipeng, director of the brand marketing team, settled on an unusual advertising strategy. He believed ads on "Double 11" should be brand-oriented, highlighting the JD brand. During this important sale period the company would get peak traffic levels without spending a penny, so it didn't make sense to run ads designed just to increase traffic.

JD, as the marketplace underdog, chose to attack its competitors' weak points. It had to be a bold, overt scheme. On "Double 11" in

2012, Tmall's logistics faced strong criticism after some customers had still not received their purchases after a week. And so, the tone of JD's "Double 11" push in in 2013 was set: "Low Price is One Thing. Fast Delivery is Another." Marketing rolled out a sequence of ads with themes like a young girl who bought sunscreen online, but when she opens her door to take delivery her face is burnt. Another featured a man with a beard who bought a shaver online, but when the delivery comes his beard is so long it brushes the ground.

This sharp advertising was a big hit. Other e-commerce companies stuck with standard marketing ads. Only JD released this flavour of brand advertising without explicitly mentioning the "Double 11" holiday promotions. It had been a bold move. If it had failed, the loss would have run into tens of millions yuan. Senior marketing VP Xu Lei trusted Men Jipeng and had granted the necessary freedom of action. "This kind of aggressive advertising is very risky," said Men. "I tell Xu Lei what I am thinking. He shares my views and is willing to gamble. If we stick to convention, there will be little risk, but little positive effect either."

Who would have thought that one day JD could compete with Alibaba? In 2009, Alibaba had assessed the top ten e-commerce companies. JD was on the list, but was in no way Alibaba's equal. Now JD and Alibaba were true competitors.

That competition derived from the B2C platform. There were four pearls in the internet industry. The first was the search engine. The second was the social network. The third resided in the combination of hardware and software. The fourth was the enterprise B2C retail platform, which directly connected production with consumption, with the underlying platform as the basic architecture. Tmall followed this model. JD POP (point of purchase) business was doing it too. Theoretically speaking, it was of great commercial value. In theory, e-commerce could account for 15% of a billion peoples' purchases.

In 2000, Amazon launched the e-commerce platform Marketplace. By 2012, more than 2 million third-party sellers worldwide were moving products on Amazon and the platform turnover accounted for 40% of the sellers' total. In 2011, Amazon's revenue was $48 billion. As much as 12% of that came from the platform.

For B2C self-support business purchasing, warehousing had ceilings. For instance, general merchandise encompassed too many non-standard products and too many brands. It was too slow to organize teams to purchase and market. If an e-commerce company opened its platform to third-party sellers, then it could quickly increase the scale of its categories. Platform unit sales were low in cost and high in profit. The self-support business attracted traffic, capital flowed with low prices, and money was made through logistics, technology, e-books and other services. This was Amazon's model and something JD planned to emulate. Liu hoped that in the future JD's platform sales would add up to 50% of its total.

Alibaba started platform services much earlier, unmatched in the Chinese domestic retail space. As JD placed more focus on the self-support business, its operational capacity on open platforms remained inferior to Alibaba's.

Like Amazon, JD had tried to expand its scale in an earlier phase, and to maximize its direct-sales product quantity. But ultimately it would join the open platform tide. The ultimate competition between e-commerce companies would be platform-level competition and rivalry on services such as delivery efficiency, bargaining power with suppliers, and so on. The decisive factor would be the basic ability of IT, including order management, storage management, data services and customer management. Tmall's advantage was in front-end sales, page display, promotion activities and user interaction. In the short term, Tmall had the widest inventory and was most sensitive to the pulse of the market. JD's advantage was in the back-end. Its organization of the supply of goods, supply chain management, logistics and delivery were superior.

JD had achieved a thorough transformation to the offline environment, a move that cost a fortune. Taobao was more like a peasant rebel army that had completely broken with the old order. But the new order it created was chaotic. JD was more like a warlord. It paid a high price but established a new order. In contrast to Tmall, JD had a large volume of point of purchase business, but customers still came to JD if problems occurred. Liu hoped sellers could turn out the best products and leave storage, delivery and customer service to the experts at JD.

In 2012, JD, Tmall, Amazon.cn, Dangdang, Suning E-Commerce and Tencent all had platform dreams. But the market could not sustain so many platforms. In 2015, only two contestants were left: JD and Tmall. Liu and Alibaba's Jack Ma are the two heroes of this epic fight. The success of millions of people depended on them.

There were four people successively responsible for POP in JD. Ma Song was the first leader of the platform. It took him nine months to build the back-end system. As for the R&D behind JD POP, the system had to be embedded into the self-support structure. Sellers had requirements of various kinds. Some had their own storage systems. Some needed JD to handle delivery. Some wanted to use JD's warehousing and delivery service directly. Some wanted to send the goods to the delivery station and let JD make the delivery. To help get a handle on all this, in September 2010, POP was put online.

Ma Song completed his mission. Later, Zhang Shouchuan took over POP. He used to work for Metro and had a wealth of experience in offline retail. In August 2012, when I saw Zhang in his office, he had just suffered a nosebleed. He was overloaded with work, day after day. "I have achieved economic freedom," he said. "I am only fighting for my ideals: changing the consumption habits of the Chinese people, which may even influence the business pattern of the world."

While Zhang was in charge, POP sales increased from 2.3 billion yuan in 2011, to 10 billion yuan in 2012. The growth came from a staggering choice of products. In June 2010, the company had 100,000 SKUs. By August 2012, the figure was 2.39 million. Consumers wanted to feel as if they were walking down the street and shopping. You needed to give them a wide range of choices and, at the same time, provide selected items so they could zero in on products they liked. And this could only be achieved with the optimization of search engines and good associated recommendations.

However, Zhang tended to think more in offline retailing terms than from an e-commerce perspective.

In 2012, JD opened the platform to the public. A seller who used both the Taobao and JD platforms complained that the JD platform was still too primitive. A seller had to pay a 5% fee to open a shop on Taobao. In addition, Taobao provided more than 80 kinds of marketing tools to sellers at different prices, which they could select based on their needs. If you aimed for top sales, you could buy the marketing tools. If you wanted to save money, you could attract shoppers by marketing on your Weibo account. But the JD platform lacked the platform operation concept. It was more like a department store where a seller could only get a storefront, nothing more. Also, as JD's consumers developed a higher consumption threshold, JD's quality control became more carefully managed. Sellers had to check each of the goods to be shipped out manually in order to avoid mistakes.

Despite the inconvenience, sellers still wanted to expand business scale through JD. The JD platform had great traffic, the gross margin was higher than Taobao's, and the business could be very promising if the scale was large enough. In 2012, JD's open platform was still in its early stages.

Seller support for JD was driven by the expansion instinct, as well as the fact that sellers felt a sense of crisis in the face of such a strong platform. It was dangerous to put all your eggs in one basket. An entrepreneur who provided back-end services to Taobao said: "The Taobao sellers that I've contacted both love and fear Taobao. For many sellers, more than 80% of their turnover comes from Taobao. They obviously love that. But Taobao is both a player and a referee, which in turn makes them fear it."

After sales were promoted by increasing SKUs, POP experienced a new set of problems. As the seller cited above complained, JD was too stiff. The operating philosophy of the open platform was different from that of the self-support operation. Employees who were used to issuing instructions to suppliers were at a loss. After Zhang's tenure, two other leaders were responsible for POP, each for a short time. Those changes highlighted internal management problems.

Staff complained that leadership did not read or reply to emails. In June 2013, Liu asked Kate Kui, who came from investment banking, to lead the POP business. It was a bold move. Kui was totally new to the industry. "Are you sure?" she asked. "Yes. It can't be worse than it is now," said Liu.

Investment banking was like hunting: once you identified and located the prey, eventually you'd get a break. But retailing was an endless game, day and night. When Kui took over POP, she saw that internal management was indeed a mess, with unclear business lines and undisciplined staff. Yet she was confident JD could develop an effective POP model. With financing for the self-support business completed and the growing scale of business, the threat of capital chain rupture was ever present. Meanwhile, something was awry in Alibaba's ecosystem. Sellers were making less and less money. Kui confirmed JD's POP market positioning and convinced sellers they should spread the risk by giving JD a try. She spent three months combing through the sellers' back-end systems and building the traffic path. With a sound, functional back-end, traffic would grow quickly.

POP is an ecosystem that manages tens of thousands of pieces of merchandise. JD was new in this business and had to keep an open mind. "Open" was the operative word. The idea of an ecosystem itself was open. In essence, the self-support business was like a planned economy, while an open platform was more like the market economy.

It was by no means easy for those who'd been successful in a planned economy to replicate that success in a market economy. "This was why Liu asked me to do the open platform," said Kui. "I don't have the obstacles in my background. I approached it entirely from the perspective of the internet, not purely as a retailer would." She first had to gain the support of Liu and Lan Ye, or she could not move forward. Secondly, she had to explain the POP concept to employees. Previously, they'd managed the self-support business. A stock problem could be immediately solved with a command to the seller. But in POP, sellers wouldn't listen to your commands. Why should they? Their sales in JD were no more than a tenth of those in Alibaba. They needed a compelling reason to follow you.

Business operations, the logistics system, marketing planning, product promotions, back-end systems and other pieces all needed to be advanced and open. Early on, sellers complained that JD had a terrible system. In fact, the issue was not that the technology was poor, but that the overall approach was foreign to the sellers. JD hadn't anticipated opening the system to sellers, and thus hadn't built it to meet their needs.

The essence of a market economy lies not in control but in making the rules. When US President Bill Clinton was in office, the economy needed to be revived. Thinking that Silicon Valley could be a big help, Clinton set up a new incentive mechanism for technology start-ups, the greatest fruit of which was construction of the information superhighway. Kui believed POPs must set the rules and build the road, offer attractive incentives and let the sellers do businesses.

"You can't be the only sales channel," she said. "You should be part of multiple channels. And this part should be valuable so the businesses can last a long time. You'll make money after others make theirs."

Kui's management style was not based on issuing orders. Instead, she raised questions. She told her employees what she observed and asked them to think about it and suggest solutions. She oversaw every detail. When the leader focuses on details, employees must do the same. Retail itself involved intense attention to detail. Kui had to worry about whether a page showed that a certain product was out of stock, if shoe sizes weren't visible and whether the name of a new store was correct. She hired many workers from Alibaba to bring new blood to the team. This competitive recruitment was a big move that upset many people, but she did it anyway.

In March 2014, after the merger of JD and Tencent e-commerce, Kui became president of JD's Paipai.com business. There were a lot of small sellers on Paipai.com and they might not be strong enough to win traffic from bigger POP players. And mall sellers might have had their own unique way of operating. JD separated Paipai.com to allow it to become a bigger and more independent C2C eco-system. WeChat and the mobile QQ eco-systems provided a huge social traffic space.

The bottom layer of Paipai had been idle for years. After being integrated into JD from Tencent, the fundamental architecture was modified, and in July 2014 it went online. At the end of September the Paipai WeChat shops were officially launched. On "Double 11" orders exceeded 200 million yuan, showing substantial growth. By January 2015, orders placed in Paipai.com topped 60 million yuan a day.

Sources for Paipai.com included former Taobao sellers looking for other platforms due to Taobao's poor performance, traditional wholesalers testing the internet channel and some individual sellers. There was risk in their trading. Paipai guided them through the process.

Xin Lijun, JD Group VP and GM of the POP open platform business division, succeeded Kui. He suggested to Liu that JD should not make yearly assessments as it had always done. JD had to be patient, comb through the internal environment, create a good architecture, and arrange the eco-system order to pave the way for POP's success.

After taking over, Xin first reconstructed the internal environment, and trimmed brand and pricing models so users could locate categories in the shortest time possible. In 2014, the POP growth rate was more than 200% year-on-year, and the platform's trading volume exceeded 100 billion yuan.

Xin also positioned JD clothing as high quality and collaborated with Bazaar magazine to do fashion shows twice a year. Men were the biggest JD customers. POP menswear traffic was a breakthrough, starting with the Men's Wear Festival in 2014.

Liu Shichao, general manager of e-commerce and internet marketing at Gloria, a women's clothing brand, sensed the changes in JD. He used to have a purely purchasing role, but now he had operational responsibilities. Purchasing was about ordering and payment on delivery, and discounts came with quantity. However, clothing was a non-standard product that emphasized variations and tones. It needed more sophisticated soft operations, rather than a simple price war. Liu Shichao found that JD employees learned the operational rules of the apparel industry by combining the front-end operation with the merchandise to find the themes that interested consumers. This was great progress.

What consumers buy does not necessarily represent only product value, but also the value of perception. Communication was important in selling clothing. Sellers needed to communicate with consumers to sell value beyond the physical textile. Buying non-standard products was a process of emotional communication, unlike buying a standard product, which was based on a direct functional appeal. What consumers wanted was not cheapness, but an opportunity to buy a seemingly high-end product at a relative low price.

Gone were the days when discounting was the decisive factor on the internet. Price was still important, but not paramount. Consumers were willing to pay for quality and convenience.

Gloria used JD delivery services, and Liu Shichao never saw a single complaint about delivery. The challenges across the entire platform dealt with flexibility, general merchandise and the JD brand. What could be done to make consumers think about JD as the department store, not just as Computer City?

Did a seller value JD's POP? That could be determined in various ways: if the new arrivals came as fast as from Tmall; if management assigned a special person for the docking; if there was exclusive model supply. JD classified the sellers in a pyramid. Growth in POP volume represented the synchronized growth of sellers at all levels of the pyramid. Those at the top couldn't always win all of the traffic and endlessly expand without fresh blood coming into the bottom layer. POP aimed to help sellers at the bottom rise to the middle and the middle to the top. The pyramid was thereby in equal proportions.

Open Logistics

E-commerce generated huge market demand. Logistics had been redefined. Express service became a fast-growing industry. Sellers and buyers raised the bar on the express industry by demanding lower prices and faster speed, as well as better service quality. The core competitiveness of a courier company lay in delivering the best service at the minimum cost.

With warehousing, transportation and terminal included, JD wanted to be the all-round big whale. The big whale required more food to survive and thrive. Achieving economies of scale was an inevitable trend. JD logistics opened not only to third-party sellers on the JD open platform, but also to independent vertical e-commerce, offline stores and others. Building an e-commerce delivery system was largely investment-driven. The traditional logistics company usually expands after it has revenue and gross margin to allow for sequential, phased development. JD placed user experience first and cost second. If it compared logistics costs with its counterparts, how could it ensure a balance between user experience and cost? With orders from the outside, there would also be contradictions between the internal storage system, transport system and delivery system. For instance, if goods are damaged or missing, who took responsibility?

In August 2013, JD began receiving orders from the outside. The company built into its network economies of scale. Customers supported the base cargo volume, which in turn guaranteed that the logistics network could operate at break-even. The advantage of JD logistics was in its nationwide reach. The delivery capability to the end user was now comparable to that of the benchmark company in the industry, S.F. Express.

Reducing costs was enough for self-support orders. For outside orders, good service and profitability both needed to be taken into account. Peng Yuxuan, deputy director of business expansion in JD's delivery division, joined the company in October 2012. At the time there were only nine workers engaged in outside orders, and some spent part of their time in other departments. The operating system was incomplete; it could not even generate an offer sheet. Peng began building the system, defining customers and determining pricing policy.

In 2013, JD launched "Double 11" free shipping offers, which promoted cooperation between JD delivery and more than 1,000 POP sellers. Sellers made use of JD logistics by stocking goods in their warehouses and asking JD to deliver for them. It was quite efficient. JD's POP had to distinguish itself from Alibaba. JD could differentiate itself by constantly improving the seller experience via its logistics capability. After surveying POP, Peng turned to the vertical e-commerce website.

Which market could JD logistics successfully occupy outside of e-commerce? A key advantage of JD logistics was its inter-city delivery capability. This meant that O2O was also JD's potential market. A rice noodle takeaway start-up had completed the first round of financing and partnered with JD. Customers placed orders via WeChat, and JD delivered the start-up's noodles to customers.

In 2010, Jiang Huixiao, director of the delivery division in JD's North China Region, joined the company. At the time, a space of about 200m² near the warehouse packaging platform was used for picking. Workers picked merchandise manually. There was no independent express operating system, and there was a shortage of working tools and talent. The employees previously worked for the warehousing system and had never done express shipments before.

In March 2012, JD's first second-level picking centre was set up. This was a new venture and it met with resistance inside the company. It was natural for an express company to set up a picking centre, but JD was not an express company. Supporters argued that it would be impossible to connect so many points into a network without a picking centre, while sceptics thought a picking centre would add one more step and reduce the efficiency.

But the network could not be built up without it. If there were no picking centre, every day dozens of trucks would have had to travel back and forth from Beijing to Tianjin. It would be more efficient and less costly if goods could be shipped in a large truck and then distributed to the delivery terminals through picking centres.

If JD's logistics network was to become an organic entity, it had to have its own trunk line. If the picking centre was the heart, self-built trunk lines were the blood and the delivery terminals the cells. The cells could only absorb nutrients when the veins functioned properly. The biggest problem for outside orders was the trunk line. Sellers wanted to distribute the goods from one region to places all over the country, which required adjustment to the organizational structure. In May 2013, JD started building a trunk line transport network. At the time there were only 20 trunk lines, and JD had 3,000 private vehicles. At the end of 2014, JD had 3,210 outlets across the country, including delivery terminals, self-collection spots and self-collection containers. The railway administration began running special e-commerce trains from Beijing to Shanghai, and from Shanghai to Guangzhou.

JD wanted to give brand sellers solutions for the whole supply chain. Its warehousing utilized the WMS (Warehouse Management System) and WCS (Warehouse Control System), the former of which owned intellectual property for the system. Flow lines were designed automatically. The picking staff used RF guns and sorted goods along the line. Li Yonghe thought JD warehousing could solve countless problems, such as the integration of global business planning with information systems, warehouse layout plans, shelf display planning and flow design. "The highest aim for the supply chain was for products to be directly sent to the warehouse from the factory, and then directly sent to consumers," said Li. "This was the most economical way. JD needed to rely on its influence in the industry to remove waste from the supply chain and create a more cooperative spirit."

Tencent
E-Commerce

Ma Huateng and Richard Liu Joined Forces

On 10 March 2014, JD and Tencent announced their strategic partnership. JD bought Tencent's QQ online shopping business on the B2C platform and Paipai.com on the C2C platform, as well as a minority interest in Yixun.com and the right to purchase the rest. Tencent was to provide an entry position on WeChat, mobile QQ clients and other key platforms to JD. Tencent got 15% of JD's shares. Tencent President Martin Lau joined JD's board of directors. China's e-commerce landscape was changing once again.

At 9:30 am on announcement day, Liu appeared on stage at Tencent's headquarters in Shenzhen. "It is a special day, and I am very happy to meet you all for the first time," Liu said. "Tencent is a great company – the most successful internet company in China. After so many accomplishments, it is still full of energy and innovation, and is still growing quickly. But one day China's biggest internet company will be JD. The largest private enterprise in China will be JD!"

The acquisition plan was hatched by Zhang Lei, an investor in JD and chairman and CEO of Hillhouse Capital Group, Asia's largest investment institution. In 2011, Zhang had brought Liu and Tencent co-founder Ma Huateng (Pony Ma) together for a conversation. In 2012, he pulled them together again. During that period the two executives had different views. Tencent was not prepared to yield in e-commerce. JD was on the rise and it didn't have a strong need for the alliance. The two were accustomed to going head-to-head on the battlefield.

But Zhang Lei did not abandon the idea. He was looking for the right time to make it happen. In 2013, he recognized the trend from internet PC to mobile internet, which was happening quickly. At JD's board meetings Liu was pointedly questioned by investors. What about mobile internet? Where's JD in all of this? Each time Liu replied that JD was supportive of it both in terms of technology and traffic. Zhang was glad to see that Liu realized this; he felt there was hope for something big between JD and Tencent.

It was evident that e-commerce was going mobile in a big way. Tencent owned a big traffic on-ramp in the form of two mobile platforms: WeChat and mobile QQ. This represented a major opportunity for JD. From Tencent's perspective, it was an ideal time to invest in JD, whose valuation at the time was about $8 billion.

Tencent was a company that excelled in many ways, including entrepreneurship, entrepreneurial culture and user experience. But the word "inventory" was not in Ma Huateng's dictionary. He had been in business for half of his life, but he didn't have a clue about inventory management. He thought his Yixun.com was experiencing rapid growth, at a rate of more than 100% a year. It was to hit 100 billion yuan over the next several years.

Zhang Lei told Ma that when Yixun reached 100 billion yuan there might be 20-30 billion yuan of stockpiled inventory. Every day the inventory would need to be checked to ensure it wasn't lost or stolen. Ma had never considered this. He created an internet empire that dealt only with virtual goods. Nobody could picture him physically checking warehouse inventory.

Zhang told Ma his problem was not making money, but expending unnecessary time and energy. He finally agreed.

In late January 2014, Liu met Tencent President Martin Lau and they began the planning process. After a meeting of the JD and Tencent teams, Zhang was asked to offer his perspective. "Life is short," he said. "Try to make something big. When it is big, make it eternal. And you must innovate constantly, no matter how big it is."

When the talks ran into difficulties, Liu called Zhang Lei seven times, asking him to return to China from a ski resort in the French Alps. "You can't leave the thing half-done," he argued. "Come back quickly or this will become thoroughly screwed up." There were disagreements in the negotiations. There were also too many voices on both sides – intermediaries, lawyers, bankers and executives. Dozens of people focused on their pieces, with little thought to achieving the bigger objective.

Zhang flew back from France the following day. He cleared the meeting room and barred middle-level managers, lawyers and investment bankers from the talks. Only the decision-makers were allowed to directly take part in the negotiations.

The Tencent side had Pony Ma, Martin Lau, Wu Xiaoguang, Zhang Xiaolong (senior VP and founder of WeChat), and James Mitchell (chief strategy officer). JD had Liu, CFO Sidney Huang and Zhang Lei. Zhang Lei told the team there had to be a decision that day or no one was going to leave. In four hours they settled 35 questions, such as arranging payment, how WeChat and QQ could support JD, the number of shares changing hands and so on.

In 2014, JD's mobile orders in the fourth quarter rose to 36% from 29.6% the preceding quarter, and the year-on-year increase topped 370%. "Could JD have done it without WeChat and QQ?" asked Zhang. "Tencent made a net profit of $7 billion in this investment. Most importantly, its energy became more focused. This is a rare win-win in the history of the internet in China."

JD Benefits from Mobile Terminal

On 26 January 2015, the former offices of Tencent's e-commerce business in Shenzhen became home to the new JD WeChat and Mobile QQ business division. The work environment was spacious and quiet. I saw three folded beds in the hallway where employees could rest after working overtime. Many employees of Paipai.com had worked at Tencent over many years. After the partnership was formed, they also joined JD.

Feng Yan, operations director of the JD WeChat and Mobile QQ business division, joined Tencent as an intern in 2005. In Tencent, when the employees wanted to work on a project, they had to hammer out details every step of the way, from tendering and product selection through operations, since the chain was quite long and disorganized. JD's supply chain models offered countless advantages. Feng was able to negotiate with suppliers and quickly launch programmes that would have been impossible in the old Tencent.

Brands including Huawei Honour, ZTE Nubia, OPPO, GAP and others may never have been attracted by JD's PC-focused resources or Tencent's e-commerce capabilities alone. But after the merger these brands flocked in. The WeChat channel hosted the first-day launch for many brands. For example, when OPPO released a new model, the JD WeChat sector designed the SNS (social networking site) games marketing programme. The click rate was 100,000 at first. In the end, the new model was exposed to more than 100 million people.

In second- and third-tier cities, mobile QQ usage was much higher. In cities with factories, mobile QQ was even hotter than in the capital cities. People with a high-school education were the largest group using mobile QQ. Its advantages in targeted advertising in different regions brought large numbers of new users to JD. According to JD's 2014 annual report, the active user population grew by 104% year-on-year, topping out at 96.6 million people.

Tencent had launched Paipai.com in 2004, soon after the birth of Alibaba, but there was a world of difference between the two companies' levels of determination and professionalism. Alibaba applied the best resources to the challenge. Tencent was less prepared; it just jumped in and took a chance.

Liu Yi (later VP of JD's user experience design division) was responsible for the user experience in the Tencent partnership. Back then, JD needed to establish a uniform user-experience standard. The pages were loosely organized and at times manufacturers' promotional pages were simply loaded onto the site. The reason, according to Liu, was that there was not much time – sometimes just a few hours – between when negotiations were finalized with suppliers and their products went online.

It was easy to adjust the categories on Tencent's home page, but JD's approval mechanism was very strict. Liu Yi didn't know why his proposals were rejected time after time. Liu discussed this with him and explained the concepts of A Class and B Class. Only then did Liu Yi realize how disciplined JD was in these matters. The classification experience came from the user experience and the design absolutely had to be in line with users' expectations.

Liu Yi was most impressed by three things after he joined JD: the focus on user experience, which was well beyond his expectations; the emphasis on empowerment; and the painstaking process for home page and channel page revisions.

The Boundaries of E-Commerce

Consumption Upgrade for Chinese Users

Those who could hold consumers' attention for the longest period of time were in a position to create the most value. Consumers had the impression that Gome and Suning were the places to buy home appliances, while Wal-Mart, Wumart and Carrefour were the destinations for commodities like toilet paper. They didn't spend much time in Gome and Suning stores because they didn't buy home appliances and digital products every day. They spent much more time in supermarkets, making routine purchases. JD had abundant categories and a wide range of services, making it ideal for meeting the shopping needs of most consumers.

Liu Yongming, founder of Nala, published an article while he was studying in South Korea. He described preparing to get married and buying a colour TV set from JD. Unfortunately, it arrived broken. JD called Liu Yongming to apologize. In his article he called South Korea the most developed country in e-commerce. Richard Liu arranged for Assistant President Liu Shuang to research the market in South Korea. Upon his return Liu Shuang wrote a detailed report, entitled *The General Merchandise Category is Greater than the 3C Category*. Richard Liu forwarded the report to all JD executives and investors. Soon general merchandise began to move online on a large scale.

Today Capital once conducted a survey with home visits to 3,000 households in China, with the middle class as its primary target. The survey was conducted in two first-tier cities, two second-tier cities and six third-tier cities. After the survey, Xu Xin grew more confident about holding JD stock for the long run. The survey revealed that the post-80s generation spent an average of five hours a day on the internet. Some 50% of that group's shopping was done online. The survey also found that consumers were willing to pay a premium for mother and baby products, and food and cosmetics if they could be assured of getting high quality goods, and this was JD's strength. Consumers' comments on JD included: "Authentic goods." "Fast delivery." "Trustworthy after-sales service."

In third- and fourth-tier cities, nuclear families with more than 5,000 yuan in monthly income were relatively free from pressing financial burdens. Bridegrooms had houses bought by their parents, and the bride's family bought furniture and a car. Between 500 and 800 yuan was spent on a child. One thousand yuan could cover the cost of living, 2,000 yuan was saved in the bank and that left nearly 2,000 as disposable income. Where that money was spent was extremely important to these consumers. But it was no big deal for them to buy things for 100 or 200 yuan. When Vip.com lowered the per customer transaction to 100 yuan or so, its sales went through the roof. Middle class customers paid attention to fashion. They liked comfortable things. They turned to Li Ning and Anta when they couldn't afford to buy Adidas or Nike.

For JD, there were still great opportunities in the mother and baby space, in food and in other categories. The market for the mother and baby category was 300 billion yuan a year. Parents in the post-80s and post-90s age groups were more interested in on-line shopping. Their demands relating to mother and baby products were quite rigid. The parents could do without laptops, but children could not do without milk powder. Meanwhile, the audiences were limited. Advertising and promotions in this category were simply wasted on people who didn't have children. Online shopping in the mother and baby category could account for more than 50% of the market. The key point in winning this category was to sell quality goods by cooperating with manufacturers to successfully control and leverage the supply chain.

The food market was gigantic, but the market for online grocery purchases remained limited. There were two reasons: e-commerce lacked the time effectiveness of offline purchases that allowed the public to buy and enjoy food immediately; and if one bought via e-commerce, he'd lose the flexibility that came with a single purchase as he usually had to buy a lot of groceries.

The price sensitivity of the food category was very low. It was already a big deal to cut a few cents off a Coke, but the consumers wouldn't really feel the difference. They'd just buy a beverage when they were thirsty. Food promotions were often half-price offers. The sales volume had to rise exponentially in such instances. Where could big growth come from? From an increase in users? Through the concentration of user sales volume? The former was a reliable growth driver. The latter could be a problem – it meant the same group of customers was buying half a year's food supply at one time. Only 9% of JD's users had bought food on the site. That posed both a challenge and a monumental opportunity.

Rural E-Commerce

In August 2013, Wang Zhijun, VP of customer service, was named VP of the delivery department. (Later he was appointed president of door-to-door delivery in JD Group's O2O subsidiary.) Liu wanted to make a breakthrough in delivery and roll out innovations in end-user services. He looked to Wang to make it happen.

Liu's ambition was for JD to be present in every inch of the map of China. He asked Wang to plant 100,000 red flags on the map. In other words, he literally wanted JD to reach 100,000 villages.

The retail market was extremely weak in rural areas, with too many unreliable circulation links, high-priced goods and an abundance of substandard and counterfeit products.

Urban dwellers thought fruit and vegetables were too expensive. But farmers weren't profiting. From the place of origin to the consumer, agricultural products moved through long, circuitous delivery chains. Rural e-commerce could dramatically shorten the upstream supply chain. Pesticides and other farming products could go from the manufacturer directly to farmers via JD. Seeds from reliable providers could go directly into farmers' hands via JD. To help ensure sustainable business benefits, JD could help flatten channels and reduce prices. Meanwhile, farmers themselves were also consumers like everyone else. Rural consumption was high, especially in electronics.

Mobile internet jump-started the e-commerce market in rural areas. Because a computer cost about 3,000 yuan and the monthly internet access cost 80-100 yuan, computers were not big sellers in rural areas. But with the emergence of smartphone and mobile internet, a farmer could order a 400-yuan product while working in his fields and the delivery was soon en route. For e-commerce companies, the rural market was still in its infancy. Villagers trusted their eyes more than anything. You could tell them e-commerce was a good thing, but they wouldn't believe it if they could not see or touch anything along the way. Many even suspected it was somehow one big pyramid scheme.

For rural e-commerce, JD relied on the entire logistics network. There were 2,860 counties and districts in China. JD's delivery network eventually covered 1,862 of them. According to the rural development plan, JD's delivery terminals in the counties were to be transformed into service centres. There, display areas would be added to showcase selected merchandise and demonstrate to locals how to shop online. Next, there would be rural cooperation centres for people of certain social status and reputation in their villages.

JD established rural campus business centres. There were 20-30 village supervisors in each region responsible for the establishing County Services Centres. Liu named Wang Zhijun leader of JD's rural working group, which amused him. Wang set a budget for 50,000 villages. Liu thought that wasn't nearly enough and had him broaden it to 100,000 villages. Wang said he would have to spend more than 100 million yuan a year to make it work. "Don't worry," Liu replied. "That's small change. Will 100 million yuan be enough? How about 200 million?"

Wang predicted that in the first half of 2015, JD could set up 3,000-5,000 village cooperation centres. There were more than 10 towns per county and a dozen villages in each town.

On the morning of 21 March 2015, in Zijin County, Guangdong Province, some 250 kilometres northeast of Guangzhou, the JD Zijin County Service Centre held an opening ceremony. The local drum corps was invited to perform, and hundreds of people came to watch. Lin Hongkun was responsible for rural promotion in the east and north of Guangdong in southern China. He stepped up to the task the previous December, when he arrived in Heyuan City. He first looked over the site and then asked local promotion managers and deliverymen to distribute recruitment flyers. On 21 January 2015, the Zijin service centre formally opened for business.

Gan Jianlou was a teacher at the Jingzi Town middle-school in Zijin County. He spent more than 1,000 yuan a month shopping on JD. He also helped his colleagues place orders. "My most familiar stranger is the JD express delivery man," he joked. "Almost every day there are parcels delivered to the school." Gan had high regard for JD's delivery speed and after-sales service. He never had problems shopping on JD.com, where, for example, Wyeth milk powder sold at 138 yuan a tin, 90 yuan lower than the price in town. "For lower-end wage-earners," he said, "even one yuan saved can make a difference, let alone 90."

There were two core lines of e-commerce in rural areas. The rural strategy was closely tied into e-commerce and finance. E-commerce to villagers mainly involved purchases of electronic products, clothing, hats, shoes, industrial products and agricultural supplies. Conversely, JD helped farmers sell quality agricultural products directly to consumers. In the past they needed to go through four or five middlemen before their fruit and vegetables reached an urban consumer. E-commerce helped make that a thing of the past. JD was instrumental in moving fresh goods directly from the field to the dinner table. Fresh food e-commerce was a game-changing innovation. So far, no other Chinese company had achieved any of this on such a large scale.

Fresh Food via E-Commerce

JD partnered with the agricultural co-op of Tangyin County, Henan Province, which cultivated pollution-free vegetables. JD made regular deliveries to Zhengzhou of the co-op's produce. In the negotiation stage, Zhang Jianshe, director of JD Group's policy research office, even went to dig in the farmers' fields, looking for earthworms. The purchase price of vegetables at the farm was 1.8 yuan per jin.

Jianshe traveled with the vegetable truck from Tangyin County to Anyang City's wholesale market. The price was raised twice, each time by 0.5 yuan. When it got to Zhengzhou, the price was raised twice again and finally was sold at 4.8 yuan per jin. The gross margin for the co-op was only 2-5%. The profit probably was only 0.1 yuan per jin – just over one pound in weight – because there were too many intermediate links. JD could help the centre reach consumers. Selling organic vegetables at the price of conventionally-grown vegetables, they could make a profit.

The circulation channel of fruits and vegetables generally worked like this: Purchase from the place of origin → local dealers → local wholesalers (such as Beijing Xinfadi) → small wholesalers → community retailers → and finally, consumers. Each level added costs, so urban consumers thought the prices for fruit and vegetables were high. In fact, the high costs were mainly the result of too many channel links.

Fresh products represented the last fortress to be conquered by e-commerce. The fresh food e-commerce penetration rate was less than 1%. Food was of course a necessity and the Chinese market was worth trillions of yuan. The gross margin on fresh food was high. The per-customer transaction could be as high as 200 yuan and the gross margin nearly 100 yuan.

But in China, fresh food e-commerce was still at the stage of market cultivation. No e-commerce company was making money in the space. Fresh food was the chronic pain point for all e-commerce platforms. It had enormous market prospects, but everyone was crossing the river by feeling the stones. There was not a single set of good operating procedures. What were the challenges for fresh food? First, there was an extraordinarily high loss percentage. For instance, the rate of waste in China was 25%, compared with only 5% abroad. Second, there was the high cost of the cold chain. A cold chain network with nationwide coverage needed at least hundreds of billions of yuan of investment. No single enterprise could afford to play alone, without making use of social resources.

The business of fresh food depended on the transport capacity of the cold chain. In the socialized logistics system in China, the cold chain was a significant weak link. The cost of input and output in the cold chain was quite high. The equipment was expensive; delivery efficiency was lower than with ordinary goods; there was a short shelf-life and significant waste; and if produce was rejected by customers, reverse logistics were troublesome.

According to JD Logistics, the construction cost for a general warehouse of 10,000m² was about 5 million yuan. The construction cost for cold storage of the same size topped 10 million yuan because refrigerators had to run constantly. If the transformer was more than one kilometre away, cables had to be laid across roads. The workforce cost was higher than with common storage, because workers had to move in and out of cold storage in appropriately insulated clothing during different seasons.

Fresh food handling involved different levels of temperature control: low temperature storage (-18°C to -25°C), high temperature storage (0°C to 4°C), quick-freezing storage (-25°C to -35°C). The cold storage temperature could be different for different categories of fresh food. For example, for salmon and ice cream it was -25°C; pork, -18°C; vegetables, 4-6°C; chocolate, 18-22°C. Pork was also divided into two types, warm air pork and frozen pork. The former was to be delivered at 4°C to ensure quality and taste. The latter was to be stored at -18°C and defrosted at the time of eating, though it was considered less tasty.

In building cold storage, the first consideration was designing different temperature layers based on the categories to be stored. For example fruit and vegetables, fresh milk, and pork each need separate areas.

Huang Xing had nearly 20 years of experience in the warehousing industry. He said converting a normal truck into a refrigerated one involved installing an independent engine to power the refrigerator. And that burned a lot of fuel. Refrigerated vehicles relied on sophisticated temperature controls. A carriage temperature might be set at 4°C but that obviously changed whenever the door was opened. Let's say a deliveryman did 50 orders a day, at a rate of five per hour. That translated into the door being opened every 10 minutes, making if difficult to maintain the optimum temperature.

A converted vehicle had two temperature layers at most. The freezer was -18°C and the outside temperature was 0°C to 4°C. On certain delivery routes the goods required different temperature zones and the quantities were beyond one's control. How do you handle that? Logistics systems required powerful scheduling and data research capabilities.

Besides, what if customers who bought fresh goods one day wanted to have them delivered on another day? For normal-temperature products, the delivery usually moved from a distribution centre to delivery terminals and then on to the customers. If those customers wanted to delay delivery, the goods could easily be sent back to the delivery terminal. But perishable items had to be handled differently. There would have to be a freezer if items were going to be held in the delivery terminal. What if there were many returns and insufficient space in the freezer? Even if there were only one or two orders of meat to return, a special refrigerated vehicle had to be arranged to send the pork to the picking centre. The cost became extraordinarily high.

But with a market worth trillions of yuan hanging in the balance, the business was critically important. JD couldn't sit back and do nothing.

The company decided to build the cold chain in 2014. In the pilot phase, in order to save costs, the logistics system put cold storage containers of 70-80m3 for sea freight in the picking centres. The operation was done when there were only a few hundred orders. The picking centres' transport vehicles were also equipped with small ice chests to keep the temperature low for 24 hours. In 2014, ice tanks began to be installed in the three delivery terminals in Beijing, Shanghai and Guangzhou.

Fresh food e-commerce companies had to sell high quality, high price products in the early stages to help offset the high initial costs of the cold chain. In June 2014, Huang Ling, director of the VIP client department for JD open platform, began to work with international fresh food. He dealt with rarer food, such as white shrimp from Ecuador or prime durian from Malaysia. The target audience for these exotic foods were people between 27 and 40 years old. They demanded safe and healthy food, and were willing to pay higher prices.

In August 2014 JD held a semi-annual summary meeting to discuss e-commerce and concluded that there were three priority areas: fresh food, cross border e-commerce and O2O. Others were trying to do O2O, but not many knew how. Fresh food depended on specialized hardware and cross-border e-commerce depended on policies. If the problems of equipment for fresh food and the legal issues for cross-border e-commerce could be addressed properly, these two areas could develop very quickly.

Huang Ling had witnessed fresh food waste. A supplier bought cherries from Shandong. To meet schedules, the cherries were picked in hot weather and stored and transported without proper cooling. When they were delivered to consumers the rate of waste was up to 40%, causing heavy losses and strong customer dissatisfaction. But cherries from Chile had no such problems. They were washed, cooled down in water and stored at about 2°C. When they came to consumers in China, even after a long ocean crossing, they were still fresh.

JD also did direct selling of foreign milk. The best milk sources were Australia and New Zealand because they offered good quality and cost. Many of their brands were new to the Chinese. International milk purchase needed a minimum order quantity and had to meet air transportation capacity minimums. If the capacity of a plane was 4,200 cartons, then the order had to be 4,200. A smaller order would not be accepted. The difficulty was rooted in whether the milk could be consumed within the designated shelf life. For milk with a shelf life of nine months, the sales period was only six or seven months. Consumers were unlikely to buy the milk in the last one or two months. The shelf life of Australian A2 Milk was 21 days. It took 10 days for it to pass from the factory to the airport, and through domestic customs clearance. The actual sales period was only seven days, because no consumer would buy in the last three days. By the end of 2014, JD had imported four or five batches of A2 Milk in tens of thousands of tons, and sold out in less than a week.

According to Zhang Li, Liu was keeping a close eye on fresh food. The business was still small but there was room for massive growth. "It will be no problem in the future for the food category to achieve 100 billion yuan," said Zhang. "But when will this be reached? In five years or 10? It's hard to tell." Liu often asked him via WeChat: "Any fresh food to recommend?" Or: "How many people are there in the local specialties team?" In order to handle specialty items, Liu wanted to mobilize students in 1,000 universities and colleges across the country by encouraging them to become independent and join the working world as soon as possible. College students came from many different places across the country. They knew their local specialties and could help with sales. "We can offer payment so they can earn income and join the work community earlier. That will help JD quickly promote local products."

Fresh food and local products were inseparable. The point was to deliver fast. And one had to have a sharp eye for product selection, or the volume of waste would be immense. In addition, the products sold on the e-commerce platform had to be difficult or impossible to obtain in normal supermarkets.

Yan Xuhong, senior manager of the food business department in JD's general merchandise business division, joined the healthcare products department of JD open platform in March 2012. At the time, monthly sales were 4 million yuan. This had grown to 60 million yuan by the time she left the department in July 2013. In August 2013, Yan took over two groups in the food business department. One was tea products and instant drinks. The other was fresh food. In the second half of 2014, JD underwent a sweeping internal reorganization. The original fresh food department of POP was transferred to general merchandise. In November 2014, Yan took over domestic fresh food and tea, as the ninth successor to that position. Monthly orders at the time topped out at around 1,000.

Yan was miserable when she left the healthcare products department, and was in tears because she was reassigned soon after she'd shown significant results. Moreover, she was being assigned to the two worst business lines. Over time she came to be grateful to the

POP leader, Xin Lijun. She used to think she could only do well in the medical business. Her education, contacts and resources were all in the pharmaceutical industry. She wondered whether she'd succeed away from it, and she knew little about tea.

According to Yan, there were two types of good leaders. One constantly pushed you at work and carefully monitored your progress. The other trusted you and gave you space to play. As for the team, the post-85s and post-90s hires had a sense of security. To them, money was not the only thing. Careers and values were also important to them.

Tea represented culture. When Yan first took over the tea category she didn't know what to sell. She just followed in the steps of Tmall. By 2014, she had a clearer idea. From the tea garden to tea cups, JD had full traceability so they uniquely could guarantee that products were safe and of the best quality.

Luochuan apples were the specialty in Luochuan County. The apples were mainly sold through the wholesale market. But dealers adulterated the supply with lower-quality fruit. The local government began brand-building and opened retail apple shops. When Zhang Jianshe contacted authorities in the Shaanxi fruit industry, they did not know about JD and were hostile toward e-commerce because large volumes of fake Luochuan apples were for sale on the internet. They found that just 3% of them were actually Luochuan apples.

They soon came around because JD operated entirely by the book and always included proper invoices, which could drive suppliers to pay taxes that supported local economic development. JD promised to sell only real Luochuan apples, and Luochuan County vowed to help the company with certification. JD began by offering 1,000 cartons, each containing nine apples, for 99 yuan.

"Over the years, one JD's biggest contribution has been to build confidence and trust in e-commerce," said Zhang. "The concept of consistently reliable, quality goods has been welcomed by the public. In a country where people pay extra attention to food safety, this is a first-mover advantage. Through JD, farmers can benefit from quality industrial products, and urban people can enjoy high-quality agricultural products. A virtuous circle is created."

The invoicing process helped guarantee that consumers received quality goods through JD. The business credit system in China was rife with counterfeiting and scams. False invoicing was a common problem. JD produced 500 million sheets of invoices a year. The cost was 150 million yuan and there was a team of more than 1,000 people directly involved in the process.

In order to save costs, JD embraced e-invoicing. Cai Lei, who joined JD in January 2012, was vice president of tax and finance for JD Group. On 27 June 2013, his team's efforts culminated in JD issuing its first e-invoice. Born in 1978, Cai was a workaholic. His life revolved around work and sleep. "I came to JD from Vanke simply because I wanted to do something big. JD can give me the stage," he said. "If it was not for JD, I couldn't have created the country's first e-invoice, no matter how capable I might have been." At that time, five provinces were working on e-invoicing, but JD made it happen first. "We want to be No. 1," said Cai. "As Richard Liu said, the growth of JD over the past ten years shows you can make the impossible possible. And I firmly believe it when he says peoples' inabilities are at the root of every failure."

In the process, Cai gradually came to realize the value of e-invoicing. It not only saved costs for JD, but by invoicing and paying the appropriate taxes, JD also compelled suppliers and partners in related industries to pay their share of taxes. E-invoicing disrupted invoice counterfeiting. It had the potential to encourage fairness and business integrity across China. It did bring tax increases, but when online sellers of all sizes were incorporated into the system, tax fairness could be achieved. Tax reduction also requires standardized measurement tools.

In addition to electronic invoicing, JD was promoting e-commerce regulation to bring fairness to the market. Fraud was rampant in online shopping. Individuals or small shops often cheated by moving from one place to another. If they were reported for selling fakes and had their shops closed down, they opened a new one elsewhere. These street sellers could be better supervised and regulated through e-invoice and e-commerce registration.

China's Financial and Economic Committee drafted a legislative outline on e-commerce. A completed draft of the bill was due at the end of 2015 and was to be submitted for deliberation at the 2016 NPC Standing Committee.

JD Finance

The 280 billion yuan IT industry has experienced a downturn in recent years. Laptops and cameras, the main categories, saw negative growth. Du Shuang, JD Group vice president and GM of the IT digital business division, was constantly searching for new opportunities. She saw great promise in smart devices. But she wanted to change the rules of the game.

Previously, in discussing partnerships, manufacturers would ask how JD planned to promote their newest products. Du told them she did not want to passively wait for manufacturers' product releases. She wanted to get ahead of the game.

Du launched an innovation acceleration plan and established creative new teams that consulted on JD Cloud for technology, raised money through crowdsourcing, orchestrated trial sales prior to massive production, and exploited the power of digital marketing.

Liu proposed a "ten-section sugar cane" theory for the consumer goods industry. The thought was to interconnect design, R&D, manufacturing, pricing, marketing, trading, warehousing, delivery and post-sales. The first five pieces belonged to brand sellers and the latter five to retailers.

The length of the section of sugar cane could be changed in the short term, but it was fixed over the long term. When there were too many brands in the market, competition became intense and profits shrank; the cane stalk became shorter. M&A activity and industry realignment usually took place in this context. For instance, at one time there were more than 40 viable companies in the Chinese e-commerce industry, but the number contracted to about a dozen.

"The ten-section sugar cane theory suggests that the first five sections are manufacturers' and the latter five belong to retailers," said Du Shuang. "My idea is to go deep in the five sections of the production and manufacturing chain to gather first-hand information. That will help ensure that my five sections are healthy and fresh. If you hold everything to yourself, you'll have no friends and many enemies. Everyone has his specialties. But I want to see what you have and what you're doing. It is not that I will drink the juice you've squeezed. But I want to know what fruit you used and whether the juice is fresh."

Du relied on JD's supply chain system as well as a variety of other services, including crowdfunding products provided by JD Finance.

Other changes were afoot. 2013 was JD's first year as a financial services provider. In October, the JD Finance Group was established. The former CFO of JD Group, Chen Shengqiang, was named its CEO.

At the end of 2013, Chen and Liu had talked in New York about the prospect of a finance business. "Doing that sort of business over the long term is very tiring," said Liu. "No one wants to do it. Second, don't try to have it all. If you can earn 100 yuan, just take 80. Leave the other 20 on the table." Chen also set forth his requirements. "If this fails, it will be my fault," he said. "But if we succeed, my core team must achieve financial freedom. That's an absolute prerequisite." Liu agreed.

JD Finance wanted to create an open, cross-category financial platform by leveraging JD's advantages in industry ecosystems and the supply chain. JD Financial's first proprietary offering went online in October 2013. Called Jingbaobei, it was a supply chain financing service that provided loans to suppliers. There was a predetermined repayment period after JD purchases from suppliers. The suppliers could raise the money in advance through Jingbaobei, to ensure cash flow, and pay it back when they settled accounts with JD. In 2014, JD supply chain finance provided small loans to POP sellers with a limit of 1 million yuan for a single shop, and 2 million yuan at most for a company with several locations.

Unlike with traditional banks, this financing process was conducted online and depended on data exploration. Yao Naisheng, vice president of strategic studies in the JD Finance Group, said there was no existing model for internet banking. Ten years ago, Chinese entrepreneurs could say they wanted to create the next Google, Amazon or eBay, but there was no point of reference for digital financing.

A post-80s recruit, Xu Ling became the head of the consumer finance business division of JD Finance. On 1 January 2014, JD Blank Note ran an internal test. After JD users filled in their name, employee ID number, credit card information and other details, the company made a risk rating based on the users' purchase record, delivery information, rejects information, shopping evaluation and other data. Each user was eligible for a line of credit, up to 15,000 yuan. As with standard credit card payments, they could choose to defer payment for 30 days after a purchase, or go on an installment plan for up to 24 months.

Some 150 employees from the 180-member R&D team were transferred to this project in November 2013. On 1 January 2014, the service began internal testing. Previously, JD had launched Xiao Jin Ku, similar to Alibaba's Yu'E Bao service, as a defensive offering. JD Blank Note represented an original, offensive move. It was the first of its kind.

The best point to extend to other industries from retail is payments, but JD Finance got a late start. In 2013, Yu'E Bao was an Alibaba success story that drew attention to JD's weakness in online payment. Liu was the first to admit that his neglect of the payment side of the business was a mistake. "The safest way is to pay on delivery or by swiping a card," he said. "For more than ten years we never had problems with cards or money stolen. Today, as we develop financial products, we find payment is particularly important to financing. There's no way to carry on without a reliable payment or account system. This will not kill us, but the main reason JD Finance is losing money is the payment system."

In October 2012, JD took over Chinabank Payment, founded in 2003. "JD payment is three years late," said JD Financial Group VP

Ding Xiaoqiang. "The team has to shoulder the heavy responsibility of catching up." Over the past year and a half, the Chinabank Payment team, a group of 100 or so people, introduced Xiao Jin Ku, JD Blank Note and internet Bank Wallet. It also undertook online payments for JD on "Double 11".

Money management represented a big opportunity for Chinabank Payment. Alipay had revealed its strategy too early, banks reacted negatively and customers were not adequately served. Now Alipay and WeChat were both vying for the prize. Chinabank Payment needed to find its own entry point.

JD launched its crowdfunding platform in July 2014. Although companies like Alibaba had introduced crowdfunding earlier, no one could match JD's control of the supply chain.

Crowdfunding advanced the supply chain. It linked designers, producers and users at the design stage, lowering communication costs for everyone. Let's say an entrepreneur wanted to make digital smart bracelets. He could post his design image on the crowdfunding platform. If a user liked it, he could invest 500 yuan to support the project and receive the product once it is produced. If it failed, the original 500 yuan would be returned to the user. JD's crowdfunding platform focused on smart hardware and related products, though not exclusively. Leveraging JD's extensive supply chain, the company's crowdfunding site went on to make a name for itself among entrepreneurs. JD was the undisputed choice for smart hardware crowdfunding.

On 20 March 2015, Liu and I exchanged ideas on this book for the last time. Just a few days earlier JD had introduced its O2O product, JD Door-to-Door Delivery. It introduced services like the delivery within a range of three kilometres of fresh food and supermarket products like fresh flowers and take-out meals. It provided quick deliveries by making use of mobile terminal positioning. The O2O business subsidiary JD Door-to-Door Delivery was also officially established on 31 March.

"Innovation can be divided into two categories," said Liu. "One is business model innovation, which is top-down, relying on the founder and the senior executives. Separately, bottom-up, grass-roots innovation looks at things like packaging quickly and safely while saving money. How do you stockpile more effectively to be more efficient? There are also problems concerning the delivery routes and much, much more. All these require that employees innovate from the bottom up. They can't count on me for such innovation. This bottom-up innovation is often driven by incentives. That inspires people to be creative. And these innovations are like the rain that moistens things silently. The top of the company may not even know about them."

As for business model innovation, Liu said he does not expect everyone in JD to have brilliant ideas. "I don't ask for quantity on business models," he said.

JD used to sell two kinds of goods: those stocked in its own warehouses and others from sellers' warehouses. From a larger societal perspective, most products were scattered across shops on countless streets and lanes. This represented a big opportunity for JD. Think of all those shops as warehouses, with JD cooperating with them to sell their merchandise. JD Door-to-Door Delivery was tested in March 2016 and formally launched at the end of April. It was, in fact, a global business model innovation.

Liu learned that business model innovation should not be promoted by senior management alone. In the past, JD Door-to-Door Delivery was ranked below JD Mall and hadn't really thrived. But this wasn't a business model problem. Whenever Liu asked what the problem was he received different explanations.

"Actually, it was my mistake," he said. "I should not have asked JD Mall to do it. It should have been handled by an independent team. JD Mall didn't have the motivation to do it, and the Mall develops new business so quickly. It identifies a business category, sets up cooperative agreements and drives 1 billion yuan in sales a year. Implementing a whole new business model generates cost, not profits."

With growth of 100-200%, JD Mall had no need to do something new and different. Besides, the JD Door-to-Door Delivery concept conflicted with the Mall's key objectives. So, on 1 January 2015, Liu decided to separate JD Door-to-Door Delivery from JD Mall.

Business model innovation needed hands-on care from senior management. Meetings of JD Door-to-Door Delivery meeting were held daily, for weeks and weeks. Liu personally dealt with matters relating to merchandise, purchasing and delivery. He even got involved in selecting specific on-screen images.

"If someone can implement a business model, start his own business and make it a success," Liu said, "why should he come to JD? Do you think the world is short of money? If you have a good existing model and effective execution, you can hire someone to create an innovative new business model. But it has to be validated. Will it help create value and profits, and deliver value to shareholders in the future? Until we can find a CEO to carry forward, this has to be managed by me."

———

The World's JD

———

On 17 January 2015, the JD Group's annual meeting was held in the gymnasium of Beijing University of Technology. The slogan projected on the screen was eye-catching: "The World's JD." Liu looked to be in high spirits, standing on the big stage in front of an audience of thousands.

He expressed pride in this company and said he hoped it one day would become an enterprise with sales revenues in the trillions, with 600,000 employees, the largest private enterprise in China and in the top 20 worldwide.

JD always had its ups and downs. Each year brought new crises and a new crop of rivals. It fought with internet companies, with traditional retailers and with itself. There were always new, seemingly insurmountable problems. It had not been a smooth ride.

What should an entrepreneur look like? What are the defining characteristics? For one thing he needs foresight, to see what others didn't. This does not come from simply earning an MBA. He has to be able to lead a team to victory and share the wealth. He needs the ability to learn.

In his autobiography, Sam Walton asked: "Will the legend of Wal-Mart be repeated in this age? My answer is, of course, yes. Perhaps right now someone is trying. If someone is very eager to pursue his dreams, although he will experience a lot of failures in the process, he should stick to it. Ability and attitude are very important, besides which, he has to continuously study and explore the secrets of business management."

In just two years, the company that was said to suffer from "capital chain rupture" went on to be ranked among world's top ten internet companies in terms of market value. But Liu wanted to go further. The Chinese market alone was not enough for JD. In 2011, with the help of Merrill Lynch, Liu went to Brazil and India to visit local e-commerce companies.

In 2012, JD made its first foray into overseas markets. Liu had been unsure which market was best for JD: the well-developed European and American markets, or the emerging Brazilian and Indian ones. The former had a mature business environment, but there were strong competitors. The latter were low-threshold markets, but the infrastructure was poor.

"The sales channel for Chinese goods to the rest of the world is quite smooth," said Liu. "Our government supports export rebates. Retail merchants sell goods abroad. But hardly any big companies are selling goods on a large scale. There are limited prospects in B2C, as it may impact local tariffs, employment and investments. The government will neglect it when the scale is small, but when the scale grows larger it will interfere. If we really want to sell Chinese goods overseas we have to build local warehouses and make appropriate investment plans."

Over time Liu has become more settled, peaceful and even-tempered. Nothing seems to make him react with extreme anger or overt joy. Even major company events don't seem to evoke much emotion. Just one thing remains unchanged: Liu's childhood dream of taking fleets of vessels across the ocean.

Liu still arrives at the office at 8:20 am and he attends morning meeting. He never goes to bed before 11 pm. With the help of We-Chat, his communication with executives has become increasingly informal. Through social media he can address business matters anywhere, at any time. He can get hundreds of work-related messages the moment he steps off a plane. He can handle them in order of importance in the car to the hotel.

American, European, Japanese and Korean companies operate all over the world. They bring wealth back to their home countries. But many Chinese enterprises only make money from Chinese customers, not foreigners. That effectively short-changes the home team. Liu admires Lenovo and Huawei, which extended their businesses worldwide. If more Chinese enterprises could go global, he figures, the Chinese economy will benefit.

In Liu's eyes, making money in China merely requires a capable company. He wants JD to be a great, world-class company that conducts business around the globe.

Nothing can stop a man with ambition, no matter how many mountains and rivers he has to cross.

Afterword and Acknowledgments

I hope my efforts over nearly a year present readers with an accurate understanding of the JD story. As Richard Liu told me: "You may write about the experiences and merits of JD, and you may also write about the company's stumbles and mistakes. But everything you write must be true."

I would like to express my extreme gratitude to Li Xi. Without her support this book would not have been possible. Thanks also to Kang Jian, JD's director of public relations, for arranging these many interviews. Thanks to Chen Mengying, a key management trainee, who played an important role in my five years of interaction with JD. I'd also like to thank Yan Yuelong, GuXiaoman, Ma Lianpeng, Chen Peipei, Zhang Lin, Li Wei, among many others, for their cooperation and support.

Qi Shanshan, a public relations management trainee, acted as overall liaison with JD for this book. From August of 2014 to March of 2015, Qi Shanshan and I visited many JD locations in Beijing, Chengdu, Wuhan, Suqian, Shanghai, Hangzhou, Guangzhou and Shenzhen. Qi Shanshan spent a lot of time on contacts, logistics and fact checking. Thanks to Miao Xiaohong, assistant to Richard Liu, who helped me arrange interviews with selected JD investors.

Thanks to JD Secretary Chen Yu for his assistance, as well as to Yang Haifeng, Zhang Ge and Zhang Benrong for their help.

I'm also grateful to staff from subsidiaries in the following regions for their collaboration in the interviews process: Southwest: Zhang Lan, Yang Tao and Li Zhen; Central China: Wang Jun, He Bing, Zhang Yali and Meng Debiao; East China: Mu Yuanqing and Deng Lunxuan; North China: Liu Dingling; South China: TangXiaomin, Mo Zhengchun and Liao Jintao; Suqian: Wu Jie, Sun Boqiu and Ding Dandan.

Li Zhigang
April 2015
Beijing

Selected internal speeches and memos by Richard Liu

"Glory and Dream
— Accelerating the 100 Billion (RMB) Target"

- 2012 keynote speech at JD's annual employee meeting

Several years ago I dreamed that someday I would rent out the Bird's Nest — Beijing's National Stadium — to hold one of our annual meetings. JDers have had many dreams over the years. And since many of these dreams have been realized in the past, this one also will come true sooner or later!

Just now, our six major regions gave detailed reports on last year's performance and outlined their expectations for 2012. Now I would like to make a few comments.

In 2011, we made history once again. Over the past year, we proved to the whole world with our actual performance that a company with a sales volume of more than 10 billion yuan can still grow rapidly. Back in 2004, we started from scratch and it took six years to reach the 10 billion threshold. Whether you look in China or anywhere else in the world, only one company among those starting from scratch surpassed us. That was Amazon. So in the past six years, in terms of speed, we were number two rather than number one. However, our slogan is: "To be only first, not second." I don't like being number two. Last year we reclaimed first place in speed of growth after hitting the 10 billion yuan mark. Thus we spent only one year — 2011— creating a record in the retail industry worldwide.

In the past year, we faced three major challenges. The first challenge was about our team. For the first time ever we recruited more than 15,000 new employees in a single year. The second challenge came from our competitors. 2011 was the craziest year yet for the e-commerce industry, because nearly every one of our competitors went all out and spent extravagantly, launching ad campaigns and price wars seemingly without regard to costs. Some of them even competed with us in the 3C markets, resulting in deep losses for the year. Their huge investments in advertising, however damaging to them, were good for the advertising industry. That industry was up about 40% as a result. The third challenge, as I mentioned earlier, was how to keep increasing our growth rate once our sales volume hit 10 billion yuan. This had never been achieved by any company before, much less a company having more than 15,000 new employees, and it was beyond our experience. Yet, we made it! Therefore, the past year is one we should be proud of. We have the reasons and the results here to bring the past year to a perfect end.

Every year I spend a whole day reflecting on what regrets I have, for myself and for the company, during the past year. Looking at 2011, my greatest regret is that I failed to fulfill a promise to our delivery brothers. At the 2010 annual meeting, I promised more than 100 deliverymen that I would treat all of them in the eleven delivery stations to dinner so that I could chat with them. I tried to fulfill this promise, but was able to go to only seven of the delivery stations. I feel very sorry that I didn't honour my promise. So today I hope all our deliverymen will accept my apology: To you, I say I'm really sorry. I'm willing to make up my unfulfilled promise with practical action. In 2012, I will invite the deliverymen from the four other stations to dinner, and our company will allocate four million yuan as relief fund for our deliverymen to help those injured during work or who may suffer family misfortune or great difficulties.

Someone may ask, you call the deliverymen brothers, but where are the sisters? Today let us make it a rule that everyone in JD should call each other brother. I know that female employees in JD are even more capable than their male counterparts, but when I say brothers, I mean all the JDers.

Our sales target for 2012 is to exceed 60 billion yuan. It's our dream and will be our glory to move towards the target of 100 billion. It doesn't mean we have to reach it this year, but this year will be the year that determines when we will reach this target and when JD will become the largest retail enterprise in China. Therefore, in the future we will not just compete in measurements such as online, offline or self-support platforms, etc., but rather on revenue. Our goal is to be the largest retail enterprise in terms of sales revenue in

China. "To be only the first" is in the blood that flows through the veins of every JDer. So how do we reach this target?

I hope there is always only one answer: to rely on our team. And there will never be a different answer. In 2012, for JD, one of our most significant strategies is training. The company's strategies won't be realized without a proper training system.

Someone may say: just recruit and poach new talent! But I assume all the senior employees in JD should know that this is not our way. Some may think that poaching costs less, because the experienced employees can hit the ground running. Why do we insist on so much training, some ask? Why do we spend so much money, time and energy on it? And even those who complete the training may not be able meet the requirements of the company. We have to allow them to try and make mistakes during the training; otherwise they will never improve. Hence cultivating and training personnel is the most time-consuming and the most costly choice, but it is also the only choice to ensure continued success of the company.

There is no doubt that we will be joined by more new colleagues in 2012. And bringing in 15,000 employees doesn't mean we will develop 1,500 new managers. This is unrealistic. But we have been making efforts to make sure 60%–70% of the managers are developed internally rather than introduced from outside. In 2012, I hope to send all our colleagues at director level or above to the top domestic universities in groups to take MBA courses. In addition to the tuition fees, we will also grant 20,000 to 30,000 yuan to each to cover other university fees. There will be no conditions imposed upon those who go for training, and those who might leave the company after taking these courses, or even during the courses, will not be required to repay the funds expended on their behalf.

Someone may say: isn't it silly? Are you paying to cultivate talents for others? This is not silly! Aren't we always talking about being grateful? Being grateful is not only about good pay, benefits and shares, we also hope our colleagues can raise their personal career, occupational abilities, insight, vision, knowledge and competence to a higher level after several years' work in JD. What's the big deal if they leave? They have been working for the company for many years and have made great contribution to the company. If they choose to leave, their training can be regarded as a gift, a recognition of the hard work and contributions they made to JD. We also have training classes for the managerial staff at lower levels. In 2011 we offered two sessions, which worked very well according to follow-up surveys. So this year we will continue to offer such training classes, and we will offer off-job training to managerial staff for at least 100 days. Those completing the training don't have to return to their original positions, they are eligible to seek new ones in the same or other departments. We hope to develop them to be at least middle-level managerial staff through two or three years' training.

In 2012, for our delivery system we also have a "ten / hundred / thousand project", which means that we intend to develop ten staff at the director level who can manage a larger area and at least 10,000 deliverymen; cultivate hundreds of city managers to coordinate the delivery stations within the city; and train more than one thousand new delivery station leaders.

Fortunately, after dedicating significant resources in 2011, we have successfully trained many deliverymen to become delivery station heads. Not only did they receive higher salaries, they also learned new skills and became more competent and productive. We are a company with a large body of grass-root labour forces. Without a training system, a deliveryman will still be in the same position after five years and this would be the management team's fault. Today we have to admit that we are not able to raise every employee's income, but we have the ability, responsibility and duty to train them and provide them with such opportunities. Accordingly, we will work out a detailed training system for each business unit from 2012 and will continue doing so.

But real training comes from more than formal programs. It comes from our daily work. A truly cultured company and a truly excellent training system should provide training to employees every day. Have the delivery station heads advised our deliverymen to be careful and put on skid-proof shoes? Have they reminded our brothers to take their raincoats with them? Have they taught the deliverymen how to answer questions that our customers ask them? If the answer is no, it means they have failed to live up to these basic responsibilities as a JD manager.

Therefore, in order to ensure our entire group receives the right level of training, we will set an unalterable target for each of our managerial staff: if you want to get promoted, you have to tell me who you have trained, and who will succeed your post if you move on. Those who can't answer these questions appropriately will lose the opportunity for promotion. This may sound harsh, but you should remember that as our team grows ever larger, without such a training system we will fail and our youth and perspiration of one, two and even ten years dedicated to the company will go down the drain. So everyone, middle-level managers in particular, think carefully: who will you cultivate?

The year 2012 will be crucial. The world will give us another opportunity to make history. Reaching a sales volume of 100 billion yuan is a key goal for our domestic business. Someone asked, "If we do domestic business only, as long as we work hard, we will undoubtedly be number one and earn lots of money. Then why do we pursue international business?" Whether or not we pursue international business, our entire company will be fine for the next ten years. But without becoming more international, we will certainly face great challenge beyond those ten years.

Don't forget that globally we have our largest competitor — Amazon. If one day Amazon is profitable worldwide everywhere except China, where we are its largest competitor, Amazon will concentrate its global power to beat its last "enemy" here. And if China is our only market and someone else prevails, we will lose. That's why internationalization is decisive to our future, and could determine whether JD will win glory or suffer disgrace in ten years.

JD's achievements that we see today come from the hard work and perspiration of every JDer. Maybe after ten years I will have retired. But this doesn't mean I will no longer pay attention to the company. I will absolutely not allow the company to fail just because the management lacked strategic insight. Taking these into full consideration, I decide that we must pursue international business and do it well. Though we haven't shown profits on large-scale international business as yet, we must do our utmost to cultivate our own international talents from now on. This also manifests our principle of viewing our employees as more valuable than the company. Because I believe as long as we have the best and most motivated team, no matter which country we enter, we will achieve success.

In addition to the hard work of all JDers, JD's rapid development to today's scale owes much to great support from the entire society and to having the good fortune to be part of the development trend of the times. Now we have already become a company that influences the entire society, and our every word and action will draw intense scrutiny from many quarters. Yet we can still be motivated, confident and passionate, and keep a fervent heart and the strong belief in "being only the first". In the meantime, we must also be modest, low-key and prudent, so that JD will enjoy a more stable and safer development for a longer term. This is not only the responsibility of every one of our managers, but also the responsibility of each and every JDer.

JD's Strategies and Values
- Richard Liu lecture at JD's first Director Workshop in 2012.

Two years ago, when we discussed a goal of hundreds of billions in revenue, it was just a dream. But now that goal is no longer a dream. Based on our performance so far this year, our entire platform sales next year are set to exceed hundreds of billions in GMV (Gross Merchandise Volume). Our company has been running about wildly for nine years. So we have determined that our core priorities for next year should be, "Repair, Raise, Revive and Rest".

"Repair", as in to fix and adjust. Many problems during our last eight or nine years arose because of our rapid development. These problems need to be fixed by examining the systems, the processes and the roots. "Raise", meaning to cultivate and develop. For the businesses that are small today but very important for the future, we will devote more concentrated effort. "Revive", to create and bring new life. We will enter into new areas and new businesses and create new models. "Rest", to stop and review. We might have made some mistakes or entered into the wrong areas. We must take decisive actions to suspend or entirely give up some businesses.

I. JD's Strategic Management Model

For the JD company, strategy is not empty talk or a slogan. Our strategy tells us what to do, how to do it, where to go and what is most important.

1. Basic Level – Team

The success of a company is the result of many factors, but the most important and most crucial element is always the team. Motorola, once the overlord of mobile phones, was acquired by Google and is suffering through mass layoffs and cutbacks globally. Products from the Japanese brand, Sony, used to represent "high-grade, precision and advanced". Every new model released by Apple seems to be snapped up by immediately by avid customers….Why? The hidden factor is the team.

The success or failure of the future of JD has nothing to do with our competitors, the media or investors. It is the team that matters. If the company succeeds, 99% of the credit goes to our team. I take 1%. If the company fails, 99% of the responsibility is on me and the team, only 1%. We send the executives to earn MBAs, recruit management trainees, train new managers, launch the "ten / hundred / thousand" delivery project, develop our "Great Wall" customer service plan and so on, all because "team" comes first.

2. Supply Chain – Information System, Logistics System, Financial System

After building an excellent team, we'll continue investing in the three critical systems for our supply chain, specifically: information, logistics and finance. I will explain each of these three key areas.

First, information. The information system is a line that links the huge businesses, numerous suppliers and the 311 cities across the country where we have teams. This is vital. What I feel proud of is that today in our system, we can still find all the data going back to when we started the company: Our first transactions, first wage statements, first customer etc. While other sellers in Zhongguancun still operated manually, we were already using scanning guns that we had bought at high prices and we were recording serial numbers and customer and transaction information.We also developed our own employee payroll system. Despite being ridiculed, we stuck to it. As it turns out, apart from our most excellent team, JD's success is inseparable from our attention to the information system.

Second, logistics. In 2007, after we received our first VC investment, we said we wanted to use the funds to build out logistics. It felt to me like the entire world laughed at us for this. Today, our delivery teams are in 311 cities, and will be in 360 cities by the end of the year. Some said JD's delivery represented excessive service, saddled with excessive costs. But now Amazon is copying our model in the US. In the e-commerce field around the globe, we are the first company to provide same day delivery. More and more e-commerce companies began to see that the logistics system is a major constraint of the e-commerce industry. Our same-day and next-day service has set an industry benchmark.

The third key component is our finance system. We think of JD as a supply chain service company. And the exchange between cash flow, material flow and information flow in the supply chain is the most important, because their quick exchange is the root for us to gain profit. Thus retail companies in the world also attach great importance to the financial system.Cash flow can be far more important than profits. With positive cash flow, the company is less likely to collapse; if the company has net profit, but it does not maintain the cash flow, then the money will run out, and the capital chain will rupture sooner or later.

3. Key KPI – Cost and Efficiency

What are our core assessment indicators? We have only two. The first is cost, and the second is efficiency. Every year, we make horizontal comparison with others and vertical comparison with ourselves. The purpose is to see whether each of our systems operates at minimum cost and highest efficiency.

For example, we are very excited about the trend in logistics cost. The cost of our entire supply chain logistics has dropped by almost half over four years but is still not yet optimal. We must continue to build our "Asia No.1" project and strive to bring the 13 warehouses in Beijing together to improve our order processing and work efficiency.

In addition, our IT system and financial system also must address the challenges of cost and efficiency. We need to achieve the lowest cost and highest efficiency of the three core systems of the company and become the world's leading experts on retail supply chain management.

4. Brand – Product, Price, and Service

We believe that the vast majority of customers are most concerned about three things: product, price and service.

Regarding product, we mean two things: first, availability. With the constant efforts of our direct sales and marketplace businesses, we aim to facilitate all the daily necessities to meet customer demand. Second is product quality. We are committed to selling only authentic goods, quality goods. That means no fakes, no smuggled goods or refurbished goods.

For price, that means offering consumers low price. Through eight years of hard work, we have successfully established a reputation of consistently offering low prices. This must be cultivated and maintained through cost and efficiency control.

For service, we are referring to the pre-sale, sale, and after-sale experiences. We have pre-sale advantages, because below each item on our platform we feature many consumer reviews and photos. Even consumers who do not shop on JD will visit our site to browse these reviews. The advantage we offer is the logistics system, same- or next-day delivery guarantee, and so on. In contrast, our after-sales does not have as many advantages. That is why we need to build out our Customer Service Center to concentrate all the after-sales services in one place. We must do it for our customers.

We are constantly trying to innovate on services. In the past, we competed for the customers who shopped in large malls and chain stores, but now we also want to win over the customers in community convenience stores. If we can succeed here, then we can have a huge and positive impact on the daily life of the common people. We believe there will be innovations on other services as well.

5. Users – Customer Experience

Users are at the very top of our list of priorities. That is, our highest concern is for the customer experience. Everything will be very simple if we only pursue the customer experience.

We can stock all the goods in a warehouse and have everything ready; we can employ the best express delivery system and guarantee 24 hour delivery; we can offer returns on any rejected products. These services are good, but no enterprise can survive doing only this.

Cost and efficiency have supported the user experience in JD and these are supported by our three systems, and these in turn are supported by our team. So, this is an inverted triangle, from the perspective of system development. From the bottom up, it starts from team – system establishment – efficiency assessment – user experience. And from the top down, the visible one on the top is the customer, but the three layers below it are invisible. So it is the invisible that support the visible.

6. With Regard to Profit

We strive to ensure each of our categories operates with the lowest expense ratio in the industry so as to significantly reduce the supply chain costs. This is our power and is the core that powers future earnings. It's not the pursuit of profits, but the pursuit of low costs and operational efficiency that will remain our focus and determine our success. The profits will follow naturally in the process. We have a basic business belief: as long as we can control the cost and develop the efficiency to the best of our ability, as long as our customers are satisfied, then we'll continuously be able to acquire new users, and our business will continue to develop rapidly. Sooner or later, we will get the margins we deserve, higher than in traditional chain channels, because we create more and bigger value for the society, the users, and the supply chain.

So JD's strategy is not a fantasy. Each of our strategies is down-to-earth and closely related to every one of us. It is the goal and direction of our daily routine work, efforts and endeavors.

II. JD's Core Values

From the JD strategic management model, we see that team is the root cause of the success or failure of any company or institution. The two most important aspects of a team are culture and capacity.

In JD, we value culture more than ability. If a person is very capable, but is culturally incompatible with our culture, then he is like "rust", and needs to be eradicated right away. A person of strong competency but different values can be more damaging than one who shares the company values but is less competent.

Culture contains three aspects: goal, vision, and values. Values is the innermost core, and a most important aspect of the culture. We can always adjust our goals and vision. But regarding our cultural unity, with the constant expansion of our team, it is faced with a growing challenge.

Values determines behaviour. Our words and deeds in daily life derive from our values. What do I mean? I think values is an attitude of a person towards others, to himself and the environment. That is, the way you see others, yourself and the environment.

Environment can include the interpersonal environment, natural environment, the environment between humans and animals. Attitude can be very individual. People with different values may have very different perceptions and come to different conclusions about the same thing. For instance, two alcoholics suddenly encounter a bottle of the world's best liquor, but only half remains in the bottle. One might become very angry, thinking, why do we have only half a bottle of such good stuff? The other may think, how lucky I am to have half a bottle of this very special drink.

How can we guarantee a large team to be aligned in their goals, direction and execution so as to maximize our cost and efficiency? The company's disciplines, rules, regulations and processes are only part of the answer, accounting for only 10% at most. The bulk of it, the other 90%, is our enterprise culture. Many employees choose to stay in JD even after receiving offers of more pay and better packages. I think it is our team culture and our values that they identify with and want to remain a part of. They believe a team with such values will have a real future and they are willing to sacrifice some short term benefits to remain a part of it. Our values can actually be summed up with one sentence: Take the right path, be a good person and create a better life with our own wisdom and sweat! Many older employees remain with us today because they feel that they've made the right choice.

1. Integrity

It is nearly impossible to change a person's values. Many of our managers have made the mistake in the past of believing that one's values could be changed. For instance, a certain colleague shares different values with us, but he is very capable, very young, and full of potential and loves learning. The manager believes that in time, or with continuous education, he will change. But this rarely happens. It is very unlikely for one to alter his fundamental values after reaching adulthood, unless he encounters some major stimulus, such as a domestic calamity or major disaster, that makes him suddenly change his world view. If he has not experienced anything like that, normal education, talking and training won't fundamentally alter his core values. Even if he does appear changed, it is most likely a facade. His values, deep-rooted inside him, still contradict ours.

So we have always placed integrity above all. Integrity is not empty talk, but concrete action. During our start-up period, our company sold CDs in Zhongguancun. All the other vendors there sold fakes except JD. Later we became China's largest optical-magnetic products agent, having 60% of the Chinese market at the time. Selling fakes could have brought us higher profits, but we insisted on selling authentic goods. As a small company with annual sales of tens of millions of yuan, all of our products were sold with proper customs declarations and VAT invoices. The best test for integrity is whether, when one is faced with temptation or shortcuts, he can stick to his chosen path.

Integrity is not something to give lip-service to, not a slogan on the wall for decoration, not the words written in the employee handbook, but something to be implemented in the practice of the company and conducts of each individual.

2. Customer First

When we say customer first, we mean we focus on the complete customer experience. I can say we've done a pretty good job on customer experience, but there is still a long way to go to meet our own goals. Some of our individual members in some individual matters still subvert the "customer first" values by emphasizing a short-term financial objective over the customer experience. For instance, when we introduced JD gift cards, customers could neither pay for them with cash on delivery nor pick them up at our self-service collection stations. These restrictive measures were meant to protect the company from losses but they did not facilitate the customer experience. This is misguided, because we cannot put our financial interests above the interests of customers.

It is easy to say something, but to do it for decades with perseverance and consistency is much more difficult. We need to discuss whether a decision we have made is in violation of our values, in violation of our "customer first" ethos. If yes, then the decision will be invalid and we have to think of other solutions. We shall never lower the user experience for the sake of financial security and information security.

3. Passion

Passion is the greatest attitude towards life. A man without passion is like a zombie, a sad individual who doesn't know why he lives and why he dies, or where he is from and where he will go. A man with passion has a kind of wealth and experience, whether or not his is considered successful.

No one can guarantee his entrepreneurship will be 100% successful. But one should not stop trying for fear of failure. All successful people are passionate, even if they appear really quiet and reserved. But if a person has passion and strong faith, he can tolerate setbacks and difficulties and he'll never give up the pursuit of life.

I went through my toughest time soon after my college graduation, with a debt of 240,000 yuan. To many people, I was doomed for life. How could one pay such a debt at my age? On my birthday at that time, I just ate instant noodles and a pickle. On Chinese New Year's Eve, I had only porridge. Still, I never felt miserable. I never complained about life. I believed one day I would make a comeback. In no circumstance should we complain about everything and about ourselves; in no circumstance should we give up on ourselves, give up on others, including our families, our colleagues and our children. Love them, care for them and be tolerant to them. At the same time, love ourselves, care for ourselves and build self-confidence. You should firmly believe that you have wisdom, brains and hands and that you have qualifications and opportunities. With your arduous work, sooner or later you will lead a happy life. The most terrible thing is that one day you stop thinking, stop trying, stop sweating.....

Passion is also faith. Without faith, it is impossible to have passion. The world's great statesmen and artists and so on are all full of passion. Some of them were jailed, some faced threats and intimidation and the possibility of death. Did they give up? Why did they carry on? Because they had faith. Without passion, one would long have been a zombie. Without faith, it would be impossible to survive the struggle of decades.

4. Learning

Wisdom is not innate but learned. In no circumstance should we forget to learn. We should not look down on our subordinates, on others. Everybody has something we can learn from. In the process of learning, maybe you've spent a lot of time reading a book and later remembered only one sentence. But if that one sentence, or one interaction, affects your whole life, then it is worthwhile.

Progress is also made through learning. If I had had to manage 26,000 employees six years ago, I could never have succeeded. But how did I acquire the management ability now? Through learning. As long as I keep learning, I believe that one day I will be able to manage 100,000 employees, or perhaps 1 million employees.

5. Team Spirit

Just as many companies around the world advocate "team spirit", we also advocate "team spirit" in JD. What is team spirit? In essence, it is to sacrifice yourself to adapt to others.

Complaining is the largest natural enemy of a team. I hope you can keep these two points in mind:

First, don't expect a self-centred person to have team spirit. When a problem occurs, he blames anyone but himself – the boss is an idiot, the colleagues not cooperative, etc. How can he be an effective, contributing, team member? Second, don't expect the one who always complains to have team spirit. Some people spend 90% of their time complaining, and only 10% of their time working. They have no team spirit and must be removed.

6. Eliminating Waste

Eliminating waste lowers costs. But we can't reduce costs by sacrificing proper treatment of our employees. We can reduce costs by improving efficiency and eliminating waste. We've talked much about improving efficiency. How shall we eliminate waste then?

Take a look at the expense approval forms I am signing every day. Almost all of them are for purchasing cars, storage racks and other goods and equipment. But if we conduct a detailed analysis and strict examination, we will find there is a lot of waste. Some is the waste of money and some is time. The waste of time is the biggest problem.

Why is Wal-Mart so successful? It has zero tolerance for waste. Next year we aim to "Repair, Raise, Revive and Rest". We will address the waste problem too. If we can truly eliminate waste, we can at least reduce the cost by one point, and that means a billion yuan saved. Waste is our natural enemy. If we do not eliminate waste, the company will go nowhere.

Success is never easy. Our life in this world is short, several decades maybe. But if we don't pursue success, what is the meaning of our life then? Today, history has given JD and each of us a huge opportunity, an opportunity that would not have been possible 10 years earlier, and that is not likely to exist in the same way in the future. It is a great opportunity now for us to achieve our dreams. If we lose this opportunity, it will mean a lifetime of regret for every one of us.

I hope we can seize the historic opportunity, work hard to realize our dreams. When the day comes, I believe what we harvest is not only the success of the company; it means that our families and our parents will be very proud and content and will lead a better and happier life as well!

Constantly Transcending and Challenging Ourselves
-January 1, 2013 keynote speech at JD's annual employee meeting

Dear colleagues and friends, Happy New Year to you all!

2012 is gone. I'd like to report briefly on our achievements last year. As of December 31, 2012, JD's GMV exceeded 60 billion yuan. Based on our strategic plan for 2013, our GMV is sure to exceed 100 billion! Also, I believe, by the fourth quarter of 2013, we will be able to realize profits in the real sense.

JD's History is the History of Continuously Excelling "Giants"

This decade of our history is a period of continuously vanquishing "giants". In 1998, when I started the business in Zhongguancun, I had only one counter. After almost three months, I had my first helping hand. At that time, the company was called JD Multimedia. Beginning on June 18, 1998, we faced "giants" like Huitian Huaguang and others in the magneto-optical storage industry. These "giants" reported turnover of at least tens of millions a year. We had only one counter and just 12,000 yuan in hand and no other resources. But three years later, in 2001, we became China's largest magneto-optical agent and had captured 60% of disc burner sales across the country.

Also in 2001, we began to think about what direction the company should take in the future. We decided to quit the wholesale business and to open retail stores, to expand the channels and to face the customers ourselves. There we saw "giants" like Gome, Sunning and Hisap ahead of us.

In 2003, we stumbled into the e-commerce field due to SARS. In 2004, JD Mall was officially launched online, offering only IT products. We were faced with the "giant" Newegg in Shanghai. Newegg's global GMV was $1.2 billion at that time, and its annual net profit was $20 million. It had the world's best information system. On the other hand, we had almost nothing, except people – JDers.Still, by the year 2008, we succeeded in surpassing Newegg.

In 2007, we began to enter the direct sales B2C e-commerce industry. The two "giants" before us were Dangdang and Joyo. Most internet users knew Dangdang and Joyo. Very few knew JD. It sounded like chasing a rainbow then to say JD would excel Dangdang and Joyo. But by the year 2012, we not only exceeded all independent e-commerce companies in the industry, but also captured half of the direct sales B2C market nationwide.

Certainly, we are still facing "giants" now. We have to admit that Taobao is doing better than we are. But JD has never hesitated to stand up to the industry giants. Actually we are challenging ourselves every day, challenging ourselves to constantly refresh ourselves and set new records. Our growth process has had us overtake one competitor after another to arrive to where we are today. So what is our strategy in 2013?

2013 Strategy – "Repair, Raise, Revive and Rest"

JD's strategic theme in 2013 is "Repair, Raise, Revive and Rest". "Repair, Raise, Revive and Rest" is not rehabilitation, it doesn't mean we will stop. It does not mean that our sales growth will slow. I will explain what I mean about "Repair, Raise, Revive and Rest".

"Repair" acknowledges that in the past nine years, our average growth rate is above 200%. At such a high rate of growth, it is inevitable for us to face internal problems in our systems and processes that have been stretched by our growth. By "repair", we mean we will fix any problems accumulated over the past 10 years. It is necessary so as to lay a solid foundation for the growth of our second decade. This solution has to be one time, thorough, and it can't leave any flaws for the future development. This is the so-called "repair".

The so-called "raise" is to make ongoing investments to JD's strategic businesses, to nourish their growth. Of course, all of JD will be centered around our main business of e-commerce. We will not stray from this core path and undertake activities irrelevant to e-commerce. We may continue to lose in some of these strategic businesses. It is not that we cannot earn profits, it's that we're not willing to lose sight of future investment and long term gains just for the sake of some immediate objective. So we have reasons, qualifications, and capabilities to make sustainable strategic investments to these businesses.

"Revive" means to stop and think whether, after more than 10 years of development, there are any businesses we haven't done and any fields that we haven't entered? We need to expand unceasingly. Needless to say, all our businesses will support our core, which is e-commerce. We need to continue to expand on the value chain and supply chain services of e-commerce. In the fields of data and finance, for example, we'll generate a lot of new business. For all the e-commerce businesses representing the future direction, we are to build up one after another in the year 2013.

The "rest" element refers to the reality that as we examine our existing business modules, we may find that some have no future. No matter whether these businesses are making or losing money now, if they don't have a future, we will have to end them dispassionately. We shall not waste resources, energy, and time on such businesses.

Since launching online in 2004 to today, JD has experienced its first 10 years. Now, we are about to usher in the second decade. How shall we advance in the next decade? What is our aim? Where is our direction? How shall we achieve transcendence again? These are the important topics today.

Three Directions for the Next Decade: Direct Sales E-Commerce, Open Services, and Data Financing

After 2013, we will enter the second 10 years of JD Mall. We will focus on the following three directions for the development of JD in the next decade.

First direction: Technology-driven direct sales e-commerce business. We will continue to adhere to the direct sales e-commerce business, which in essence is the technology-driven supply chain service. Our model is completely different from Taobao. We not only provide information, but also provide supply chain service. Our supply chain service is to bring products from the factory gate to the consumer's door. Therefore, we must continue to invest in technology and logistics. As we want to provide supply chain service, we have to build our modern warehousing system, "Asia No.1", in all regions. In the future, we will achieve large-scale, mass SKU, low cost and high efficiency in supply chain service, and continuously create value for our consumers and brand owners.

Second direction: Technology-driven open service business. With the completion and operation of "Asia No.1", we have enough capabilities to offer our warehousing and delivery services to a large number of third party sellers. By 2015, 20% core sellers on our marketplace platform will represent 80% of our overall sales. And the vast majority of the sellers will use JD warehousing service. The service price we offer will be far below the fees of warehouses rented by the sellers or the third-party delivery services they find. By that time, the consumer experience using our marketplace can fully match what they find today on our direct sales platform. We will also offer other services, such as after-sales, call center, data and payment and so on, all of which will be known as JD's open service businesses.

Third direction: Technology-driven data financing business. In 2012, we bought Chinabank Payment. But payment is only a small part of our financial services businesses. The acquisition of

Chinabank Payment isn't just to run an online payment company. In 2014, we will be setting up a financial company within JD to offer a variety of financial products. JD has the access to the most real, the most effective order transaction information. JD has no false turnover, no false transactions, no money laundering, no fakes, and no smuggled goods. Therefore, our consumer data are also the consumption data of the highest quality in China. With these data, we can not only provide loans for sellers, but also provide consumers with personal loans.

So, in the second decade, we will surpass the concept of doing only e-commerce as we did in the first decade. All of the three new business directions are technology-driven and all will bring huge profits. As I have said, a loss-making enterprise is shameful. But if a company is too eager to make money and dares not to invest, and it has no ambitions, no dreams, then it is an ignorant, pathetic and stupid company.

The Assessment Objective for the Second Decade: Human-Oriented

In the second decade of JD, I have only one personal objective: to care for people, for JDers.

I view JD as a family. In the second 10 years, I hope to see more JD babies born. I hope our JD babies can grow up happily and enjoy a good education.

In the second 10 years, I hope to see the quality of life improve for the parents of JDers. Most of our employees are from the countryside. I, too, come from the countryside and I know that many of our parents have not had an easy time. They have been busy and have worked hard all their lives. Even so, too many parents back home still don't enjoy a peaceful life. In the next 10 years, I hope to see JDers' parents healthier, enjoying more love and living a better life.

In the second 10 years, I hope to see improved job satisfaction for JDers. In the new decade, I hope to see JD's culture being passed down, deepening and maturing. Within 10 years, I'm sure our numbers will far exceed 150,000, and we will be present in more than

1,000 cities throughout China. We'll be able to find our colleagues everywhere. In the new decade, our employees' satisfaction and happiness will be my important evaluation indicators. I believe that when employees are satisfied, JD will be able to provide the best user experience.

With you by my side, we've achieved our success for the first 10 years. With you by my side, I believe we will usher in the glory of the next ten years!

A letter From Richard Liu to Management Trainees

Dear Management Trainees,

It's such a pity that I haven't communicated with you for a long time. After being away from university for 17 years, I once again find myself in school as a full-time student. I feel excited and in a state of constant motion. On the busiest day, I have to get up at 5:00 a.m., leave home at 6, then preview lessons and attend classes. There is one hour for lunch and then classes continue through 6 pm, when I drive home. It seems that I only got up so early when I was at primary school. And the daily assignments also take several hours to finish...

I know that all of you, the Management Trainees of the 7th session, study harder than I do. You have more expectations, surprises, as well as confusion and frustration! I've read all of your weekly reports via e-mail. You've done a very good job, as have the previous Management Trainee groups. You have all begun your job rotations with enthusiasm and intellectual engagement. I have two requirements for you:

1. Job rotation is designed to teach you, for you to learn our internal processes. When you go to different departments, you are not

there to find faults. You can learn and develop your consideration, thinking and ideas for improvement. But you are also to fight together with your colleagues in the departments. You are one of them during the job rotation! You are no more special than the others! I've read a very good retrospection from a Management Trainee: It is impossible to learn anything at all if you hold the mentality of finding faults rather than learning, if you hold yourself above the colleagues in your area. This is useless and worthless! I can tell you: it is the easiest thing to find problems in work. An illiterate person can quickly find many problems in a warehouse. What you've seen won't give you better insights than his! The real key is how to rectify the problems, how to systematically solve the problems, how to lead a team to tackle the problems.

With the mind-set of finding faults rather than learning, you can't be modest enough and will lose the most valuable learning opportunities. I hope you can always remember: In every department you go to, even the lowest-level worker with the shortest service experience is your teacher, has something to teach you and deserves your respect!

2. Though you spend a very short time during job rotation in different departments, I hope you are not skimming the surface. And moreover, you can't hold the attitude that "I will never work in this department, I am here as mere formality!" I hope in each department you are assigned, you are a contributing member of a team that has the best fighting spirit and works hardest. Since the JD Management Trainee system was established, the members of the second session turned out to have had the most rigorous experience so far. (There were only two Management Trainees in the first session, because the company at the time lacked a formal training process.) When the Management Trainees of the second session reported for duty in the warehouse, what they heard from the manager was: Go and do the job now! The year-end sales promotions fell in November and December, and each day during that period the warehouses became overloaded, so the trainees had to help out. They had to work from 7 or 8 in the morning till 10 or 11 at night

for many days in a row. There was no head teacher. No one arranged their living quarters, their transportation or even food. Their session enjoyed the least oversight and care, yet they are the most successful, most outstanding class today. I asked two Management Trainees from that session, Yu Rui and Li Yang to take the lead and talk about the situation then to the trainees of your group, the seventh session.

When I came out of the Renmin University of China, I kept on reminding myself: My capital is my youth and my hard work. Other than that, I have nothing. Today, my youth is gone. So I have only one asset left: to work hard and go all out!

Most JDers don't have the same family background. But we share common values. We all think that only by going all out and doing the right thing can we find the way forward. This is our core value.

Today, think of all of you as lucky dogs, because you get a chance to win if you fight hard! You are given a chance to learn by the side of the delivery staff who pack and deliver night and day. I hope you can learn and struggle with gratefulness and modesty.

I hope you can succeed in learning and return early to add your unique contributions to the team!

Yours,
Richard

From "Big" to "Great"

- Richard Liu speech at annual JD employee meeting on January 11, 2014

Hello, everybody!

The year 2013 just gone was significant. It marked the end of JD's first 10 years. There is only one word to describe this decade, and it is "amazing"! Back in 2004, we were nothing. We knew nothing about e-commerce. But 10 years later, we continued to excel and achieved one after another milestone.

Is our turnover of 100 billion yuan something for us to be proud of? No!

One of our first milestones was to dominate the "IT Digital" business. In 2004, when we developed the IT digital business, we set Newegg as the target to beat. They had teams, technology, suppliers … everything. We had nothing except the spirit. We started from zero. After four years, we surpassed Newegg. But even though we gained a little reputation in IT digital after beating them, still we were very small compared with others. In 2007, I remember one of our first investors said to me: "By 2012, if you are able to do 1 billion yuan, we will be more than happy."

The second tipping point came in 2010, when we exceeded Dangdang and Joyo, a previously unthinkable accomplishment. The third major milestone will come in the near future. JD is to become China's largest retailer!

Today when we look back, we may think our achievements are nothing to be proud of. But in those days, they were truly amazing. We've completed one after another mission impossible. We had been under allied "encirclement and suppression". We not only survived, but we eventually exceeded them.

Was our signature achievement for the first 10 years merely the 100 billion yuan turnover? Is this really something for us to be proud of? No! In our first 10 years, the thing we really take pride in is our unique business structure! In the market, we haven't found who has the ability or qualifications to surpass, short- or long-term. This is because in the first 10 years we did a lot of stupid, crazy, tiring, difficult and heavy work that was ridiculed by countless people. We did the things others failed to appreciate or were not interested in doing. When they realized our path was the successful one and they also wanted to follow, they found they simply could not reach our height.

The first decade should definitely be the pride of each and every JDer. We have done so many amazing things. But as usual, we never indulge in the joys of the past. JD's dreams are far more than this. We're not satisfied, because we firmly believe that we have a great strategy, a more ambitious goal. We can do better. Working hard and constantly seeking improvements are deep rooted in JDers' bones and blood. This is the characteristic that has driven JD's development from a little-known small counter to a leading retail business in China.

What is Our Tactic to Win?

At the beginning of the second 10 years, I still want you to review and understand your company's strategy. Each and every manager and employee, including deliverymen and everyone else, must be clear about our strategic direction and know what we rely on to win. The core of our strategy for the first decade remains unchanged and it will not change in the second decade. That is the "inverted triangle" strategy. What did we rely on for the success in the first 10 years? The innermost core is us, the JD team. Team is our most valuable asset for our success, the reason behind our constant growth. The thing we are most proud of in the first decade is that we have built an excellent team. This is the cornerstone of JD's development. The primary task, especially mine, in the second decade, is still to focus on the team.

Underlying and supporting the team are our financial system, logistics system and technical system. Some say JD is "speedy". Being "speedy" is one of JD's core competencies. But if we ignore cost, "being speedy" can become a burden. JD's real core competitiveness is to be able to achieve good service quality and low cost simultaneously.

So for these three systems, our core assessment is cost and efficiency. The cost of each system must be lower than the industry average. Our operation efficiency must become the industry's highest operation efficiency.

Customers do not pay attention to these, of course. What do customers want? Very simple. Three elements: product, price and service. Consumers come to JD because JD has no fakes; only authentic goods. They come to JD because we provide lower prices and better services. These are things that customers can perceive. But what they can't perceive are the very complex systems underlying them.

No matter how creative we can be, we can't abandon our systems. We should never forget how we have won and survived. Who are the people we rely on for a living? No one but our customers. We should never forget the user experience. If we lose the user experience, we are bound to fail. Without quality assurance, price guarantee, and service warranty, we are doomed to fail. Therefore, the inverted triangle strategy system will still be the cornerstone of our development in the second 10 years. I hope the innovations, starting point and foothold on management of every JDer should never be in opposition to our direction. Neither should they go against the user experience, the cost and efficiency. We should recognize that our innermost core is our team.

In the Next 10 Years, JD is to Stride Forward to the World's Biggest Retail Enterprise

Now I would like to talk about Zhongguancun with you. Why Zhongguancun again? Because Zhongguancun is a great example of how quickly what looks like the natural order can be overturned. In 1998, when I entered Zhongguancun, there was a perfect ecosystem. It had everything, from soup to nuts, that an IT customer would need.

It was universally believed that Zhongguancun was indestructible, that nothing could replace it. However, it soon disappeared anyway. Why? Because business development is bound to have its own set of rules. This kind of small, flea-market style business model was doomed to decline. It is the law of commercial development that organizational circulation and standard service of goods will prevail in the end. Consumers are sure to take brand as their first consideration when they make choice. So the next decade should be regarded as the best decade, the golden age for China's retail industry. In the past 30 years, the manufacturing industry took the upper hand. But I believe that in China, the next decade belongs to the retail industry.

Operating today in Europe, the United States, Japan, Korea and in most other developed countries are Wal-Mart, Carrefour, Costco and many other giant retail enterprises. They introduced the massive, organized and managed circulation of commodities and reduced countless intermediate links. With minimum costs and highest efficiency, they helped brand owners deliver products to consumers, and thus reduced costs and upgraded the efficiency at every step of the commercial chain.

In the next 10 years, I believe that China will transition to an age of consumption. The disorderly, non-standard, brand-less flea-market style retail format that can't give brand owners and consumers added value will gradually decline. It will be replaced by the emerging retail enterprises, which will capture 60% to 70% market share of the standardized commodities in China.

I believe that in the next 10 years, three things will appear. First, there will appear several retail enterprises with the sales of hundreds of millions, or even trillions in China in the days to come. Second, in the next 10 years, 20 years at most, the number one retailing business in China is sure to be the world's number one retail enterprise as well. Third, JD will become a world class retail enterprise!

"My Initial Dream to Start the Business was to Make a Great Enterprise!"

I want to share my latest dream with you. After my dream comes true, I should retire and go home to enjoy family life. This dream is internationalization. It is said that countless companies in China have attempted to achieve internationalization, but 99% of them were beaten black and blue, some even wiped out.

Why should we want internationalization? My dear colleagues, I have always held the belief that the real pride of a country or a nation must stem from the commercial success, the cultural success, and the institutional success. As part of the commercial world, we should advance with full courage and daring dreams. Why are the profit margins of Chinese companies so meagre? That's because over the past 30 years of China's economic development, we concentrated mainly on manufacturing, on OEM in the middle link. The more valuable and profitable positions — the brand at one end and the retailer at the other end — were occupied by foreign companies. JD's internationalization goal also is for the good of the country. We hope to sell quality products made by China's powerful manufacturing industry to all corners of the world through JD so that others can discover the Chinese brands and the products made in China that have the same quality as international brands, but are sold at lower prices.

No matter how successful we are in the country, in China we are still just a local company. In the past 10 years, we've made great achievements. In the next 10 years, we'll make greater achievements. But no matter how successful we are, we are still far from being a great enterprise. And my dream when I started the business was to create a great enterprise; an enterprise that can represent this country, this nation, an enterprise every Chinese person can feel proud of.

This is the last dream in my heart. I hope we can represent China as a global enterprise. We have the ability to serve customers worldwide. We can win the trust and confidence of consumers in the world. We can continuously win the world's wealth for the country and the people. If there are more companies like this, the country will be much more prosperous and the people will be much better off. Of course, to achieve this dream, we have to work 10 times harder than we did in the past. We may have to work overtime for countless days and nights. We may still have many difficulties to overcome. We still have so many unknown things to learn. We need to unite numerous friends, family and colleagues, unite the talents in the world for our use to strive for the same goal, for the same dream!

The first decade is gone. The 2013 "Repair, Raise, Revive and Rest" is over. Dear friends, last year we talked the least, but we did the most. So far, around the world, no company with revenue of 100 billion yuan can be like us, with a CEO that could pick himself up and walk away, could just go to the US to study for half a year as he wished. No one could do that. I did this because I wanted to test the base of JD's management system at the end of the last decade. Of course, we withstood the test. It was reflected on our speed increase, on the innovations of all our systems, on the introduction of our new products and on everything else.

Goodbye to 2013. In 2014, we shall lead ahead and keep on moving! I hope that everyone can release the JD passion and unite together to lay a better and more brilliant foundation for our second 10 years!

Thank you all.

Dreams Coming True, Embracing the New Beginning
- Richard Liu memo to employees at the time of JD's NASDAQ listing

Dear JD family, friends and colleagues:

After 10 years of hard work, our company officially went public on NASDAQ today! It is a day with milestone significance in JD's history. From today on, the entrepreneurial spirit with JD brand will be displayed to the world; from today on, the concepts and propositions of Joy [JD's mascot] will enter into millions of households around the world with us; from today on, JD has a brand new beginning!

Recalling the time when I started the business, although I was just a college student from the countryside, I always had a dream. That was, to create a great enterprise that can contribute to society and create value for the society. Even when I was in the most difficult time of my entrepreneurship, I never had the least doubt or hesitation. Today, my dreams have come true! Thanks to the great age of reform and opening up in China, we can have a chance to realize our dreams without having to rely on our connections and influential family members; thanks to our customers for tolerating our imperfection and consistently urging us to grow; thanks to all suppliers, partners and investors for appreciating our "stiffness" and stubbornness and trusting our persistence and pursuit.

But I feel most grateful to my colleagues. When you abandoned the comfortable life, rolled up your sleeves and trouser legs to do the hardest, dirtiest and most tiring work in e-commerce, you didn't doubt, didn't complain, but you took JD to a higher stage with JD's spirit of never giving up, never settling!

What made me feel proud is that over the last 10 years, we have succeeded in three things.

We have reshaped the "credibility" of China's e-commerce. From the first day of our start-up, we have been holding to our core principle of "authentic goods, no fakes". Behind that is our reverence to business ethics and the respect for consumer value. One cannot stand without credibility and an enterprise cannot prosper without credibility. By being consistent and credible, we have gained the trust of the community and our customers.

Today we have redefined the e-commerce experience in China. Today, when JD's distribution systems have made "last mile" the most important factor affecting the quality of user experience, the taunts and jeers we heard so often in the early years still linger in our ears. More often today consumers use words like "cool" and "delight" when they describe our business and their experience, instead of words like "stupid" and "persistent" that they once used.

We've redefined the "value" of China's e-commerce and what it stands for. A company's values no longer depend on how greedily it has grabbed huge profits, but on what ecological progress it has made as a whole. Over the years, we have constantly invested in e-commerce infrastructure construction, continued investing in research and development and big data, on open logistics system and internet finance. Now, with investments, we have got the effectiveness and efficiency of our partners.

Today, we stand at a new starting point. I think in the next 10 years, we still need to accomplish a few other things. We must reinforce our international strategy and make JD an enterprise respected by the world.

After the listing, we need to own our mission as an ambassador of China's new economy. We need to have the sense of responsibility to help China's manufacturing industry go global. We need to have the sense of honour to participate in international competition on behalf of Chinese enterprises. I hope, through JD's platform, we can continue to deliver high quality Chinese products into the hands of consumers all over the world. We hope numerous Chinese enterprises will reach the scale of 1 billion, 10 billion or even 100 billion RMB with the help of our platform. These will be the greatest achievements of JD in the future.

We need to build more diverse e-commerce ecosystem, and help entrepreneurs and the small and medium enterprises to grow in a fair and just environment.

By properly operating in B2C, C2C, finance and other business sectors, JD will be able to meet all the demands of consumers. We will uphold JD's core values through open and transparent rules. We will build a thriving business ecosystem where hard-working people have important work to do and can make a good living by their hard work. We want to make it easy for every entrepreneur and seller to earn money with dignity on JD's platform and to create values for society.

We are determined to become the leading technology-driven enterprise, and enhance social and commercial civilization through internet technology.

Compared to the traditional economy, the internet itself represents revolutionary and innovative productivity. Over the past few years, we have made many innovative attempts to enhance the efficiency of the way goods move from manufacture to customer by making use of information technology tools. In the years to come, we will further strengthen the investment in R&D, with a focus on in-depth innovations in cloud computing, data exploring, mobile application and other areas. We will help traditional industries transform themselves into internet-enabled business so as to enhance the circulation efficiency of the whole society and promote socio-economic development.

Finally, I want again to emphasize the importance of management and culture. After the listing, the company will share JD's success with our excellent employees through various forms of equity incentive plans so that everyone enjoys a decent and stable living and so that our parents and families who have long supported us can feel reassured and proud. But allow me to remind you that one prospers in worries and hardships, and perishes in ease and comfort. Going public is far from our ultimate goal. We need to maintain the initial intention as we started the business and the reverent attitude of learning from our excellent partners and even our competitors. Especially with our business penetrating in different fields of different length and depth, our scope of services spanning to different countries, we will be deeply involved in global competition and will face global partners and consumers directly. Only management and culture can keep ensuring the development of JD. The future stock price may fluctuate and the future capital market reaction may vary, but no matter what, we will stick to our mission and values. Please always keep in mind our commitment and responsibility to users, partners and the society at large!

As the poet wrote, "Eagles soar undauntedly in the sky. Fish hover in the limpid water. All the creatures are struggling to live free life in autumn."

My dear friends, we are going to stand on the world's stage to create the next 10 years of JD. This is a historic opportunity for all of us. Let's create a great world-class enterprise with our hands. We will and we can!

Yours,
Richard Liu
May 22, 2014

Heading for Trillions
- Richard Liu speech at annual JD employee meeting, January 17, 2015.

Dear colleagues, Happy New Year to you all!

What was the theme for 2014 annual meeting? Do you still remember? Yes, it was "Leading ahead, Moving forward". Some people wondered why we chose to go public in 2014. Our finances become transparent after the listing. Today, as a company with 30 billion RMB in cash, our company has one of the largest cash reserves of any internet company in China. The rumours that kept circulating about "capital chain rupture" at JD have proven to be unfounded. With the listing of our company, we have released our financial data to tens of thousands of partners, which has not only helped them feel relieved and more comfortable about cooperating with JD, but it has also brought us a lot of other changes as well.

Last July, when I went to Germany, I was discussing business with our investment bankers in the car. "Are you from JD?" the driver asked me. He said that he had invested 3,000 Euro in shares at JD's IPO.

A month or two ago, we visited one shareholder at his home. Many founders of the internet companies around the world were also present that day. I discovered for the first time, at this international gathering, that almost everyone knew JD.

In 2013, some invested in India, some invested in Southeast Asia. Both the Indian e-commerce platform Flipkart and Mr. Oliver, a famous entrepreneur in Germany who has been engaged in e-commerce in more than 10 countries around the world, told everyone that they were copying China's JD model.

Therefore, I came to realize that after listing, we are no longer unknown. We are standing on the world stage and we have been saddled with a lot of expectations, which come not only from our shareholders and investors, our employees, our partners, but millions of entrepreneurs who want to enter the emerging field of e-commerce in various countries. Taking our success as an example, entrepreneurs from more than 10 countries also selected the direct sales e-commerce model that JD is executing and received very good valuations, very good financing and achieved their dreams as entrepreneurs.

Let's look at our achievements in 2014. First, after reaching 100 billion RMB turnover in 2013, in 2014 we achieved 100% growth. In the third quarter of 2014, JD became an e-commerce company that had captured more than 50% of the direct sales e-commerce market in China. Five years ago, I said publicly that I hoped that JD could obtain half of the market share in the direct sales e-commerce market in the whole country. We have achieved it in the third quarter in 2014. But that is not the key point. The key point is that our growth is still twice the industry average growth.

I firmly believe that we will capture even better market share. In 2014, our city penetration strategy achieved a big breakthrough. As of last night, JD's delivery stations and teams now cover 1,880 districts and counties across China. We have become China's largest retailer in the computer and branded phone markets, both online and offline. By the end of 2013, we have had over 50,000 business partners. We've offered services to over 100 million different users cumulatively with our hands and sweat. It means that one out of every 14 to 15 people in China has received JD's services.

In 2014, our total employee population exceeded 70,000 people. We bear the expectation of tens of thousands of families. By December 31, 2014, if we raise our voice and shout "Any JDer here?" in any lane or street of Beijing, Shanghai or Guangzhou, it is likely that someone nearby will answer, "Yes!" This morning, on my way here, I wondered how many JD express vehicles I would come across. Guess what? Five trucks! Five red express vehicles with JD logos! And this was in the short distance I traveled from the north 5th-Ring Road to the east 5th-Ring Road.

Some may wonder how we could be so successful in 2014. Why JD? Outsiders also ask this question. Let me tell you, it is because of our team! A few days ago, I read a message of a colleague in his friends' circle on WeChat. It was about how one of our deliveryman encountered an old man in his 70s. He was sick and had wandered away from home. His family tried to find him everywhere, contacting police stations and police bureaus, but were frantic after 26 hours with no success. Without food or water, this old man had passed out in the street. A large crowd of people surrounded him, but no one dared to lend a hand to support him up for fear of getting into trouble. At this time, our deliveryman happened to be passing by. He pushed through the crowd and carried the old man on his back to the police station so he could be reunited with his family. This colleague is also with us today. Please stand up! Let's give him a big hand!

Stories like this in JD are quite common. I remember a few years ago, Beijing was struck by a major storm on July 21 that paralyzed the whole city.. But our couriers still braved the storm to deliver goods for our customers. Power failures occurred in many households. They were out of food and water and were expecting our deliveries. On that day, all of our couriers in Beijing not only delivered to our customers, they also spontaneously participated in the relief work in Beijing on their own initiative, before receiving any instructions from the company. Some carried older people, some helped push stranded cars and some salvaged goods. In one night, I can tell you, our JD Express colleagues did a lot of good things for Beijing.

Two years ago, there was a high speed car accident in Beijing. The car overturned at a busy intersection and the driver and the passenger were unconscious inside. Some citizens saw but, fearing an explosion, dared not try to approach the car and save them. At this time, our deliveryman passed by. Without a second thought, he went up and broke the car window and dragged the two wounded people out of the car and onto the road. He then called emergency services and helped the two onto the ambulance. Then he continued on his way so he could make the deliveries our customers were expecting. To this day I doubt that the two men knew it was our JD Express colleague who saved their lives.

We have done many things, but we rarely publicize them. In recent years, our country suffered several disastrous earthquakes. In 2013, we went to the southwest for help with the relief efforts. We did a good job, a timely job. On the morning meeting then, I issued a command to all our executives all over the country: when the country and the society are stricken by disaster and in need of water, or in need of any products available in JD warehouses, I empower all regional General Managers so that they do not need to ask permission from Headquarters and have the right to send each bottle of water, each tent, and each share of food to the stricken areas in their regions. What is a JDer? This is us. This is the value of JDers.

This has been the most essential cornerstone for JD's success in the past. JD is believed to be successful, believed to be capable, but JD is also widely said to be losing money. Some of our couriers even asked me, "Mr Liu, our parents have asked us if, as good as our company is, is it a concern that it is still losing money?" I told them, "Brothers, trust me and believe in yourself. If we want to show profits, we can do this anytime, just by changing some little things."

Some Chinese factories and express companies recruit workers through labour dispatching and cooperative chains and thus save money by not paying into employee insurance and housing funds. Some companies pay employees only the minimum social security amount as required by the local government. We could take this approach, save a lot of money and easily show a profit. But we don't operate that way. Based on our current ranks of about 100,000 colleagues, we pay more than 2.5 billion RMB into the Social Security Fund.

Every JD employee, every courier, every packaging team member has signed a contract with JD. We cover everyone with full payment of five kinds of insurance and housing funds. If a courier earns 8,000 RMB, we will pay into the appropriate insurance and housing fund accounts based on that number. Today each courier, each colleague who has worked for more than a year in JD can feel he is living with dignity. But I also hope that after we are over 60, or after we lose our labour power, each of our colleagues can still live in as dignified a way as they do today. I cannot tolerate the thought of any JDers living miserably when they lose the strength to work. In addition to salary, the five insurance and housing funds, the benefits under the state's *Labour Law*, JD also offers substantial additional benefits to our colleagues. Each warehouse provides beverages, and a wide variety of labour supplies. These are additional benefits, not legally required, not signed in the labour contracts, but all represent extra spending.

We also have other ways of making money. In 2013, I decided that every year, the company must invest in a new business, not a small one, a significant investment which perhaps can really generate income or return profits within three to five years. In 2013, we set up the Financial Group. In 2014, we cooperated with Tencent and established Paipai.com so it could develop as a separate wholly owned subsidiary. These two companies are still in the investment and fostering period. To achieve great success, we need to increase investment and give them strong support. If we didn't invest in these subsidiaries, our JD Mall business alone would allow us to show overall profitability, according to U.S. financial standards. Even while paying the full taxes and covering employee insurance and housing fund payments, JD Mall is still profitable. But that should not be the goal and dream of JDers. The single model cannot provide a full range of services to our customers. If today we don't invest for tomorrow, for the coming five years, then after a few years, the company will no longer be a company we can feel proud and excited about. So we insist that in 2015, we continue to invest. Each year we will invest in a new business.

If we turn a blind eye and allow those who sell smuggled goods and fakes to flock onto JD, we can instantly make lots of profits. If we issue fewer options to our employees, we can also make money. Since the first time we issued options in 2007, the entire value of options granted to Group employees, if calculated based on yesterday's closing price, exceeds 10 billion RMB.

So, it is quite easy for the company to show a profit. However, we will never think of making money unethically, and will never try for a second to avoid paying legitimate taxes that benefit our colleagues. If we make money through these channels, we'll never feel proud and superior but only a deep sense of shame instead.

What is the theme of the 2015 annual meeting? "Innovation and Breakthrough". Many said that JD had not made any large business model innovation in the last few years. We spent 10 years in the Mall businesses by making ongoing business innovation, product innovation, and service innovation. Speaking of which, JD Mall already has the best model and doesn't need significant change right now. We have introduced many innovations, such as same- and next-day delivery guarantees, the Jingdongbang home appliance service center, the O2O project, our villager agency and campus agency program, the decentralized mobile shopping and WeChat shops of Paipai.com, all of which have achieved great success. Since the WeChat shops launched in October 2014, in just over two months, the single day trading volume broke 20 million RMB and the single day trading peak exceeded 60 million RMB.

Today, to open up your thinking, I will talk more about JD's innovation in financial products. We opened JD Baitiao, Jingbaobei, and have reached tens of billions in lending. We don't know the users' names and we have no lending officer. All the suppliers and sellers can get the loans in three minutes. This is a great start. I believe that this can bring great value to our suppliers, sellers and customers.

Several months after the launching of our crowdfunding product it exceeded 60% of the market share of the crowd-funding products and it has become the absolute first in the industry. In 2013, there were three products that had received more than ten million each in JD Crowd-Funding.

What is the social value of JD's equity crowdfunding? It aims to achieve capital equality one day so that the people with 10,000 RMB and the people with USD 10 million can have equal investment opportunities. Otherwise, the world's poor can only put their money in the bank to be devalued while the rich can invest in companies such as JD to get great returns and become richer, leading to more serious disparities in social wealth. So I want you to keep this in mind, JD brothers and sisters, the real promise that equity crowdfunding has is to create a chance for ordinary people to make money in ways that only the wealthy could do previously.

For a rural family, particularly in poverty-stricken areas, if we give them thousands of RMB to buy a tractor to ship rice, wheat or provide some simple transportation for others, this may change the fate of a family. So from today, our JD Baitiao will not only promote to urban white-collar workers based on big data analysis, but also enter villages and campuses in 2015. At present, JD has opened a lot of county service centers, through which we can go into the villages and establish local agencies. In the future, we will not only have more than 100,000 employees, but also tens of thousands of farmers in China acting as our country promoters, taking charge of order placing, payment, delivery, aftersales, and credit business for all the residents of their villages.

I'm from the countryside and was exposed to rural life for 18 years. I know too well the rural status quo. Almost every farmer has borrowed money at exorbitant rates. Numerous farmers are unable to repay these loans in five or 10 years and have brought disasters onto their families. The money they earn each year is barely enough to cover the interest, and the principal is left unpaid, perhaps for their lifetime. Every year, many farmers buy seeds that turn out to be counterfeit, sow them, and fertilize them with painstaking efforts. But by the harvest time, they get nothing in return or what they get doesn't cover the cost. Nearly 70% of our JD colleagues come from rural areas. I believe each of you, including myself, has seen farmers standing in the field in despair for having bought counterfeit seeds, fake pesticides, and fake fertilizers and reaping nothing at the harvest time. Today I hope that many farmers will use JD Baitiao so they can get the funding to buy authentic seeds, pesticides, fertilizers, electrical appliances, clothing and food.

It's common lately to read or hear about "state enterprises", but this doesn't sound proud enough. An enterprise that can really win respect and pride should be called "national enterprise", which belongs to the country and to all people in this country. What is a national enterprise? For a national enterprise in any county, it is never one that traffics in fakes or smuggled goods within China, or gets involved with exporting fakes to the world; it is never one that doesn't pay its taxes; it is never one that makes money at the expense of its partners .

There is an American enterprise named Wal-Mart. Its market value today is just average. But nearly every American, including the US President, it seems to me, is clear: they view Wal-Mart as their country's national enterprise. I can tell you, the US Government couldn't bear the risk and the loss if Wal-Mart were to shut down. The founder of Wal-Mart is one of only a very few American entrepreneurs to have won the Presidential Medal of Freedom, a supreme honour in the US. So, a national enterprise as we define it is not a company that has the largest market value at a certain time, but an enterprise that can create maximum value for the society at any given time. Only by doing this can it be qualified to become China's national enterprise.

My dear brothers and sisters, one day, sooner or later, China will see such an enterprise whose sales revenue exceeds 1 trillion RMB. Such a company will become the largest private enterprise in China, and 70% of its employees could be a bunch of simple young men and women from the countryside. The company will rank in the top 20 companies in the world through the hard work of its employees. The company will have trade contacts, business contacts, partners, or customers in more than 100 countries all around the world. As long as this company firmly adheres to our values, adheres to creating value for the society, adheres to what we have been adhering to today, one day it come to participate in or even to develop the rules of global trade flows.

Dear colleagues, if a company like this appears in China, I can tell you, it must be ours! Immersed in the things we are doing, let us create a great, proud, respectful, reliable enterprise with our hands. Let's do it for the Chinese in the world, for the Chinese people, for this country and let's build a "national enterprise" in China. This is our new dream. In 2015, my dear brothers and sisters, let us continue to fight side by side! Thank you all.

BEYOND THE
WRITTEN WORD

AUTHORS WHO ARE EXPERTS

LID Speakers are proven leaders in current
business thinking. Our experienced authors will help
you create an engaging and thought-provoking event.

A speakers bureau
that is backed up by the
expertise of an established
business book publisher.

years

building on our success

- 1993 Madrid
- 2007 Barcelona
- 2008 Mexico DF & Monterrey
- 2010 London
- 2011 New York & Buenos Aires
- 2012 Bogota
- 2014 Shanghai & San Francisco